DEADLIER THAN THE MALE

Terry Manners, forty-eight, is Assistant Editor of the *Daily Express* and was formerly Night Editor of the newspaper for five years. He is a Barker of the Variety Club of Great Britain and a member of the Advisory Panel of Editors for the Press Association. He has published five books and lives with his family on the Essex coast.

DEADLIER THAN THE MALE

Stories of Female Serial Killers

TERRY MANNERS

PAN BOOKS

First published 1995 by Pan Books

an imprint of Macmillan Publishers Ltd
25 Eccleston Place, London SW1W 9NF
and Basingstoke

Associated companies throughout the world

ISBN 0 330 33711 4

3 5 7 9 8 6 4 2

A CIP catalogue record for this book is available from the British Library.

Typeset by CentraCet Limited, Cambridge
Printed and bound in Great Britain by
Mackays of Chatham PLC, Chatham, Kent

TO MY late grandfather, William Saunders, a gentle man with a belief in fair play, who instilled in me a love of history. To my wife Carol and daughter Sarah, for their endless hours of typing and research. To Gemma in America for her tireless efforts in newspaper libraries. And to those colleagues who showed absolutely no interest in the book. They just made me even more determined to write it.

I would like to acknowledge the following sources:

Washington Post, Toronto Sun, Toronto Star, Albany Herald, Albany Sunday Herald, Tallahasse Democrat, Associated Press, Reuters, UPI, *Daytona Beach News-Journal, The New York Times, Newsweek, USA Today, Orlando Sentinel, Tulsa Daily World, Dispatch* (Lexington), *People Magazine, Life, Time, Oklahoma City Times, County Record, Oakland Press, The Voice, Sacramento Bee, The Times* (London), *Daily Express, Daily Telegraph, Sun, Daily Star, Guardian, Independant, News of the World, Daily Mail, Sunday Express, Mail on Sunday, Sunday Mirror, Daily Telegraph.* Dr Eric W. Hickey, California State University (his book *Serial Murderers and their victims*), Ian Stephens, consultant forensic psychologist, Lanarkshire. *The Allitt Inquiry* (HMSO). Gemma Saienni, Los Angeles. The Long Beach Public Library, The Press Association. The Department of Health. CNN. The Home Office (Public Records Office), North of England Newspapers, the *Face* magazine. Administration of Justice, Pennysylvania State University, the State of Alabama Records Office. Stephen Holmes and Ronald M. Holmes, *Journal of Contemporary Justice* vol. 7, no. 4, December 1991. Sue Russell (her book *Damsel of Death*) published by True Crime.

CONTENTS

FOREWORD

It was early in 1992 that, as night editor of the *Daily Express*, I orchestrated coverage of the woman we had headlined the Damsel of Death – female serial killer Aileen Wuornos. The thirty-five-year-old hooker had shot dead seven middle-aged men in an eighteen-month murder rampage on the Florida highways. What particularly interested me, during her trial, was her background story. Wuornos never knew her father or her mother. Abandoned as a baby, she led a lonely, cold life where offering sex was a means of obtaining the things that gave her comfort – a packet of Marlboro cigarettes or a can of Budweiser beer. She always dreamed of being a movie star and now she was as famous as one. Film companies and agents were rushing to buy her story, publishers were planning books, friends and even detectives were desperately trying to get in on the act in a bid to make megabucks from Hollywood, and she was incorrectly being billed as the world's first female serial killer. In court psychiatrists told how her sad life had left her emotionally scarred. She was 'self-destructive, and impulsive with roller-coaster emotions'. She was unhappy and tended to project that unhappiness on the world.

I began to research other female serial killers, women such as Christine Falling, the babysitter who killed children in her care in 1982; Velma Barfield, who in 1984 murdered husbands and lovers, and Dorothea Puente, the landlady who buried her down-and-out lodgers in the garden in 1988. All of them had the same sort of sad stories, and they were so completely different from their male counterparts. But not all women who had a bad start in life go on to become serial killers. Why then did they?

Perhaps no one really has the answer, but taking their stories together I began to see a pattern, a global picture, almost a common bond between them all. I went back in time even further to Victorian Mary Ann Cotton, who poisoned twenty people with arsenic, including her husbands, lovers and children. Behind the horror, her story along with the others was fascinating. Most of the women had managed to gain sympathy from either the public, their attorneys, gaolers or the Press. There was a feeling of disbelief among many of the people who crossed their paths that they could have committed such awful crimes. The lawyers, the reporters, the friends, the victims' families became part of the female serial killer's horrific but sad story.

In a recent American study of female serial killers, the average woman killed for 9.2 years before the murders stopped. Most were homemakers (32 per cent), and the next biggest group were nurses (18 per cent). Ninety-seven per cent were white, and the average age was thirty-three when they began their killing careers. Almost without exception, the females, unlike their male counterparts, did not travel to more than one state in their quest for victims. Their motives and methods also differed from the male. Women tended to murder for material gain by using poisons or pills. Some women who killed serially did so because of their involvement with cults or disciple relationships, like those who were associated with multiple murderer Charles Manson in the 1960s.

The female serial killer has been broken down into several categories in a report compiled by Stephen T. Holmes, Dr Eric Hickey and Ronald M. Holmes and published by the *American Journal of Contemporary Criminal Justice*. Here are their findings:

The Comfort Serial Killer

She is motivated to murder for material reasons. This tends to be the most prevalent motive among female serialists. There are no voices or visions from God or the devil demanding that anyone must die. The offender will usually kill persons with whom she is acquainted. The material gain is typically money or the promise of money, such as insurance benefits, acquisition of business interests or property. In 1901 Amy Archer-Gilligan opened a rest home in Connecticut. During the next fourteen years she disposed of at least twenty-seven men and women by poisoning them. Of the men she nursed, she married five, insured them for substantial amounts of money, and then poisoned each one. In other instances she killed elderly women after she had helped them rewrite their wills.

During the mid 1970s, Janice Gibbs of Georgia killed her husband, three sons and an infant grandson for $31,000 insurance money. Mary Eleanor Smith trained her son in the art of killing to rob men and then dumped their bodies in acid beneath their home in Montana. Dorothea Puente of Sacramento was charged with seven counts of murder after the authorities found bodies in the garden of her rooming-house. She killed her lodgers for their social security cheques.

The Visionary Serial Killer

In this type of murder, the perpetrator has a severe break with reality. This break can be demonstrated by the person's admission that she has spoken to God, an angel, a spirit or Satan himself. In such a case, the attack tends to be spontaneous, with the killer selecting a victim following a description outlined by the message-giver.

Priscilla Ford heard the voice of God as she walked down the streets of Reno, Nevada. The voice demanded that she kill those she met along the way because they were 'bad people' and deserved to die.

Another visionary serial murderess was Martha Wise. The forty-year-old widow from Medina, Ohio, killed her family simply for revenge. She used arsenic to poison her mother after she had been ridiculed for being involved romantically with a younger man. She later administered arsenic to her aunt and uncle but bungled an attempt to kill the rest of her family. Wise claimed the devil had followed her everywhere and forced her to do the killings.

The Power Seekers

Power is the ability to influence the behaviour of others in accordance with one's own desires. Power may also be defined as the ultimate domination of one person by another. For example, Nurse Jane Toppan is believed to have killed between seventy and 100 victims. She proudly exclaimed that she had fooled the authorities, 'the stupid doctors and the ignorant relatives'. And she was quoted as saying: 'It is my ambition to have killed more people, more helpless people, than any man or woman has ever killed.'

Some female serial killers, however, will repeatedly poison their victims and then nurse them back to health. When the patient finally dies, the offender moves on to another victim.

Genene Jones, a pediatric nurse in San Antonio, was arrested for the murders of young children admitted to hospitals, often for minor medical problems. Thought to be responsible for the deaths of as many as sixteen infants,

Jones felt a sense of importance working in a hospital setting as a primary medical caretaker. Recently Munchausen's Syndrome by Proxy has been used to explain individuals who fabricate and induce medical problems in children under their care.

Some individuals temporarily boost their feelings of low self-esteem and worthlessness through involvement in life and death situations, such as those found in an emergency room, operating room or critical care unit. Jones was such a personality.

The Disciple Killer

Some women kill when they are under the influence of a charismatic leader.

In 1982 Judy Neeley and her husband, Alvin, were involved in forgeries, burglaries and robberies. Eventually they began to seek a greater thrill by abducting, abusing, raping and murdering their victims. Judy claimed that her husband forced her to commit tortures and murders because she was completely dominated by him. While in Alabama they abducted a thirteen-year-old girl and held her captive. Judy watched while Alvin repeatedly raped, tortured and abused the child. Finally, Judy injected liquid Drano into the girl's veins, but when that failed to kill her, she shot her in the back and threw her over a cliff. The final number of their victims was never discovered.

The Hedonistic Serial Killer

This is the least understood and least reported of all female serial killings, says the report. Hedonism is a striving for pleasure. In this sense the hedonistic offender is someone who has made a critical connection between fatal violence and personal, sexual gratification. Carol Bundy of California was allegedly involved in the killing not only of a male victim but of several young women, who were runaways and prostitutes. She is believed to have helped her male accomplice abduct and decapitate victims and then place their heads in her refrigerator. Later the heads were taken out and used in sex acts.

The female serial killer is one of the most frightening human predators of our time. As a child she seeks love. Instead she may suffer sexual abuse from a father, brother, uncle or family friends. The guilt inside her is a timebomb ticking away: guilt that the offence took place and guilt that she could have stopped it happening. That morbid secret haunts her throughout her life but she manages to sweep it away into a dark cupboard in her mind. When it manifests itself she must relieve the stress, and sometimes murder is what follows.

Cunning and intelligent, the female serial killer is sometimes weak and gullible but always merciless. She uses her sexuality to lure her prey, and when she is caught, trades on sympathy with her male prosecutors and the public.

In some ways she is like her male counterparts: Jeffrey Dahmer, Son of Sam David Berkowitz and Yorkshire Ripper Peter Sutcliffe. She too is in the grip of a deadly compulsion. Just as heroin addicts must have more of the substance that gives them a high, so must the femal serial killer find another victim to feed the fantasy world she has made real. The first killing gives her the best high, for she has at last broken through the thin veil between her evil thoughts and reality. But she will never achieve quite the same emotional thrill again. Now killing becomes an obsession. The murders are self-perpetuating. The original meaning loses its significance. The murderess invents reasons for her trail of evil. She will convince herself that she is putting the sick and infirm out of their misery or that she needs money from a will or insurance policy in order to survive in a harsh world. It is her right, especially if she has always had to fight to survive from a childhood of poverty. In fact, research shows that money is the most common motivator for a woman to murder.

The female serial killer is an even more complex creature than the male. Just like Dahmer, she craves bloody murder, a psychological revenge from childhood. That revenge can only be satiated by the complete and utter possession of another human being's life – in her case usually a weak man or child. In this way she experiences at last the feeling of dominating the male.

But she cannot kill like a man, she doesn't have the strength. She is the poisoner of husbands, the suffocator of children, the drug injector of hospital patients. She uses potassium chloride, which attacks the heart, strychnine or arsenic. Arsenic has been popular among female killers since the 1800s, when it was readily available from the alchemist. Husbands would buy it to kill rats in the garden. Wives would buy it to kill bed bugs. Young men and women would sip it in small quantities to heighten their sexual desires. Arsenic does not mix well with cold water but it is almost undetectable in hot food and drinks like cocoa or coffee. A large dose can kill within a few hours, but death may be prolonged by using small amounts. In such cases the victim may live in agony for weeks or even months. Doctors were often fooled into thinking the vomiting and stomach cramps were the result of gastro-enteritis, a common complaint in the days of poor hygiene and rotting food. The female arsenic poisoner would often nurse her unsuspecting victim until death. There was no reason for an autopsy – most doctors were too busy even to consider the possibility of one. Death was commonplace. Had the body been exhumed, traces of the poison would have been found because it was a strong preservative. Today, however, pure arsenic is difficult to obtain. The female serial killer will use potassium chloride, which is difficult to detect after burial. Pesticides, too, are another favourite.

But not all female serial killers act alone. In some cases they are so besotted with a lover or husband that they follow his will, either fearing his retribution or believing he will shield them from harm . . . an excuse perhaps to live out their childhood fantasies. In these cases the killings are often violent. Victims may be bludgeoned to death or strangled and raped at the same time. Where a female serial killer has a male partner sexual drive will enter the compulsive mix.

The one thing, though, that all female serial killers have in common is that unlike their male counterparts they never taunt the police. No phone calls to detectives giving them another clue, no anonymous threats to victims or newspapers. Neither do they trawl for their victims like men. They don't hang around bars and follow their intended victims home, they don't lurk in dark alleyways waiting for their prey. Neither do they mutilate their victim's corpse, a common ritual among male murderers. The female serial killer often uses caring to kill. She trades on her womanhood. She uses trust as a weapon and kills in her own environment – her home, her hospital or her guest-house.

From Aileen Wuornos, Florida's hard-drinking, chain-smoking killer prostitute who loved God and her lesbian lover to white-haired granny Dorothea Puente, who drugged boarders to death at her old people's home and buried them sometimes alive in the garden, the compulsion for a sadistic kick and material gain is the same. At no time did any of them believe they were doing wrong.

That same compulsion drove Victorian Mary Ann Cotton to poison twenty people with arsenic, including her children, husbands and lovers, between 1865 and 1872, and it gripped the tortured mind of nurse Beverly Allitt, who murdered four children, attempted to kill three more and caused grievous bodily harm to six others on Ward Four of the hospital where she worked. Allitt, of course, was found to be suffering from Munchausen's Syndrome by Proxy, a condition where sufferers repeatedly draw attention to themselves through the creation of injury or drama. The search for the reason why female serial killers begin their trail of terror consumes the state and its armies of psychiatrists and psychologists. Depression, repressed guilt, alcohol, drugs, menstruation cycles, hormonal imbalances, even women's liberation are offered as explanations. One wonders what the explanation for Victorian Mary Ann Cotton's trail of death would be. Perhaps a psychiatrist could have saved her from the gallows.

It was an obsessive compulsion that gripped Karla Teale, Canada's Barbie-doll blonde, whose trail of terror with her lover and later husband was a mixture of torture, rape, butchery and fear of him. And, like Aileen Wuornos, there were sickening mementos of her crimes. Wuornos handed out her victims' possessions as gifts for her lover. Teale and her husband captured their victims' last moments on video.

Christine Falling was a trusted and caring babysitter, but time and again she killed the babies in her charge by squeezing their tiny windpipes. She couldn't stop herself. Nevertheless mothers kept entrusting their children to her – they just couldn't accept that she was a killer.

Nannie Doss, America's Giggling Grandma, poisoned her husbands by mixing rat poison into their stewed prunes. Her jokes and good nature made her a media star. She was everybody's favourite grandmother. No one believed she could stand and watch as the men in her life twisted, turned, vomited and screamed in pain until they died.

Velma Barfield couldn't handle life. She never got over the sexual abuse and hardships she suffered as a child. She blotted out the harsh realiites of her existence with a daily cocktail of drugs, then went on a murder spree that ended in her own execution and tears from her attorneys.

Terri Rachals was the perfect nurse, loved by doctors and patients alike. But she was secretly at war with herself, riddled with guilt that she had been sexually abused as a child. When she was led away from hospital facing six murder charges and twenty allegations of assault, medical staff cried. The Bible-reading nurse, whose husband had cerebral palsy, could never have done such a thing, could she?

These women had been without power all their lives. Murder and assault gave them power for the first time, a chance to control something in a world that in many instances had dealt them a rough hand. But when a female serial killer has power and wealth the trail of death is often more difficult to stop. Such a female is able to manipulate others to act out her fantasies for her.

The common factors, then, in the cases of most female serial killers are that they suffer emotional, physical or sexual abuse as a child, usually under the age of three. They are deprived of love from their fathers. They have been verbally abused, abandoned or humiliated sexually to the point where they plot to survive. They grow up surrounded by domestic violence, cowering in a corner as their father beats their mother. They see all men as domineering, powerful, lustful and aggressive. Psychiatrists say that at an age when most youngsters begin to develop consciences these young girls are too busy devising cunning schemes to care for others. Their emerging consciences are replaced by rage. They seek revenge for being abandoned, for being abused, for being shamed in front of others. They strive for material gain to make up for the things they never had in childhood. They were born guilty.

When the embryonic female serial killer grows to womanhood, she begins to punish victims who represent the pain of her early years. Some of her victims may look or act just like she did at their age. The victims, however, are just objects. There is not the slightest trace of love, for example, between the female serial killer and the husband she will kill. Men are there just to perform a function – to bring in a wage, to have children, to provide a nest. Remember, statistics show that most female serial killers are homemakers. Few have legitimate full-time employment. Those who do are generally nurses in charge of the weak and vulnerable.

The female serial killer is always promiscuous. Sex is just sex, it is nothing to do with love. While planning to kill one husband Nannie Doss was already bedding the next. Mary Ann Cotton used her body to acquire a better roof over her head, and was even seen dancing with joy the day after one of her husbands died in excruciating agony from the arsenic she had poured into his milk.

Such women must have absolute physical control over their victim, so that things do not go wrong. Aileen Wuornos's victims were middle-aged men whom she believed were weaker than herself and easier to fight if the going got tough. Now the thirty-five-year-old hooker admits to doctors that she was like a huntress looking for trophies to prove she was stronger than her prey. She kept souvenirs of her killings . . . a badge from a retired police chief, a truncheon from another officer, playing cards, razors, alarm clocks, a fishing reel, even a Bible.

Her story begins in childhood. She was abandoned by her mother as an infant and her father hanged himself with a prison bedsheet after raping a seven-year-old girl. The grandmother who adopted her was an alcoholic and Wuornos was beaten by her grandfather. At the age of fourteen she was pregnant, at fifteen she was a prostitute. By the time she was twenty she had slept with thousands of men. Finally, in her early thirties, she cracked. She embarked on a trail of killings, convincing herself that she was in danger from the men who picked her up on the highways. She finally confessed to shooting seven middle-aged men, ranging from a church missionary to a rodeo worker. Today, as she sits on Death Row, there is much public sympathy for her in the state that was her killing ground.

Like all female serial killers, Wuornos was intelligent and cunning. The bodies of her victims were stripped naked to prevent easy identification. Their abandoned cars were found up to 100 kilometres away, cleaned of prints, and the licence documents and log books were missing. Once she even pulled out the teeth of a victim.

She was nothing if not practical. She would go touting with a bag containing a change of clothes, a bottle of household cleaner to wipe away fingerprints and a seven-shot .22 calibre revolver. It was her kill bag. Wuornos showed no remorse over her bloody trail, only regret that the men she killed had crossed her path.

Psychiatrists say women like her are not mad. They are sane and organized. Very rarely is the female serial killer medically and legally psychotic. Nor will she look like a monster. Karla Teale looks like a movie star, Beverly Allitt like the girl next door, and Velma Barfield was described by a lawyer as the kind of woman you see on a honey jar label.

Often such women work hard to perfect that safe look. They plan their lives so that their secret identity is never revealed. They keep their schedules compartmentalized and often their partners don't know where they go when they leave.

In all cases of female serial killers the addiction has grown until they are out of control. Then they take chances. This makes them careless and finally detectives pick up on a pattern. If they hadn't been careless or finally admitted their bloody crimes in a moment of weakness, many of these women would still be on the loose. Perhaps then they really wanted to be caught.

Their ability to act out a completely normal life in the shadow of such terrifying bloodshed is one of the most chilling things about them.

Dr Eric W. Hickey, of California State University, Fresno, who has researched female serial killers, says: 'They tend to be insincere, amoral, impulsive, prone to exercise manipulative charisma and superficial charm, without conscience and with little insight, since they fail to learn from their mistakes.'

Take Karla Teale. She was married on 17 June 1991. As she kissed her husband at the altar, police frogmen were lifting the body of fourteen-year-old Leslie Mahaffy from a deep lake. The blonde high school pupil with braces was just one of their victims. She had been hacked to pieces and her remains entombed in concrete. The next day the Teales flew to Hawaii for their honeymoon.

The seemingly perfect couple met in October 1987 in the quiet Canadian town of St Catharines, near Niagara Falls. Karla was seveteen and Paul a twenty-three-year-old accountant.

The local community loved them both. But behind the scenes was a world of violence, bloodshed and lust.

Their reign of terror might have gone undetected but for an argument in which Paul hit Karla with a flashlight. In a moment of hysteria, she called the police to their neat suburban home, broke down and confessed in front of astonished officers.

She revealed how teenage victim Kristen French, fifteen, was put through thirteen days of hell during which time she was repeatedly raped and tortured before being murdered. Karla had sat on her chest while her husband raped her. The schoolgirl's naked body was discovered on a lonely country road two weeks after she vanished on her way to school. Police were also shocked to find videotapes in the house showing Karla in lesbian orgies and victims being tortured.

Today Karla shows no remorse, only regret that certain victims came her way. She blames her husband for the killings. She claims she feared him.

Files were reopened on the death of her own sister Tammy, who died, aged fifteen, on Christmas Eve 1990. Karla had sex with her before she died.

For Karla Teale, Aileen Wuornos, Beverly Allitt, Dorothy Puente, Mary Ann Cotton, Velma Barfield, Terri Rachals, Christine Falling, and Nannie Doss, fantasy exploded into the dull world of reality with their first murder. It perhaps shocked them, because they did not suspect they could go so far with all their hatred. But their first killings fed their depraved imaginations. That first murder was addictive. Once they had tasted the fruits of their fantasy they sought more and better trips to repeat the pleasure.

They have all talked of compulsion, and in fact it was no idle excuse. They have all struggled with it. But they have all struck a chord of sympathy somewhere in the public eye and that perhaps is why they have sometimes fared differently in sentencing to their male counterparts.

Hickey argues: 'Even those few female killers who have received national attention do not instil the fear that male killers do. This is not unexpected, because males do most of the killing and are usually responsible for most of the sadistic and perverted acts committed against victims. Our underestimation of the ability of women to commit murders as heinous as those that males commit may be a factor in the perceived differential treatment of women in the criminal justice system.'

Ian Stephen has worked in forensic psychology for twenty-six years. For ten years he was Director of Psychological Services at the State Hospital, Carstairs, where in conjunction with the University of Edinburgh he developed a training programme for clinical psychologists who wanted to work in prisons. He holds an Honorary Senior Clinical Lectureship at Glasgow University and is an Honorary Fellow of the University of Edinburgh. Recently he has been developing an independent forensic psychology consultancy for the Scottish Prison Service and the Health Service. He has devoted years to studying the behaviour and mind processes of serial killers both male and female.

He has discovered a pattern in the profile of the female. She usually comes from a broken home, has a deprived childhood and is abused at a young age. She may have some form of neurological abnormality, possibly the result of a head injury. There is usually evidence of bed-wetting, arson and cruelty to animals. She is sometimes intelligent but usually an under-achiever with lots of resentment. She blames others for her failure to achieve and longs to be important.

Female serial killers are shallow, and seem to have no feelings. Love is something they have read about in women's magazines. They see men only in terms of sexuality. They have learned from early childhood that relationships between men and women are purely sexual and aggressive. Men do not offer comfort. They are not friends. They are the abusers. They are to be feared and hated. However, sometimes, for these women, the more they hate a man the more exciting the sex act can be. They achieve a thrill because for a few moments the aggressor is in their power. He has a moment of weakness.

The male serial killer, however, is driven by his macho instinct. It is part of the domination syndrome that has been with him since time began, since caveman killed the tiger. His violence is usually sexually based. He is mostly strong and aggressive. Male serial killers are stalkers, the torturers, the blood lusters. They will even have sex with corpses or leave a tell-tale mark on the body. Female serial killers, however, rarely leave ritualistic clues. Superficially they have a caring personality which throws the police and neighbours off their trail. But something has happened to them in childhood which detaches them from reality. They induce a pseudo-empathy. They use their sexual and motherly skills to throw people off the scent and they can be totally believable, for they create a rational logic to their trail of death. They convince themselves they are doing something good, like euthanasia to relieve the pain of dying. The murders they commit relieve their stress and tension and they come to terms with the killings by telling themselves they are really mercy killers or that they are doing society a good turn by sending down-and-outs to their maker. They wonder why their captors and prosecutors are against them.

Ian Stephen described the female killer as having the mind of a three-year-old in a playgroup. The child goes over and snatches a toy from another youngster because she needs it to play with. When she gets thumped she is amazed. She can't understand why. She needed the toy, the toy was there, why couldn't she have it? Most children would learn from that experience, but not the girl who will one day grow up to be the serial killer. She can't understand it and never will. It is the child who thumped her who is wrong.

He compares the female serial killer's life to Mr Ben's. Mr Ben was a cartoon character who dressed up in a variety of costumes through the ages then walked through a door to another time. On the other side he lived out his fantasies in a world that fitted his new clothes. After a while he would come back through the door again and close it behind him, reverting to his own staid world and staid clothes. Female serial killers are the same. They take on other personas, because they feel negative about their own personalities. They are seeking self-esteem. They step into a role and believe it. But they can easily revert back. Like Mr Ben they close the door on their fantasy world until a compulsion drives them to open it again. They are the only ones with the key.

In some ways the male and female serial killers are the same. The world didn't exist before I was born. How could it exist, because I didn't? I am the universe – just like the child who snatched the toy in the playgroup.

Once a potential female serial killer murders her first victim she goes on a cycle. She has turned her fantasies into reality and that is exciting. She got away with it, quietly closing the door on Mr Ben's world without anyone knowing she has been there. It is her secret. She reasons with herself that if she is found out, she will somehow be able to justify her heinous crime. She believes everyone will understand. The next killing triggers the obsession. The original meaning of her actions loses its significance. The crimes become self-perpetuating. The killings can escalate from one every three months to one a month.

In tracing the history of the female serial killer it is difficult to unearth evidence of early sexual abuse in the cases of women like Mary Ann Cotton. However, it is quite likely that some sort of abuse did occur.

Today more and more research is being undertaken into the psyche of the female serial killer. As Eric Fromm said, in *The Heart of Man: Its Genius for Good and Evil*: 'We are not created evil or forced to be evil, but we become evil slowly over a period of time through a long series of choices.'

If you could crawl into the mind of a female serial killer and examine the elements of her psyche, you would find her conscience missing. That very fact alone allows full and violent expression without hesitation, guilt, shame or remorse. The female serial killer knows right from wrong – but she simply doesn't care.

In this book I have tried to look behind the crimes that have been committed by female serial killers. Using newspaper reports, interviews, quotes and court records, the aim has been to bring a media eye to their stories, to take the reader back in time to the events that led up to their crimes and the events that followed.

For obvious reasons some names have been changed to protect the innocent, and in some cases the dialogue has been created for the situations that occurred. I have tried to be as accurate as possible with dates, times and places, but inevitably because of the timespan covered there were conflicting records and reports through which I had to sift. One can only make a final decision on which one to choose, and stick with it.

Finally, as the dead cannot speak, many of the storylines are taken from court evidence, and much of that is from the killer's own testimony on trial. The rest we must imagine for ourselves.

This is not a book that focuses on the crimes of the female serial killer. This is a book that tells their stories.

Chapter One

MARY ANN COTTON

'I am a friendless woman, forsaken by the world. But I hope not by God.'

West Auckland, Co. Durham, 1872

'Poor little blighter,' whispered Dr Kilburn under his breath to Chalmers. They stood side by side, staring at the body of the seven-year-old boy on the kitchen table. There was just one hour left before the inquest. David Kilburn sighed loudly. He had seen little Charles Cotton days before his death and hadn't been too worried. True, the boy had been pale and was retching, but he should have been strong enough to survive a stomach bug. He had been an energetic little fellow, even though he was thin and obviously undernourished. Kilburn's assistant for the day, surgeon Archibald Chalmers, passed him the scalpel.

'Shall we get on with it, David? There's not much time?'

It was 2pm on Saturday, 13 July, and little Charlie had

been dead thirty-two hours. Kilburn cut the skin around the stomach, noticing signs of malnutrition. The post-mortem had begun.

Next door, at the Rose and Crown in Front Street, tables and chairs were being hastily rearranged for the inquest at three o'clock. Deputy coroner Thomas Dean, a small, fussy man, was busy shuffling papers in the far corner of the bar. He kept stopping to blow his nose and curse his cold. Outside a small crowd had gathered. Charlie's stepmother, Mary Ann Cotton, peeped at them from behind the curtains of her three-storey terraced house before quietly returning to sit beside Sergeant Tom Hutchinson. The local policeman thumbed his whiskers and said nothing. His thoughts were on the post-mortem downstairs in the kitchen, where the two doctors were working against the clock. So far they had found nothing to indicate poisoning – but they were still uncertain. Kilburn discovered that the boy's lungs were stuck to the walls of his chest, an indication of a long-standing inflammation. He examined the stomach with a small microscope. It was a dark, brownish red in colour and there were particles of white powder, which he took to be some of the morphia he had prescribed for the boy when he had fallen ill. There was no time for a chemical examination; the inquest was about to start. Kilburn put the boy's stomach and some of his intestines into a glass jar and washed his hands in a bowl of cold water. 'Would you mind locking the jar in my surgery closet, Archie? The jury might want a chemical analysis.'

'I'll do it now,' said Chalmers. 'But I think it unlikely.'

As Kilburn left for the inquest Mary Ann came down the ladder from the upstairs room. For a moment he realized what men saw in her. Her clothes were not expensive but they were well tailored and she wore them well. She had an ample figure, strong, shiny black hair pulled back in a bun and penetrating eyes. She looked at him for a moment, then glanced away. Yes, he thought, her eyes did indeed hold the promise of fire. Or perhaps his mind was playing tricks because of her reputation in the village. After all, she was pregnant with her new lover's child. Strange, she showed no emotion about her little stepson stretched out on her kitchen table. Kilburn, however, didn't realize that the look she gave him was one of silent hate. He had refused to sign her stepson's death certificate and she had been unable to collect the small life insurance payment due to her.

Late that afternoon Kilburn, a member of the Royal College of Surgeons, told the packed Rose and Crown that Charlie'e death could have been from natural causes, possibly gastro-enteritis, a common complaint of the times. Coroner Dean pressed him to give a definite opinion but he could not. The coroner and the jury didn't think it necessary to request a chemical analysis. The death of a child was commonplace, as was gastro-enteritis. The jury retired for an hour, returning with a verdict of death by natural causes. They had no option, no evidence from the doctor to go on, only village rumours. In the back of their minds was the fact that many children in the village were lucky to reach the age of five because of poor hygiene, contaminated food and the cold. Kilburn glanced across at Mary Ann sitting in the back of the room. She seemed to smile at the verdict, and well she should, because now she could collect 10s.0d. from Prudential Insurance. As she left the Rose and Crown, Mary Ann came face to face with corner shop owner Thomas Riley, the village 'social worker' she blamed for her troubles. Her face went white with anger.

'This is all your doing!' she screamed. 'You have tried to bring shame on an innocent woman – but you have failed, thank the Lord!'

Riley stared hard at her. 'I still think you murdered that boy,' he said coldly, and walked away. The little Victorian pit village went back to its everyday business. But Riley and Kilburn had nagging doubts.

The next day was a fine, bright Sunday. That afternoon children beat wooden hoops along the cobbled streets and men in cloth caps stumbled out of the pubs on their way home for food and sleep. Kilburn had enjoyed a heavy roast beef lunch, washed down with port. As he rummaged through some papers in his study, looking for a thesis on lung disease from a colleague in London, he remembered the glass jar containing Charlie's organs in the closet. Was there any point in keeping it now? For some reason, he decided to give Charlie's stomach one last test. An hour later he stood in his surgery, pouring the contents of the boy's intestines into a glass bowl. They measured five fluid ounces. Putting on his boots, he strolled into the garden and reflected on the inquest as he buried Charlie's remains.

For the next two days Kilburn could think of little else.

The boy should not have died. He should easily have fought off gastro-enteritis. He had been pale and waxy and was vomiting and purging himself. Kilburn had prescribed ammonia, followed by hydrocyanic acid and powder containing morphia. He remembered what store owner Riley had told him. Two weeks earlier Riley had gone to see Mary Ann to ask if she could help him look after a friend who had smallpox. As Mary Ann stood on the doorstep of her home at 13 Front Street, Charlie sat at her feet.

'How can I help when I have him to look after?' she said, pointing down at the lad. 'If you can get him in the workhouse I'll nurse your friend.'

As the village 'relief officer' Riley had the power to grant workhouse orders. But he admitted: 'I can only give you one for the boy if you go too.'

Mary Ann was irritated. 'I'll never go into such a place!' she shouted. 'You must be able to help me. Don't you know how hard it is for a widow like me, trying to keep a boy who is not her own? He stops me from earning many a pound. All I get is one shilling and sixpence a week relief. I even wrote to his uncle in Ipswich, saying I'd give him the boy's clothes and all, but he wouldn't take him.'

Riley wasn't to know, but this was a cry for help from Mary Ann. In one caring moment she was trying to spare Charlie from his fate. Perhaps it was because she and the boy now slept together in the same room and had become close since his father's death, as close as anyone could be with her.

'Can't you take a lodger to help with the money?' asked Riley.

'I've got someone very respectable who would come – but not while he is here. The boy is simply in the way.'

Charlie sat on the step staring at the ground as Riley joked with Mary Ann. He knew that she must mean her lover, brewery excise officer John Quick-Manning. It was the talk of the village.

'You might well be getting married, I hear, Mary,' Riley said.

She smiled: 'Maybe. But not while the boy is here. Still, perhaps it won't matter because I don't think I'll be troubled long. He'll go like the rest of the Cotton family.'

Mary Ann's fourth husband, pitman Frederick Cotton, had died of gastric fever, aged thirty-nine, after suffering stomach pains. Fever had also taken his son from his first marriage, Frederick, ten, and Mary's own fourteen-month-old baby Robert Cotton had died of convulsions. If only Riley had known the history of her past twenty years. Every man she lived with had tried to look after her. They cared about her more than their lives. She had sexual power over them and they literally worked themselves to death for her. Their fate was sealed when she realized they couldn't offer enough for her needs.

Riley ruffled Charlie's hair as the boy sat in silence. 'You don't mean to tell me this healthy little fellow is going to die too,' he joked.

'He'll not get up,' she said, looking down at the lad.

Riley knew what she meant. The boy would never

reach manhood. But surely it was some kind of joke – wasn't it?

Dr Kilburn's thoughts wandered even more. He was worried. What if Mary Ann was the poisoner the whole village thought she was? Riley had persuaded everyone. Kilburn was forty years old and still needed to work. Any kind of scandal that would expose him as a professional buffoon would ruin his career. He poured the contents of the boy's stomach into a saucepan, then added some hydrochloric acid. It was late on Wednesday night, 17 July, and the flickering oil lamp threw a poor light across his parlour as he boiled the fluid on the stove. He dropped in a strip of clean copperfoil and waited. Reinsch's test, developed by the German chemist of the same name thirty years earlier, would tell him what he wanted to know.

At midnight he was in a coach on his way to the police station at Bishop Auckland. Charlie's stomach was full of arsenic.

The most prolific woman serial killer in British history was about to be arrested. One day, though, she was to be eclipsed by a woman who desperately wanted to be a nurse just like her.

'You must not come here any more,' said Quick-Manning, trying to close the door.

'Don't you want me to rub your back, John, like I did when you had the smallpox?' she said softly, gripping his hand.

Quick-Manning looked over his shoulder at the staircase. It was 2am; he prayed Mrs Neasham was still asleep. The landlady liked her lodgers to be gentlemen. But Mary Ann had every intention of going in. She needed money but right now she needed comfort. The excise officer was well-off, weak and lonely, an easy target who she believed could offer her what she wanted. She was desperate to marry him. The village had turned against her. No one would talk to her. No man would look at her, in case their wives or mothers talked. Her voice grew louder, not angry, almost pleading: 'You can rub me down too, like you did before.'

Her dark eyes pierced his very soul, but sex was the last thing on his mind. He put his finger to his lips, signalling her to be quiet. He was worried, fearing that he would be implicated in her stepson's death.

'I am carrying your child, let me in!'

Quick-Manning had no option. He ushered her to his room, quietly bolting the door of Brookfield Cottage, his middle-class lodgings in Johnson Terrace. When he entered his small living area, furnished with just a double bed and two armchairs, she had already taken off her shawl and blouse, her firm round breasts waiting for him. She would take him again, it was easy now, like it had been with the others. He must marry her, she thought. He must, he must.

But everything went wrong for Mary Ann Cotton. Like so many female serial killers, life had dealt her a rough hand, although she never ceased to believe that one day it would all come right and she would find her just reward in life. In the end, as she kicked for life on the gallows in one of the cruellest executions in British history, all she had left were her own thoughts.

Mary Ann was born in October 1832 in the Durham pit village of Low Moorsley. Her father, miner Michael Robson, was seventeen, and her mother, Margaret, nineteen. Shortly after her birth the family moved to a two-room cottage at East Rainton, a mile away, where her father, a remote and religious man, worked at the local pit. Michael and Margaret were to have two other children, a son, Robert, and a daughter, Margaret, who died not long after her birth. Mary was a strikingly pretty child with fine dark eyes who captured the hearts of all the villagers. She grew up in the era of the Industrial Revolution; George Stephenson's locomotion; iron and steel works; the treadmill and the workhouse. Trams were finding their way on to the streets of America, reservoirs in Britain began to supply towns with clean drinking water, sewers were being built and gas light was on the way. But death was commonplace. So was sexual abuse of the young.

Mary Ann was a strict Methodist – it was the dominant religious force in the county. Her father was a disciplinarian who conducted the choir at the local church, where she attended Sunday school. When she was eight the family moved into a double-storey, terraced house in Durham Place, one of the first new streets to be built in the old farming hamlet of Murton, a mile from East

Rainton, where a coal seam had finally been tapped after five years of exploration and her father had a new job. The following year tragedy struck. Her father slipped and fell to his death down a shaft while repairing a pulley wheel. Mary Ann was profoundly affected by his death – and was fearful about the future. She believed the family would end up in the workhouse. But like so many widows in those times, her mother did not stay without a husband long. She needed a man who could earn a wage, something Mary Ann was to understand all her life. Along came pitman George Stott and Mary Ann gained a stepfather. Their relationship was cold and distant. He showed Mary Ann no love and made it plain that she was a financial burden to him. Stott, twenty-seven, was three years younger than his new wife, Margaret.

When she was sixteen Mary Ann got a job as a nursemaid to the Potter family in South Hetton. Edward Potter was a colliery manager and very important in the area. His wife, Margaret, had been bearing a child a year for many years and their house was known as the Hall. The family were all taken with Mary Ann's beauty, and so was a local curate, who reputedly fell in love with her and would watch in adoration as she took Sunday School classes. Rumours were rife that the extra lessons she took from the curate strayed from the Ten Commandments. Mary Ann left the Potters when she was nineteen to be a dressmaker – but her life at the Hall had given her a taste for better things than a pitman's cottage. She wanted to improve herself. Only her weakness for big, strong men was to lead her off the road to riches.

Late one summer's afternoon Mary Ann stood staring out of the window of the local grocery store.

'Is there anything else you need?' Mr Willis inquired, tying up the bag of flour and wiping his hands on his grubby pinafore.

'No, no, that will be all, thank you.'

Mary Ann seemed agitated as she handed the old man three pence from her purse. She constantly looked over her shoulder out of the window as he packed her shopping into a brown paper bag.

'That's a fine new dress you're wearing today, and the bonnet is new too, isn't it?' Mr Willis inquired.

Suddenly they both heard the sound of boots crunching on cobblestones.

'They're late today, aren't they?' said Willis, going to the window. Mary Ann hurried from the shop without bothering to answer. Once in the street she headed straight for the dozen or so men coming home from the pithead. They were half an hour late. Tired and blackened with coal dust, they eyed her admiringly. Sure enough, William Mowbray was among them. The tall, handsome labourer with a rolling gait and deep blue eyes caught her gaze before she looked away and crossed the road. He broke away from his mates and ran over to her side.

''Tis a fine afternoon, Mary Ann.'

'Yes, but I think there's rain on the way.'

'Could be, but I'll wager it will stay fine enough for an evening stroll across the hill.'

'Then I'd take a coat if I were you, Mr Mowbray.'

This was only the third time they had met. But Mowbray was smitten. He took a chance.

'I was thinking you might like to come for a stroll with me.'

'Shame on you, Mr Mowbray, you are so very forward.'

That night in an old shed on the hillside they made love as the rain pounded on the leaking wood and sackcloth roof. Twenty-six-year-old Mowbray was powerful. Mary Ann liked his muscular arms and strong legs. He would make a good husband and bed companion. There was plenty of work in him, he would be a good earner.

They married on 18 July 1852 at Newcastle Register Office, some twenty miles from her home. Mary Ann was nineteen and pregnant. Her chapel-going family were ashamed of her and she wed in disgrace, lying to the registrar that she was twenty-one. This was the turning point in her life. Her stepfather, George, washed his hands of her but Mowbray was besotted and promised he would give her a good life. The couple broke completely with the north-east and headed for a new beginning in the West Country. At first Mowbray got labouring work in Somerset and Cornwall, then he became a timekeeper for a railway construction company in Penzance. Over the next four years they had five children. But money was hard and Mary Ann was dissatisfied with her lot. One fine spring afternoon they returned to Murton, where Mary Ann proudly introduced her daughter, named Mary Ann after her, to her mother and stepfather. Then she announced that they had come back to live in the village. Sadly, she explained, her other four children had died of gastric fever and other stomach disorders.

In April 1857, things were looking up. Mowbray was a storekeeper at the local colliery and Mary Ann had another child, Margaret Jane. The following year along came yet another daughter, Isabella. But Margaret Jane later died and so too did little Mary Ann . . . both from gastric fever. Surviving Isabella was to live longer with her mother than any of her children. Then in the autumn of 1861 along came another baby, also named Margaret Jane. By now the Mowbrays had set up home in a pub, next door to Mary Ann's mother and stepfather. But things began to go from bad to worse. There were daily rows about money and in the end Mowbray went to sea as a stoker on the steamer *Newburn*, trading from Sunderland. He got the job because the master was Mary Ann's uncle. Mary Ann meanwhile did what she did best, had children. She gave birth to her first son, John Robert, and moved to Sunderland to be nearer her husband. But John was dead from gastric fever within a year. Death never seemed far from Mary Ann.

By now Mowbray was losing a lot of his early strength. His sexual prowess was diminishing. He was simply tired. One day he arrived back at the family's lodgings on a crutch, after injuring his foot on the *Newburn*. He couldn't work any more and the money ran out. Another chapter in Mary Ann's life was closing. She hadn't expected her life to turn out like this.

Late one January night in 1865, a few weeks later, Dr Richard Gammage was called to Mary Ann's home. He found Mowbray suffering from gastric fever. As the hours passed his condition grew worse. Mary Ann was distraught when Gammage told her to expect the worst. He put his arm around her to comfort her.

'How many more of my loved ones must I lose?' she sobbed. Gammage was profoundly moved. Mary Ann was shaking uncontrollably. He had never seen anyone so emotionally affected. The next morning handsome ship's stoker Mowbray suffered an attack of diarrhoea so violent that he died in a matter of hours. The following day Gammage passed their house and had a mind to drop in and comfort Mary Ann, who by now must be in the depths of despair. He looked in the window and what he saw almost choked him.

Mary Ann, a widow at thirty-two, was singing and pirouetting in front of a mirror, holding a new dress before her. That day she had received £35 insurance money from British Prudential.

Mary Ann opened the windows and breathed in the sea air. She loved the sound of the gulls and watched them drift down from the cliffs towards the coal ships in the harbour. She had rented a ground floor room, next to the Lord Seaham Inn in Seaham, a coal port five miles down the coast from Sunderland. She turned and looked at herself in the mirror. Not bad for thirty-two, she thought. But she must hurry, he would be coming down the road soon. Her daughters Isabella, now six, and Margaret Jane, aged three, watched their mother straighten her cap and ruffle her petticoat.

'Where are you going, Mummy?' asked Isabella.

'Never you mind, look after your sister, and cut that cloth like I told you. I've got to finish Mrs Evans's dress by Thursday,' Mary Ann answered, clsoing the door on the two girls and hurrying out into the street. She spent a full twenty minutes walking up and down. Finally she saw him turn the corner and come towards her.

Joseph Nattrass, twenty-eight, was big and strong, just how she liked her men. The labourer from Ryhope, near Sunderland, who was staying in a house across the street from her, was engaged to a local girl, Mary Thubron. Mary Ann had watched them together. She was pretty but lacked fire, she thought. Mary Ann would soon show him what real passion was. She headed towards him, catching his glance for a second as he doffed his hat to her.

Two days later she stood naked before him in his small room as a shaft of moonlight cast her shadow over his expectant body on the narrow, wooden bed. It was a dalliance he would not live to regret.

The Sunderland Infirmary, House of Recovery for the Cure of Contagious Fever, was a depressing place. Bed-sheets were changed only once a fortnight and patients' linen every four days. It was overcrowded and there were deaths daily, even among the nurses themselves. Mary

Ann decided to make the best of it. After all, she needed the money. But for the first time in her life she felt really free. Little Margaret Jane had died of gastric fever after being ill for two days and Isabella was now in the care of her grandmother, Mary Ann's mother, at her new home in New Seaham. Of Mary Ann's nine children, eight were dead. Her only regret, however, was that her relationship with Nattrass hadn't come to anything. Sex with him had been good. She thought he had wanted her desperately . . . but he had still gone ahead and married Mary Thubron.

Mary Ann was paid a shilling a day plus board and lodging at the House of Recovery. She washed out her ward with arsenic and soap at seven o'clock every morning and served breakfast at eight. She drank beer and gruel along with the men, women and children patients and bathed when she could in the public baths, with the patients who were taken there in cabs when enough money was made available. Doctors and nurses were impressed with her. She showed the sick and dying tenderness and compassion and she had a good understanding of medicines, although she was always keen to learn more.

George Ward lay on the small, sagging bed in the crowded corridor, not caring if he lived or died. The handsome, well-built, thirty-two-year-old engineer was drenched in sweat. He could barely raise his hand. Someone was mopping his brow, now wiping his chest, now his legs, now . . . He managed to open his eyes, just for a moment, and saw an angel of mercy. Sadly it was an angel of death.

On 28 August 1865, with her husband William in his grave just seven months, Mary Ann married discharged fever patient Ward at St Peter's Church, Monkwearmouth, on the north side of the Wear in Sunderland. It was her first church marriage. Two others were to follow. Here now was an opportunity to better herself. A new beginning. This was no coal-face worker or labourer. Here was a man with proper training. But she was to be disappointed. Ward was a poor lover, he had not got his strength back properly and his libido was low. Mary Ann did everything she could to arouse him but it was hopeless. He was frustrated with himself and she was just frustrated. All her life she had been pinned down by children. Now here was a time of release but it hadn't worked out. Ward was still unable to work. By November that year he was receiving four shillings a week parish relief and Mary Ann did not have enough food in the house. Worse, she hated housework and could not afford a woman to clean for her. By December things took a turn for the worse. Muscular Ward began to fall ill again. He suffered nose bleeds and stomach pains. Doctors were called and leeches applied to his body, a common cure at that time. Medical opinions differed and Mary Ann seemed to resent questions from the visiting surgeons. Ward began to suffer paralysis of the hands and feet. On 21 October, the following year, he was buried, aged just thirty-three. In the Sunderland cemetery register the word fever was pencilled in by his name. He had died with excruciating stomach pains, just like other members of Mary Ann's family.

Shipwright James Robinson left the bedroom and shut the door behind him. The doctor was still by his dead wife Hannah's bedside and his five children were downstairs. God, how would he tell them? How would he look after them?

A few days later, in that cold, blustery November of 1866, he advertised for a housekeeper at his home in the Sunderland suburb of Pallion. He hadn't taken to the first woman who applied, she was fat and far too bossy for her own good. The second woman seemed just the job. She had worked as a nurse, and could make dresses too. She was a good Methodist who lived near by and was damn pretty. Robinson liked the saucy twinkle in her eye.

A few weeks later, Mary Ann stood at the door holding Robinson's ten-month-old son John in her arms as he went off to work at the shipyard on the Wear. Things were looking up for her again. Robinson had money, he was even buying his own house, and she liked him. She had packed the shipwright cheese and pickle sandwiches and an onion pie for lunch. Robinson was pleased that he had hired her. He turned and smiled at her once more and she waved back, clutching little John as if he were her own. Sadly, because of his own lust, it would take him too long to accept that Mary Ann had no time for children . . . or housework. One week after James had eaten his onion pie by the side of a new wooden dredger, John was dead, killed by gastric fever.

They buried him at Bishopwearmouth cemetery the day before Christmas Eve. Rain dribbled on the little coffin lid as his brothers, sisters and father watched him being lowered into the ground. Mary Ann stood a few paces back, not wanting to interfere in the family's personal grief. That evening Robinson was distraught. The children were in bed and he sat by the fire with his head in his hands. Mary Ann came to his side and put her hand on his shoulder.

'First my wife and now my son. God, what have I done to deserve this?' he sobbed.

Mary Ann squeezed his shoulder, then knelt and stroked his head of fine, grey hair. He pulled her to him and she kissed his brow. Robinson felt fire and anger. She melted to him like honey on a warm spoon as his strong arm tightened around her waist and they rolled on to the stone floor together, almost in slow motion. By March 1867 Mary Ann was pregnant, but again her best-laid plans were set adrift by circumstance.

Her fifty-four-year-old mother had fallen ill and her stepfather simply couldn't cope with Isabella, now nine. Mary Ann went to look after them, but she was carrying Robinson's child and he was besotted with her. She must keep her hold on him. Her life now was the best it had ever been. Robinson was a careful, hard-working man. He had money in the Post Office Savings Bank and was buying his house through a building society. Mary Ann had moved up a class.

'I've seen death before and I'm afraid I see it now on my mother's face,' Mary Ann told neighbours who were inquiring after her mother's health over the bars of coal tar soap in the corner shop.

'But the doctor seemed quite pleased with your mother's progress,' said Mrs Margaret Bradley, who lived next door to the Stott family home.

'Doctors, what do they know?' Mary Ann replied.

Mary Ann hurried from the grocery store and headed for the chemist, who sold her half an ounce of arsenic to dilute with water so that she could scrub her mother's house down. That day she and her mother argued. Her mother was tired; she told Mary Ann she needed a long rest. Mary Ann, she said, would have to stay and look after her and the child. It was her duty. But Mary Ann's mind was on Robinson.

Nine days later, on 15 March, her mother died after suffering excruciating stomach cramps and sickness.

'Never darken my doors again,' screamed George Stott as his stepdaughter hurried Isabella out of the house. Neighbours had told him that on the very same day his wife died, Mary Ann had taken some of her mother's clothes and bedlinen from the house. Had Mary Ann murdered her own mother?

For Isabella, time sadly was running out. And for Robinson's remaining children, too, the future looked bleak. The besotted shipwright was desperate for Mary Ann's return. No one had ever made love to him the way she did. He cared about nothing else except sleeping with her. He would do anything for her . . . almost anything. But when it came to money he could not change his ways, and that fact probably saved him from a death sentence. He tried to persuade Mary Ann that they had to be cautious and save. She asked him about insurance for the children in case they died. He told her it was a waste of money, they had enough in the building society just in case the worst happened. But he was lying. Something in him would not let him tell her that he had insured them. Behind the scenes his three sisters were nagging him about Mary Ann. For some reason they did not like her. Perhaps it was because she was a poor manager in the house. Robinson had told them that his first wife could make a penny go as far as Mary Ann could a shilling. Funny in a way, he thought, only men seemed to like her. He had seen his workmates and men who lived around him look at her in that special way. A sort of longing. He didn't blame them, he wanted them to envy him. But he was jealous of her. They had better keep their hands off.

It was a depressing April. Things hadn't been going too well at the shipyard, work had fallen off. Robinson was tired and worried as he slowly walked down the road to his home. He wasn't much of a drinking man, otherwise he would have seen the night away in the corner pub. He had dependants and he cared about them. He needed to keep his money for them. He was a good man. Too good for Mary Ann, but he didn't know it.

Mary Ann almost ran to him as he came through the

door. James, six, and eight-year-old Elizabeth were ill. The doctor had been called to see them earlier that day. Robinson hurried to their bedsides. They were rolling about in agony and foaming at the mouth.

'For God's sake give them something to drink!' he almost screamed at Mary Ann.

'Every time they drink they are sick!' she shouted back, her eyes brimming with tears. 'It is best to give them nothing.'

Robinson hurried to the stove, where he found some broth. Filling two cups, he tried to force his children to swallow. They did their best for him, both clutching his arm, but they retched.

'It is in the house, my Isabella will get this too,' said Mary Ann to him later by the hearth. He had never seen her so physically upset. She seemed to be burning up; she told him she felt weak. 'I'm sure I have the fever,' she said.

That night Robinson wiped her forehead with a damp cloth as she tossed and turned in their bed.

'Let me send for the doctor,' he begged.

'No, no. I am stronger than the children. Just see to them.'

Robinson's son James was buried on 21 April, Elizabeth five days later and Isabella on 2 May. The cause of death for them all was put down to gastric fever. Through those long hard days of death and funerals Mary Ann was beside herself with grief. She was critical of herself and sobbed in Robinson's arms, saying she had failed him. Robinson begged her not to take her own life. They had their unborn child to think about.

On 11 August 1867 they married, against the wishes of Robinson's sisters, who were suspicious of the deaths of the children. At the wedding in Bishopwearmouth church, near the old Sunderland infirmary, Mary Ann signed her name as Mowbray and not Ward as she should have done. Days after the ceremony she hired a woman to do the housework for her.

The newly-wed couple's baby girl was born on 29 November and baptized Mary Isabella on 18 February. She was buried on 1 March . . . a victim of gastric fever. Robinson had some doubts but refused to let his mind dwell on them. But his doubts grew as Mary Ann kept niggling at him to get himself insured. He joked that he was fit and well and would outlive her. One evening their difference of opinion exploded into a full-scale row when Robinson discovered that his wife had tried to insure him without his knowledge.

A few months later in 1869 Robinson stood before a desk in Mr Trewhitt's building society. 'There has been some kind of mistake,' he told the clerk.

'Obviously, but it is not ours,' said the thin, balding man peering over the top of his gold-rimmed spectacles. The Robinson family's paying-in book showed several ten shilling entries – but the building society had no record of them.

'My wife paid you the instalments on the house and that is all there is to it!' stormed Robinson, his face so twisted with rage that the clerk felt quite frightened and had no wish to pursue the matter in the dusty, dark office. He would leave it to the police if he had to.

Robinson marched out, slamming the door so hard that the bell almost came off the wall. He told Mary Ann to withhold all further payments. But by October he was worried. Trewhitt's threatened legal action and insisted on payment for the arrears of £5. Robinson, not wanting any scandal, told his wife to settle the bill. A week later, however, he received a letter from his brother-in-law. Mary Ann had been trying to borrow £5 from a loan office and had used his name as a guarantor. It was the last straw. Perhaps his sisters had been right all along. He questioned his two remaining children and Mary Ann's fate was sealed. They told him she had been sending them to the pawnbrokers with clothes, jewellery and ornaments from the house.

Mary Ann pleaded with her husband to save her marriage. She swore she would get the £5 from her stepfather. But Robinson was adamant. They would have to separate. That night when he came home, she was gone . . . along with his youngest daughter, aged three. For a while he sat sobbing with his remaining five-year-old son in his arms. The next day he discovered that his other building society account, at Mr Wayman's, was £7 in arrears and that his Post Office savings had been drawn out. He never spoke to Mary Ann again during their lives.

A few weeks later, one dismal November afternoon, curtains quivered along the street of shipyard terraced houses as two solitary figures slowly made their way to number 14 in the drizzle. Mary Ann, with Robinson's three-year-old daughter, stood quietly at the door waiting in vain for an answer. Robinson, unbeknown to her, had moved in with one of his sisters. She had returned to ask forgiveness. Slowly she turned, and forcing her head up, walked back down the road with her child in front as peering eyes followed them from the windows. She had no money and no hope. Mary Ann was to remember that moment until the day she died. The road ahead now led to months of debauchery. Mary Ann lived in a room with a sailor, then stole his possessions when he returned to sea. A stream of men followed who were always pleased to leave a ten-shilling note or even a pound on her dressing table. They enjoyed her and she enjoyed them in her way. It was all purely functional. She needed the money. But this was not the life she was seeking. Finally, she managed to find a job with retired banker and Quaker Edward Backhouse in Sunderland. He had established a refuge for 'fallen women', and was a pillar of society. He liked Mary Ann and gave her a job in the laundry of his fine house set in its own parkland. Everyone who met her liked her. She even went to chapel on Sundays.

Then, at the end of 1869, Mary Ann called on a friend in Sunderland with Robinson's three-year-old child. She said she was just popping out to post a letter for ten minutes, leaving her daughter behind. She never returned. In the early hours of New Year's Day 1870, Robinson came home to his new lodgings from the night shift to find Mary Ann's friend and his child. He broke down in tears, hugging his daughter. As the toddler began a new life with her father, Mary Ann was finding a new life too – back in Newcastle.

She was desperate to start again. She had been caught

out by Robinson and she regretted it. In a way she missed him, his steadiness, his security. In the Victorian world of hardship for the lower classes he had offered her the chance to live more comfortably than her upbringing. Now the Victorian siren was ready to cast her net again. She had to survive, and the people who crossed her path were just pawns in the game of life. A new chance came when she bumped into an old friend in the street, Margaret Cotton. They had been friends in their teens in South Hetton.

Margaret's thirty-seven-year-old brother Frederick had faced tragedy. His wife Adelaide, thirty-four, had recently died of consumption and only two of his four children were alive. His two daughters had died from a mixture of fatal illnesses, including typhus fever. Frederick was lonely and unable to cope. Margaret had left her job as a laundry maid to comfort her brother and help him look after his two remaining sons, Frederick and Charles. Days after meeting Mary Ann, Margaret took her home to meet vulnerable Frederick. He was easy prey. The family lived in the small mining community of North Walbottle, Northumberland. Pit worker Frederick was immediately struck by the gentleness of Mary Ann, whom he saw as a quiet, pretty and unassuming woman. His sister and others spoke well of her. She was a God-fearing chapel-goer and law-abiding citizen. And there was something else – a sort of mischief about her. He wondered if she would make a good bed partner and it wasn't long before he found out. One morning when Margaret had taken the boys shopping, there was a knock at the door.

Frederick, who had been on the late shift the night before, rose from his bed in his nightgown. It was Mary Ann, come to clean. Minutes later she was in his bed too.

On 25 March 1870, Margaret was writhing on her bed in the Cotton house, racked with stomach pains. She died the next day. With a little more imagination than usual during those times, the doctor wrote pleuropneumonia on the death certificate and not gastric fever. The way was clear now for Mary Ann, and by April she was pregnant with Cotton's child. But she did not move in with Frederick. She was irritated that she had not been able to climb up the social scale and now she had other thoughts in her mind. She had been told about a doctor who needed a housekeeper in the village of Spennymoor, twenty miles away.

Dr Heffernan was a naturalized German who lived in a two-storey house. He was neither handsome or ugly. The small, rounded man had a kindly face and, just like Cotton, liked what he saw when Mary Ann arrived on his doorstep. For a while all worked well. The house was kept tidy; even his medicine room where he kept his arsenic bottles was made spick and span. But Mary Ann had other plans. She began to hire villagers to help with the cleaning, paying them with food from the larder. She was growing fatter with Cotton's child and that irritated her. Her life was easier and she didn't want the doctor to know that she was pregnant. But that wasn't the only thing that ruffled her feathers. The doctor didn't seem to notice her sexuality. She was earning good money, and with her dressmaking skills was able to wear some eye-catching silk skirts. Heffernan, however, was unimpressed and secretly irritated. He had heard whispers that she had been having sex with tradesmen who called at his house. One night as he lay in his bed she knocked at the door, asking if he would like some warm milk. He stared over the top of his book at the door handle in the flickering candlelight. It gently moved down and he held his breath, wondering if he had locked it, half-hoping he had. The door was locked. Mary Ann was not used to being rejected. Two days later the doctor had severe stomach cramp, then again the following week. He became suspicious and Mary Ann was fired. A week after she left, Heffernan discovered that a gold watch, a ring and some cash were missing.

There was only one route left for Mary Ann – back to North Walbottle and Frederick Cotton. When he married her on 17 September 1870, he didn't just sign the wedding certificate, he signed his own death warrant. Mary Ann married bigamously; she had never divorced Robinson. She signed her name as Mowbray, that of her first late husband. A few days after the wedding she insured the lives of Cotton's two sons with the Prudential. By now people were beginning to turn against her. Her reputation as a maneater was growing daily, and they were suspicious of her motives in marrying Frederick. One day she rowed with a family in the street. The following week their pigs were found poisoned. Mary Ann was blamed in village gossip. But the fact that wherever Mary Ann went death seemed to follow still did not arouse much suspicion. In the late 1800s people who died were readily given death certificates stating the case as gastric fever, a common complaint which had symptoms similar to arsenic poisoning. It was an age when hygiene was almost non-existent. Bugs and vermin lived in houses where food was left rotting and toilets were just holes in the ground. Poverty was commonplace, and overworked doctors did not have time to perform autopsies when they were suspicious. Most people were poor, with no hope of inheritance, so there was no motive for murder. Thus Mary Ann got away with being a serial killer for twenty years.

In January 1871 Mary Ann gave birth to Robert Robson Cotton. By now she hated the small village where she lived and yearned for big town living. Perhaps there, where there was money and trade, she would find someone who would give her the life she deserved. She was tired of Cotton. He was boring in bed and again times were hard. Then she found out, quite by chance, that Joseph Nattrass had returned to West Auckland. By the summer the Cotton family were on their way to West Auckland too, where Frederick had managed to find a job as a hewer at the same pit as Nattrass.

Mary Ann walked slowly down the road from her home in Johnson Terrace. It was a fine sunny day and she was wearing her best blue silk dress. She had seen Nattrass from her bedroom window several times and knew he would pass her on his way home from the pithead. She stopped and looked into the window of the grocery store. Nattrass was tired as he turned the corner and headed for his lodgings. Life had dealt him a bad hand. His wife had recently died and he was finding it hard to make ends meet. He glanced at the woman staring into the store as he passed her by. There was something familiar about the way she wore her bonnet.

'Hello, Joseph,' she said, turning to him.

In that moment all the fire from the old days was rekindled.

A week later in the darkness of his tiny room Nattrass held her close and promised to marry her. Frederick Cotton was on the road to his Maker. Two months after Mary Ann moved to Johnson Terrace, her husband was dead from gastric fever, aged thirty-nine. It was 19 September 1871, two days after their wedding anniversary. Mary Ann dressed in black and mourned for three months – then Nattrass moved in as her lodger.

Nattrass adored the late Cotton's three sons, especially ten-year-old Frederick. He was a polite, sensitive and trusting boy who missed his father terribly. He was trying to make the most of his new, lonely life. He desperately tried to make Mary Ann love him, but it was impossible. Mary Ann loved no one except herself and the boys were in the way. Often Frederick would cry himself to sleep in his bed at night. Nattrass befriended him and little Charles, aged seven. He would sing them songs from his own childhood and stroked the head of fourteen-month-old Robert. When he pointed out bruises on Charlie's body, Mary Ann would tell him the lad had been fighting with Frederick again. Nattrass believed he was bonding a family and Mary Ann seemed pleased. But sadly for the well-built coal worker, someone else higher up in the social order had arrived on the scene, Excise Officer John Quick-Manning. He had gone down with smallpox at his lodgings, Brookfield Cottage, a minute's walk from Mary Ann's home. With her nursing experience, Mary Ann was called in to look after him.

From the moment Quick-Manning, weak and ill, set eyes on her walking across the room to his bedside, he was spellbound. She talked softly to him as she dabbed his sores with a warm cloth and iodine. He grew better and looked forward to her visits, when she would still rub him down with the warm cloth. Soon they were lovers. In the three weeks between 10 March and 1 April 1872, death tore through Mary Ann's home. Ten-year-old Frederick went down with fever. Mary Ann never left his side. One morning he asked for his school cap, and he had it on him when he was laid out in his coffin hours later. A few days after his death Mary Ann collected £5.15s from Prudential Insurance.

Nattrass, meanwhile, had struggled to do his job for weeks. Workmates had held him steady as he retched and tried to be sick. Finally he was so weak that he just lay in bed. While he stared at the ceiling, baby Robert died from convulsions put down to teething problems. Mary Ann refused to have her son buried and kept his body in the house. When neighbours asked her why, she told them Nattrass would soon die and she could only take one funeral at a time. As Nattrass tossed and turned with pain in his bed she sent out for stockings and wax to lay him out. Friends who stopped by would find her sitting by his bedside; she would not let any one else nurse him.

Nattrass suffered wild convulsions and friends would watch her hold him down. One day they did help, when he crashed his head against the wall and bent back his toes in cramp. The tough miner had built up a tolerance to arsenic. He should have died days before. Mary Ann would only leave his side to prepare food for herself and to discipline Charlie, who by now was taking the brunt of her frustrations. She would repeatedly beat him with a miner's belt. Finally, Nattrass died. Two days later Mary Ann collected his insurance money and two weeks later the doctor confirmed that she was pregnant with Quick-Manning's child. The fact that Nattrass and the children died and were buried within a month did not cause much of a stir in the town. After all, a newborn child of the working classes had just one chance in two of reaching the age of five.

Cotton and Nattrass had left Mary Ann all they had, but that wasn't much and she received only 1s.6d a week relief money for her remaining stepson Charlie. There was gossip now in the village that she and Quick-Manning would marry, but the weeks slipped by. In Mary Ann's mind, only one thing now stood in the way of her next marriage – Charlie. He had been spared so far because she had been too busy poisoning the rest of the household to have time to deal with him.

The little doorbell of Townsend's chemist shop tinkled as Charlie Cotton wandered in clutching a piece of paper.

'What can I do for you, young 'un?' asked John Townsend, peering down at the lad. The boy passed the piece of paper to him. The note from Mary Ann was for two pennyworth of arsenic and soft soap.

'What's this for?' inquired Townsend.

'To clean the bedstead with, sir. It's got bugs in it.'

The chemist refused to serve Charlie and sent him back home. The 1851 Arsenic Act stated that arsenic was not to be sold to anyone under twenty-one. Mary Ann was angry when Charlie returned home empty-handed and dispatched a neighbour, Mary Dodds, who helped her with the household chores, to buy the poison. Townsend was just shutting up shop and hurriedly gave her the mixture, containing around 300 grains of arsenic. Just three grains would kill an adult. But he was patient enough to record the sale in his pocket book. When Mrs Dodds returned, she and Mary Ann scrubbed the bedstead but didn't find any bugs. What was left of the mixture was put in an old pint jug and stored in a cupboard.

There was one last chance for Charlie, when Mary Ann tried to get him into the workhouse through public relief officer Thomas Riley.

A week later Charlie died alone on the sofa, racked with stomach pains. It was a sad end to a sad little life. He was a pale and sickly boy who never got enough food. He was regularly beaten by Mary Ann, who would often pull him about the house by his hair.She would lock him out in the street for as long as ten hours – or shut him in a room with no food for a whole day. When he cried for his father, Mary Ann would punch him in the ear. When Riley had seen Charlie less than a week earlier, although he had looked white and thin he was full of energy. Riley became suspicious, remembering how the other children had died, one after the other, within a month. He went to the police and then to Dr Kilburn.

'I knew the boy had been ill with gastro-enteritis. My assistant, Chalmers, saw him three times in the week, as I did myself only yesterday,' said Kilburn.

The doctor thought about the matter for a few moments. 'In the circumstances, I'll withhold the death certificate and ask permission to carry out a post-mortem,' he said.

The first intimation Mary Ann had that for once everything was not going to plan was when the insurance agent refused to hand over any money for Charlie until he had seen the death certificate.

'I shall get one from Dr Kilburn,' Mary Ann told him confidently.

Even after Kilburn had refused to give her the certificate, it did not dawn on her that she was in serious trouble until the coroner asked her to attend an inquest the following day at the Rose and Crown, next door to her house. But the coroner acted too quickly, and Kilburn had only an hour in which to conduct his post-mortem before the inquest began. In the short time available to the doctor he had been unable to find any clue that might indicate Charlie had died of anything but natural causes. Now practically destitute and with no help from Quick-Manning, Mary Ann made it clear to everyone that she could not afford to pay for Charlie to be buried. He was placed in a pauper's grave.

After the inquest, Mary Ann thought she was in the clear, but she had not reckoned with Kilburn, who had left the Rose and Crown feeling that he had been made to look a fool for having supported Riley without any evidence to prove that Mary Ann had killed her stepson. Like Riley, he was now convinced that she had poisoned him, and was determined not to let the matter rest.

Fortunately he had kept most of the contents of the body, and after undertaking Reinsch's test, he found enough arsenic to call in the police. The following morning a superintendent, accompanied by two sergeants, arrived at Mary Ann's house with an arrest warrant for the murder of Charles Edward Cotton. Mary Ann said nothing as she was taken to Bishop Auckland, where she languished in a cell for more than a month. She finally appeared before magistrates, where she was remanded.

Her infamy soon spread as the many suspicious deaths in her past were investigated, and she was jeered outside court. Children ran ahead of her burly police bodyguards letting others know she was coming. Mothers snatched their youngsters from her path and her name was used to conjure up a bogeywoman to frighten children into obedience. People made up rhymes about her, and the black shawl she wore, fashionable at the time, was not worn any more by women in Durham.

The bodies of Charlie, Nattrass, ten-year-old Frederick Cotton and baby Robert were exhumed.

In all of them enough arsenic was found to make it almost certain that Mary Ann would soon be meeting the hangman. But that wasn't all. Now information came to light from police inquiries into Mary Ann's life before West Auckland. On 1 October a damning police report was sent to the Home Office. She was suspected of being responsible for twenty deaths: her mother, three husbands, fifteen children and lodger Nattrass. On 15 October half a dozen medical men, headed by Dr Kilburn, arrived at the St Helen's, Auckland, graveyard with Thomas Riley. Their mission was to dig up the body of Mary Ann's fourth husband Frederick, who had died thirteen months earlier. They couldn't find him. None of the graves were marked, and they were as thick and close as furrows in a lea field.

The legal proceedings, meanwhile, had to be postponed because of Mary Ann's condition. Her baby by Quick-Manning was due in two months. As she sat in jail she found herself once again down and penniless. Prison officers felt sorry for the quiet, frail killer in the black shawl who constantly maintained her innocence. Her face grew paler under her tied-back black hair. Her eyes were dead as she stared at the floor in thought, and her clothes, hanging in a closet for court appearance after court appearance, grew tattier. She tried to sell her furniture through a male friend to raise money but he pocketed most of the cash. In the legal profession there was some concern that she was not being properly defended. At one stage the absence of a defender at committal hearings was deplored by the prosecution.

Meanwhile police and doctors were putting together the jigsaw of how someone like Mary Ann had been able to murder so many people without being detected. She was hardly able to put together a letter, let alone read a book on poisons.

They decided that her knowledge came from being a housewife who knew that soft soap mixed with arsenic was the cure for most household bugs and diseases. Properly administered it could even be used as medicine. It was readily available from chemists, as were arsenic-impregnated flypapers. As a poison it killed faster on an empty stomach. This was why Mary Ann had so often refused to give her victims food or let anyone else near them. But why did she commit murder time after time? Behind the scenes the judiciary surmised that she did it mostly for the insurance money. But many pointed out that not all her victims were insured, and when they were the amounts she received were hardly worth the risk.

People who knew her believed that sex was one of the driving forces behind the murders. No sooner had she found one man than she wanted another. It was true, police officers admitted on reading her dossier, that she had a robust sex life. But Mary Ann had never confided in any one about that. In Victorian times it was frowned on for a woman to talk about sex openly. Mary Ann was a loner. Women like her were loners. They had lovers, neighbours, acquaintances and people who worked for them or with them, but they did not have friends. Even their lovers were not friends, for they never shared their innermost secrets.

This does not explain how she could kill off nearly all her own children with no remorse, but, like most female serial killers, Mary Ann had no feeling for anyone. Her own desires were paramount. Her victims were killed not for love but for gain, either monetary or because they stood in the way of her survival. Each victim was a chapter in her life. When she got bored she needed to find pleasure from new sex and gain. Not fortunes. Just a way to survive in a world where women were second-class citizens. Mary Ann was a cold, cruel and heartless creature who had blotted out lives without the slightest compunction. But even so, not even she deserved her terrible death.

Mary Ann gave birth to a baby girl, and days after she was born the legal process started in earnest. Early on Friday, 21 February 1873, carrying her baby Margaret in her arms, she was taken by train to Bishop Auckland to face magistrates. All along the route people lined stations, straining to catch a glimpse of her as she sat breast-feeding her child draped in a black-and-white checked shawl and pink satin cap. In the courtroom she breast-fed the child before passing her to a nurse. The Press benches were packed and all the reporters commented on her appearance. She had lost weight and it suited her. The evidence against her for the murder of Joseph Nattrass was overwhelming. In the absence of good legal advice she refused to talk, believing it was her best defence. The magistrates committed her for trial at the Durham Assizes.

Mary Ann Cotton came to trial the following month. Leading for the prosecution was forty-year-old Charles Russell, who was later to add to his substantial reputation by his stirring defence of poisoner Mrs Maybrick in 1889.

He was also to serve the nation as Attorney-General under Prime Minister Gladstone. The defence was carried out by Thomas Campbell Foster, a Leeds lawyer who had been approached by the court because Mary Ann had no money to pay for legal representation. Foster's experience and considerable courtroom expertise could not help much in a case such as hers, where the evidence was so overwhelming, but he was to fight gallantly to defend her plea of not guilty to the murder of Charles Edward Cotton, the first and only case to be heard.

The courtroom was packed before 10am every day. There was so much interest in the case that admission was by ticket only. Hundreds stood outside all day waiting for a glimpse of Mary Ann. When she was led into the dock a ripple of whispers broke out in the court. She looked pale and worn and supported herself with a walking-stick. Her black shawl and gown were tatty and her hair brushed forward for the first time. One by one, the prosecution paraded its witnesses before the all-male jury, and each one of them banged another nail in Mary Ann's coffin. Neighbour Mary Dodds told the court about buying the soft soap and arsenic from the chemist. Another cleaner told how Mary Ann had physically ill-treated Charlie in her presence. Mary Ann, she said, had deliberately kept him in a half-starved condition. Riley related to the court how Mary Ann had told him that the boy was in the way, preventing her from marrying Quick-Manning. The combined effect of this evidence was not conclusive, but the results of the post-mortems were irrefutable. Campbell Foster, defending, did his best to throw an element of doubt over the findings by getting Dr Kilburn to admit that arsenic was sometimes found in graveyards, and could have impregnated the corpses. The jury was visibly unimpressed, so he revealed how green pigment in wallpaper contained a large amount of arsenic. Was it not possible, he argued, that the green wallpaper in Mary Ann's bedroom had thrown off deadly fumes and had slowly poisoned the boy? Or could it not be that particles of the paper floating in the air had been breathed in by him? At this point, the judge, Mr Justice Archibald, interrupted, saying that the argument for the defence was so speculative that it was hardly worth asking the question. All the defence could extract from Dr Kilburn that was of any value was his admittance that the dead boy would have been susceptible to disease as he was delicate. The gallows moved closer for Mary Ann when the jury heard that arsenic had been found in little Charlie's stomach, bowels, liver, heart, lungs and kidneys.

Campbell Foster knew that whatever tactics he tried would be completely negated by the evidence of other post-mortems. He argued that the evidence relating to those deaths was inadmissible, as Mary Ann was being tried only for the death of Charlie. Mr Justice Archibald overruled him and from then on the verdict was a foregone conclusion.

At 3.50pm the twelve men of the jury retired to consider their verdict, and a bigamy case involving a local man with three wives was started in the court. But at sixteen minutes to five they returned. Mary Ann was led back and stood clutching the dock rail.

'Do you find the prisoner, Mary Ann Cotton, guilty or not guilty of poisoning?' asked the clerk of the court.

'Guilty,' answered Tom Greener from Darlington.

'As so you all say?'

'Yes.'

Mary Ann staggered in the dock as Mr Justice Archibald put on the black cap and the clerk asked her if she had anything to say on why the death sentence should not be passed. She muttered a faint reply protesting her innocence. As the judge ruled that her body be buried in the precincts of Durham Gaol, she collapsed and was carried out of the court. Before the judge left he agreed with the prosecution that the other charges be left on the file. Mary Ann's baby girl by Quick-Manning was taken to her death cell, where a cot had been hastily moved in. During the following few weeks Mary Ann's thoughts were focused on pleas for clemency sent to the Home Secretary. They were all rejected. She had been given the women warders' retiring room. It was well-lit with a south-facing window and had a crackling log fire. She had a table, chairs, a stool, an iron bedstead and the old wooden cot. The walls were covered in pretty paper and there were books to read. She was respectful to her gaolers but talked little. Her letters and thoughts were centred on her hatred for those people who had testified against her. To the end she protested her innocence and was to finish one letter to an old acquaintance with the words:

> 'I shall try to put my trust in God As you knone I
> Wons did And ther was non on Earth happyer then

> I wos then but He says he Will not Leave us in trouble he says if We Aske in faithe it shall be given in troubles I Will not leav th All Mine enemys Whispers together against me even against me do they imagine this evil So no more from A frendless Woman no I may say is forsaken by the World, but I hope not by God.'

As the time drew near for her execution Mary Ann would pray aloud as she lay in her bed. She would shout to God to protect her child. The two women gaolers who were constantly with her would watch with tears in their eyes as she bounced the baby on her knee and breast-fed her. Her daughter was taken from her five days before her execution. It was a distressing moment for the officials in the room. Mary Ann clung on to little Margaret, whom she had wrapped in a piece of her own, torn-up shawl. There were 150 applications to adopt her and the authorities had picked a West Auckland couple.

On 24 March 1873, Mary Ann rose at 4am. William Calcraft, the public executioner, was already at the gaol. What followed was like something out of a nightmare. Calcraft was not one of the latter-day types of executioner such as Pierpoint, who always tried to hang his victims as quickly and painlessly as possible. Calcraft was a judicial murderer whose rough methods had already led to a number of distressing scenes on the scaffold. Sometimes he completely bungled the job and was forced to grab the legs of someone he had just hanged and swing on them until they were dead. On the day of Mary Ann's execution he was to excel himself.

Calcraft had been appointed executioner for London and Middlesex on 4 April 1829, at a weekly salary of a guinea with a supplement of a guinea for every execution he carried out. He was born at Baddow near Chelmsford in 1800, and had come to his trade through once selling meat pies in the streets during public executions. He met executioners James Foxen and Thomas Cheshire, who told him there was a market for the teeth of corpses because the landed gentry wanted real teeth in their dentures. Calcraft offered to pull them out. Foxen and Cheshire were impressed. Then one day Calcraft volunteered to help Foxen at a double execution in Lincoln. The offer was accepted and he did the job well. He was immediately employed to flog juvenile offenders at Newgate. With these qualifications under his belt he later applied for the vacant position of hangman when Foxen died. Calcraft, a quiet and respectable-looking man, married with two young sons, got the job. One of his first tasks was to hang a boy of nine for setting fire to a house. He did it with the brutality that was to be his hallmark. Among his early and infamous victims were body-snatchers John Bishop and Thomas Head. But Calcraft could never get it right. Slow death from strangulation was to become his trade mark. He arrived, a surly and sininster-looking old man of seventy-three, to execute Mary Ann. He had long grey hair and a beard and was scruffily dressed in a black suit with a tall hat. He looked at Mary Ann with glassy-eyed indifference.

That fateful morning Mary Ann refused breakfast but sipped a cup of tea at 5.30. She looked out of her iron-barred window at the grey-blue sky for a few moments, then returned to her bed and prayed for her baby, her last legal husband, Robinson, whom she seemed to have missed terribly, and her stepfather. Suddenly the cell door was thrown open and the officials shuffled in. A leather belt was strapped around her arms and chest and she was led sobbing to the gallows in the east wing of Durham Gaol.

At ten minutes to eight o'clock, Calcraft placed her on the platform as she shook uncontrollably. His helper put a white cap over her head, drew the noose around her neck and set the knot beneath her right ear. Calcraft strapped her ankles, checked the rope above her with his stubby grey-haired hands and stepped away. Before getting an agreed signal from the Under-Sheriff he pulled the handle. The trap door swung open and Mary Ann plunged into mid-air. She began to kick and writhe at the end of the rope. It was meant to snap her neck but instead was slowly choking her to death. The three minutes seemed like hours to the appalled and fidgeting onlookers. Mary Ann continued to twist and swing from side to side. Calcraft tutted and lunged over. He grabbed her by the shoulder to steady her body and she hung there wriggling until finally she was still. Her adult life had been one of unmitigated evil, but no one deserved to die as she had done, at the hands of a callous executioner whose only interest was not how his victim died, but his fee and the rope he would now sell for curiosity value.

Even after her death Mary Ann stirred controversy. Jurors standing over her body during the inquest argued about the rope she died on. Many felt it should be buried with her. But Calcraft had taken it. There were also many dignitaries in Britain at the time who were against the hanging of women. The argument raged on. The West Hartlepool Phrenological Society took a cast of Mary Ann's head so that scientific knowledge could be extended. Her hair was cut off . . . but every single strand was carefully put back in the coffin. Stage plays about her began to be written.

Calcraft caught the train home leaving behind him resentment and a judiciary bitterly disappointed that Mary Ann had never confessed to her crimes. She had lived during a time when many children were at the mercy of their guardians. They suffered sexual and physical abuse, disease and hunger. It has been estimated that in the 1860s and 1870s there were over 400 child murders every year in London alone. Nationwide the figure must have been staggering. Murdering a child was easy. Poisoning anyone was easy and mostly went undetected. For Mary Ann killing was easy. She saw no wrong in it. She just had to survive. Her daughter Margaret, born in Durham Gaol, was to have a long but tragic life. She went blind from cataract trouble when she was thirty years old. She lost her first husband in a pit accident and her two sons died in the First World War. She died in her eighties – still eligible for a halfpenny a day from the state, for being born in prison.

Chapter Two

NANNIE DOSS

'My late husband sure did like prunes. I fixed a whole box and he ate them all.'

Mt Carmel, Davidson County, North Carolina, 1954

Dr David Plummer checked his watch against the clock in the Davidson County courtroom. It was a minute after 2pm; where the hell was that report? Haywood had promised him it would be delivered by midday. Damn, it was so bloody cold. What was wrong with the heating? He'd told them about it before. Guess they thought he was just bitching again. 'Dr Haywood Taylor from Duke Hospital on the telephone for you, Dr Plummer,' said the clerk. Taylor was good, damn good, but sometimes he was too thorough, perhaps that's why he was always so late, thought Plummer as he headed for the wretched little telephone kiosk near the clerk's office. He hated it, everyone else around could hear what he was saying. Taylor was the county's leading toxicologist. He and Plummer were old friends, they had dug up and investigated so many murder cases that they could fill the whole of Mt Carmel's Methodist cemetery with the bodies. The vital organs from the body of Arlie Lanning had been sent to Taylor's laboratory to check for traces of arsenic. Arlie's ex-wife Nannie was being held by police in Tulsa, Oklahoma, charged with murdering her fifth husband, Samuel Doss. But the plump, jovial, forty-nine-year-old widow who was scratching a living babysitting and housekeeping had now admitted poisoning four of her five husbands. At first detectives hadn't taken her seriously because she laughed and giggled as she confessed. However, if her confessions were true, and the body of her third husband, factory worker Arlie, could hold the evidence, then Plummer would be digging up her mother Louise Hazel tomorrow. Nannie could have poisoned her too, along with two sisters, two children, one grandson, a nephew, and heaven knows how many more.

'Hello!'

'That you, Plummer?'

'If you mean 2pm, tell me 2pm for God's sake. I've been here two damn hours.'

'You're getting liverish in your old age, want me to check your organs?' asked Taylor.

'Just get on with it.'

'OK, Lanning's organs are heavily positive for arsenic. The poor guy was saturated in it. Must have been in a lot of pain.'

'Thanks, Haywood, looks like we got some kind of obsessive killer on our hands.'

'Yeh, but what makes her kill over and over? These guys weren't millionaires.'

'Beats me, we'll leave it to the homicide boys.'

Five minutes later Plummer obtained a court order to exhume the remains of Nannie's mother Lou.

The following day they stood solemnly around the grave. Officers from three states, North Carolina, Oklahoma and Kansas. There were some officials from the funeral home, a grave digger and a photographer. Four Highway Patrol cars had sealed off the road that led to the sloping Mt Carmel cemetery, five miles west of Lexington, and officers were busy keeping sightseers away. No one wanted to be there that chilly December day, but the court had ordered it. The photographer from the Lexington daily newspaper the *Dispatch* took their picture. Men in overcoats and hats, watching Coroner Plummer conduct his autopsy on Louise by her grave. God, how he hated this job, thank the Lord he was retiring in four days time, Plummer thought to himself as he sawed through a chest bone. Someone else could do this kind of damn dirty work. Plummer removed the mother-of-four's vital organs. Hope this is enough for you Taylor, he said to himself. If it's not you bloody well do it!

An assistant carefully put the rotting organs into a yellow plastic bag before taking them away to Duke Hospital for examination by Taylor's toxicology department. Special agent Ray Page, from Oklahoma City, buttoned up his overcoat in the freezing wind and pulled his hat down tight until it sat on his eyebrows. Agents Ray Garland from the North Carolina State Bureau of Investigation, based in Statesville, and Wayne Owens from Overbrook, Kansas, stood with their hands in their overcoat pockets staring down at the gaping hole in the ground, three feet wide, eight feet long and six feet deep. Three tough cops investigating one tough female serial killer.

They were tired. They had driven down from Tulsa two days earlier, arriving at around 5am at the Piedmont Motel in Carmel. Four hours later they were up for a briefing from Lexington Sheriff-Elect Homer Lee Cox, who was heading the case. That same day they had to see Coroner Plummer. It had been non-stop ever since they arrived.

'Wanna beer?' Page asked Owens and Garland. They nodded, each man with his own thoughts.

The bow-tied Davidson County cop drove them down the lane from the cemetery and headed for the Piedmont Motel, turning the radio on. He didn't feel like talking, nor did anyone else. The news bulletin broke their thoughts. Eisenhower was warning that a naval and air blockade of Red China would amount to war action. The first duty of the United States was to exhaust every peaceful avenue to protect the rights of Americans imprisoned by the Peking regime. On Main Street, Lexington, there would be a ban on parking cars because of the Christmas parade. Someone had entered a float called Brer Rabbit and one shop owner had made a giant jack-in-the-box on four wheels. Page wondered how people found the time. Temperatures would be four to six degrees above normal and rainfall light to moderate, but the cold winds would continue. Garland hated the wind and wondered if he would be back at home with his family for Christmas. Owens reflected on the bottle of liquid rat poison he had bought in a nearby store. It contained arsenic. In Kansas, buyers had to be registered. But not here, not in North Carolina. How easy it would be for someone like Nannie Doss to kill.

At the Piedmont they had just opened their beer cans when the telephone rang in Page's room. It was Sheriff-Elect Cox.

'Just had a message from Tulsa, Ray. Nannie has been ordered by her defending attorneys not to talk to detectives about the other deaths,' he said.

Page had guessed this would happen. 'Doesn't matter, as long as she still answers questions over Samuel Doss,' he answered.

Nannie had already told detectives she had put rat poison in her fifth husband's stewed prunes.

'I think they're going to plead insanity,' said Cox. 'They want her checked out in a mental hospital for ninety days.'

'OK. Thanks for telling us. Anything else?'

'Yeh. She was woken up in her cell the other evening and taken down to the county attorney's office. When she got there she joked about being disturbed, then asked why the hell they got her up to talk to her when they'd damn well been talking to her for a week!'

'That's Nannie all right, thinks it's all a joke. Sure don't seem like she feels any remorse over what she's done.'

'Nuh. All she wants to do is read those damn romantic magazines, smoke cigarettes and chew gum, no wonder she's got such bad teeth. Keeps asking her guards if they've ever been in love. Think she fancies one of them.'

'Tell him not to eat prunes with her then, otherwise he's a dead man,' joked Page. 'Perhaps her attorneys are right and she is a nut after all. Listen, better fix us up to talk to her brother William Hazel, he can help us with her background. Make it soon, we've got to go to Alabama tomorrow.'

'Will do.'

Page put down the telephone and took a long hard swig of his beer. Nannie certainly was a romantic, he thought to himself.

'Say boys, what was it Nannie wrote on those tombstones?'

They sat around remembering the farewell messages on the graves.

On Arlie's grave her inscription was: 'We'll Meet Again.' Second husband Frank Harrelson's tombstone in Alabama read: 'God Be With You Till We Meet Again.' And the tombstone of grandson Robert Lee Higgins bore Nannie's inscription: 'Darling How We Miss Thee.'

Yes, thought Page, Nannie was either clever or mad.

It was shortly before lunch one November morning when E. E. Witherspoon, editor of the *Dispatch*, got a long-distance telephone call from Tulsa. He put his feet up on the galley pulls, page proofs and pictures strung across his desk and leaned back in his chair.

'What is it, Harmon?' he asked, loosening his tie.

Harmon Phillips was a *Tulsa Tribune* reporter. He wasn't any good at digging up graves like Plummer but he was good at digging up newspaper stories, and he had just dug up another good one, about a woman named Nannie Doss. Now he wanted to check on her background in Lexington and Witherspoon was just the man to help him – he knew everything about everyone.

Harmon told Witherspoon that a doctor in Tulsa had become suspicious over the death of Nannie's husband, highway worker and former truck driver Samuel Doss.

'Why, what was wrong with him?' barked Witherspoon, looking at his watch and thinking about his pre-lunch cocktail.

'That's just it, the doctor couldn't find anything serious enough to kill him. Apparently Doss was OK when he was sent home from hospital where he had been for twenty-three days following convulsions, but he died two days later – again after more shakes.'

'So?'

'Well, the doctor ordered an autopsy – and guess what?'

'What?'

'They found enough arsenic to kill a horse.'

Witherspoon sat up, interested now.

'What happened then?' he asked.

'It gets better. I told our local sheriff, who admitted he knew all about it. And guess what?'

'For Christ's sake, Harmon, I haven't got time for these guessing games.'

'Sorry, sir. Anyway, he tells me that they might be

digging up Nannie Doss's former husband Arlie Lanning, down there with you. He's buried at the Mt Carmel Methodist cemetery. They might dig up other people too. No one seems to know yet. But she did have five husbands.'

'How the hell did this guy Lanning die?' asked Witherspoon.

'It was put down to a cardiac arrest – after a three-day illness.'

'You telling me he was full of arsenic too? No woman could be that daft. Killing one husband I can understand, but two? And what do you mean other bodies could be dug up? What have we got here, some kind of mass killer? If so, who says and where's the evidence? Come on, Harmon, I know you're trying to make this a sensational story, but we're a newspaper based on facts, give me more facts.'

What Witherspoon then heard made him change his mind and pull out every stop to cover the Nannie Doss case in the months to come.

The reporter told him that eight weeks after Arlie died, the Lannings' wood-panelled home and all its contents had burned down. A few hours before the blaze Nannie was seen carrying away her favourite possession, the TV set. When she was asked by a neighbour what she was doing with it, she replied that she was hiding it because she would be away from home for a while and it might be stolen.

'Mmm, good, good, what else?' asked Witherspoon.

'Well, Nannie Doss wasn't left any money by Arlie and

under the terms of the will his house reverted to his sister. When it burned down the insurance company sent a cheque to "Mr Arlie Lanning Deceased" which meant as administrator of her husband's will, Nannie picked up the cash.'

Nancy Hazel was born on 4 November 1905 on a farm in Blue Mountain, Alabama. She had three sisters and one brother, William. Her father, railroad worker and farm-hand Jim Hazel, was a strict disciplinarian and she hated him. She learned at an early age that he had a mean streak, he never played games with her and there were never any treats in the Hazel household. The family were so poor they never had enough food, and by the age of five Nannie was made to cut wood, plough the fields and clear the land of weeds and debris. Ball games and seeing friends were forbidden. There was little schooling, as her father could not afford to hire help and so he used his children instead. On the few occasions they were not working the fields, their mother, Louise, would send them off to school. That was hard work in itself, for it was a two-mile walk there and a never-ending two miles walk back. It was up to the children whether they went or not, their father didn't seem to care. But their mother tried to encourage them, she wanted them to read at least. Nannie wasn't a good pupil, however, and was to remain semi-literate all her life. There was little laughter in the Hazel household, although her mother tried behind the scenes to comfort her children, teach them to read when she could and sing them to sleep. Nannie's only happy childhood memory was of the time she went with her family on a train ride when she was seven years old, but even that had an unhappy ending. The train stopped suddenly and she hit her head, suffering pains for months. In later years she suffered severe headaches and depression which she put down to that fateful day.

In early childhood Nannie, who had terrible mood swings, dreamed of love and of finding her own Prince Charming. Her only interest was her mother's romantic magazines and she would sit for hours in her bedroom just looking at the pictures of the loving couples staring out at her from the pages. As she grew older her favourite bits were the ads for the lonely-hearts clubs.

On up days Nannie would chatter on and on about anything. Often she would lie, but showed no shame when she was caught out. It was as if everything she had said was true, even when her sisters proved to her that it wasn't. The sisters' teenage years were just as difficult. Their father barred them from going to dances and, if there had to be boyfriends, he would pick them. In many ways he was right. For Nannie was molested by a string of local men of all ages in fields, barns and cars before she reached her middle teens. Her father's same rules applied to her choice of husband. Her mother didn't argue because there was nothing she could do. She was dependent on her husband and frightened of him. The cotton-field countryside of Alabama was a hard place for a woman on her own.

In 1921, as the Charleston dance craze swept America

and Prohibition opened the doors to the new bootlegging rich, sixteen-year-old Nannie married a young, handsome cotton worker she had known just four months. His name was Charlie Braggs and they had met in the Linen Thread factory where they worked. Braggs was the only son of an unmarried mother and she insisted on living with the newly-wed couple. It was a desperate situation and Nannie wasn't happy from the start. She had gone from a dictatorial father to a possessive mother-in-law who ruled her son with a rod of iron. When Charlie's mother didn't get her own way she would suddenly develop a dizzy spell and fall ill for days. Charlie would fuss around her until she was better. But it wasn't long before he began to disappear for days at a time, something Nannie was to learn to do herself. Nannie suspected Charlie was seeing other women, in fact she was convinced of it. Charlie suspected Nannie was seeing other men, in fact he was convinced of it, for there was no doubt that Nannie enjoyed the physical company of the muscular farm labourers. It was an explosive situation. In between the rows, however, they managed to patch up their differences and settle down to some sort of married life.

Over the years the couple had four daughters in rapid succession. Two of them died later, a few months apart, from suspected food poisoning. Each of them was robust and healthy when Charlie left for work, but they were crying. They died in convulsions not long after breakfast. Charlie was to be haunted all his life by a nagging suspicion that Nannie had killed them, after an undertaker gave him the benefit of his opinion at the graveside. Only small insurance payments eased the pain. Eventually Nannie's mood swings proved too much for Charlie and he disappeared again, this time with his oldest daughter, Melvina, leaving his wife behind with their other daughter, Florine. There was something about Nannie that worried him, he didn't feel safe with her any more. Nannie expected him back after his customary three-day absence but the months went by and things became desperate. She found it impossible to make ends meet as she struggled to bring up Florine. Finally she got a job in a cotton mill and took in boarders in a last-ditch attempt to hold her home together.

One bright summer's afternoon thirteen months later, as Nannie stood in the yard hanging out the washing, Charlie returned – with a woman and a child. Nannie had not been a saint but there was no way she could tolerate this relationship. She went home to share her mother's bleak world, taking her two daughters with her. Charlie and Nannie divorced in 1928 and Nannie managed to get a job in a mill at Anniston, Alabama, while her mother looked after the girls at home. Charlie later maintained that he left his wife because he was frightened of her – and suspicious of her cooking.

Things started to pick up for the chain-smoking mother who still shut herself away in the evenings poring over magazines like *True Romance*. She believed in her heart and mind that they would one day bring her the love and the material comfort that she never had and she began to write to men through the lonely-hearts clubs that advertised in the classified pages. One of them particularly interested her – twenty-two-year-old Frank Harrelson from Jacksonville. She liked the way he wrote, but more than that, she liked the pictures of him that he sent her. They married in 1929. The rains came and went, the autumn leaves fell and they made love by crackling log fires in the winter. But all the time drink was a part of Frank's life. As the months went on the honeymoon period crumbled and Nannie realized that her tall, good-looking husband, with the square chin and rugged features, was an alcoholic. Harrelson worked hard and drank hard, often ending up in jail. Time and again Nannie would spend the last of their money bailing him out. For a while they tried. They would pick cotton together, sometimes late into the evening, to earn money. They even managed to save, but when Harrelson knew there was a pile of dollars around he would find it and sneak out to the downtown bars. Harrelson was bad in drink and would often hit Nannie. She was unhappy. There was no romantic White Knight after all.

One cloudy, wet morning in February 1945, Melvina, Nannie's eldest daughter from her marriage to Charlie, went into labour at her pretty little wood-panelled house seven miles from Hartselle, Alabama. Her worried husband, Mosie Haynes, eased her into the station wagon and they sped to town, slowing down over bumps on the road for the unborn baby's sake.

'You can't be in labour, you just can't,' said Mosie, clutching the steering wheel and staring intently ahead for more holes in the ground. 'You worked out you were only seven months pregnant.'

'Just drive the damn car, I dunwanna talk,' Melvina screamed at him.

In the maternity home, Dr James Greaves examined Melvina and agreed with her. 'The baby feels developed a good nine months,' he said.

Melvina was glad when her mother arrived to help her; she was good at things like this. Nannie had a grandmotherly look about her and a comforting smile. She leant over her daughter and wiped her forehead with a towel.

'There, dear, it'll soon be over.'

A few hours later the pain was almost unbearable and Melvina screamed. Her baby girl was born but died. Melvina, groggy from the ether she had been given, was falling in and out of consciousness. The room was a blur as she looked over and saw Nannie bending over the baby. Why is she sticking a pin in my child's head? Melvina thought before falling asleep again.

Back at home several days later, Melvina told Mosie and her sister about her dream in the maternity home. They looked at each other oddly, then they revealed that when Nannie had told them the baby was dead they saw her stick a pin through the child's dress.

As the months rolled by Melvina and her husband separated. Melvina, who had a two-year-old son, Robert, began dating a soldier – but Nannie didn't approve of him. The tension grew and finally there was a bust-up.

Melvina went to stay with her father, Charlie, for a while, and Robert stayed with his grandmother.

Late one Wednesday evening, Melvina received a telegram from Nannie saying her son was sick. A couple of days later, on 7 July 1945, Robert died. The doctor put his death down to asphyxia, the cause of which was unknown. Nannie filled in the details for the death certificate and later collected a $500 insurance policy she had taken out on her grandson.

By this time, Nannie was wondering just how much more her husband Frank could drink. The older he got, the more violent he became when he was drunk. Then one night it was the last straw. Frank had been drinking all day and now he wanted sex.

'If you don't come to bed with me now, I ain't gonna be here next week,' he shouted. Nannie didn't want to know. How she hated him. Still, it wouldn't take long. He would just roll off and go to sleep. She would get him for this. It wasn't like the love she had read about in her magazines. As they had sex Nannie stared at the ceiling and vowed to get even. The next day, tending the little rose garden she adored, she found her husband's corn-liquor jar hidden deep in the surrounding flower-bed. That was enough. She liked to keep her yard pretty. She took the jar to the storeroom, poured away some of the foul drink she had smelt on his breath the night before, and topped it up with rat poison.

On the night of 16 September 1945, Harrelson died in excruciating pain, aged just thirty-eight. An hour later Nanny washed out the empty corn-liquor jar.

'Funny,' Nannie said to Melvina, 'he had the same sort of symptoms your little Robert had.'

Nannie bought ten acres of land after her husband's death, thanks to some savings and the life insurance payout. She immediately planned her own burial next to his grave. Neighbours were sympathetic. A double tombstone was erected in the Jacksonville city cemetery, with room for the vital information on herself. It gave the date of birth and death of Harrelson and on the other side said: 'Nanie Harelson [misspelt], March 4, 1905' and on the second line '19..'

The stone also read: 'God Be With You Till We Meet Again.'

Two years later Nannie's love of romantic magazines had taken her from Alabama to Lexington. By now she must have had a penchant for men who liked a drink. Perhaps they were easy prey. She had been writing to fifty-four-year-old Arlie Lanning for months, through an ad in a magazine. They married two days after she stepped off the bus and into his arms. Ironically the couple realized they had known each other when they were kids, and from that day on Arlie believed their marriage was set in heaven, where he was later to be dispatched.

Arlie, like Frank, enjoyed his drink – often to the point of becoming comatose. Nannie worked hard persuading him to go to church on Sundays and in the end he caved in, becoming a regular attender of services. For a while their marriage worked. Nannie became an active church worker and respected member of the community. The couple even held prayer meetings in their home. But

Nannie didn't like the fact that Arlie was popular with women. When she went to nurse her sister, who had cancer, she suspected he was bringing women home. She knew his previous track record. Before they were married he was known to have a fondness for loose women. Arlie wasn't too sure about his wife either; she certainly seemed to like men.

One bright summer's mornng, Arlie put the rat poison he had bought on the shelf in the garage at the little house he had inherited from his father, three miles west of Lexington, then went out into the garden to pose for a picture with friends. He and Nannie cuddled in the sunshine and smacked kisses on each other's lips as a neighbour clicked away with his camera. Those pictures would one day be seen by a world hungry to learn everything about Nannie through the pages of their newspapers. They were a loving, smiling couple for all the world to see – or were they? To their neighbours they were an ordinary couple with ordinary ups and down. Nannie was well liked and a good cook who kept a neat and tidy house. She was also known to be a very capable nurse to those who were sick. But Nannie was hiding her growing anger. She hated the fact that Arlie, tall and smartly dressed with thinning hair, still seemed to be popular with women, and she suspected he was having several affairs. It seemed to be all right for him – but not for her. As the years passed she began to disappear just as she had done during her marriage to Charlie, except now the vanishing spells were longer. She would take off for months at a time, finally wiring her husband for money to come home. The telegrams came from as far away as New York and Oregon. Later there were reports that she had even married other men there, but no proof was ever found. While she was away, lonely Arlie began to throw parties and find comfort in the bosoms of new friends.

It was raining on the Wednesday night when Arlie got home late from work. He was angry, tired and hungry. He suffered from bronchial asthma and it was playing up. He was coughing and spluttering and breathing heavily. It had been one helluva day. All he wanted was a hot coffee, a huge supper and plenty of drink. That evening he particularly enjoyed the stewed prunes Nannie dished up, then he fell asleep in the chair. A few hours later he sat bolt upright and was sick. The stomach cramp was almost unbearable. Nannie told him it was a bug. For two days he turned and twisted in his bed, sweating profusely. Nannie appeared by his side and made him sip coffee. Friends and neighbours who looked in on him always found his caring, attentive wife by his side. They all agreed there had been a nasty stomach bug going around. But if anyone could get him well, it would be Nannie. She was a caring and clever nurse. Everyone said so. On the third day an ambulance was called but it was too late. Arlie was dead when the medical team arrived. His last words to Nannie were: 'It must have been the coffee.' Dr Carlton Mock put the cause of death down to cardiac failure. Nannie, alone at last, poured the rat poison Arlie had kept in the garage down the sink.

For two months she continued to live at the house even though she desperately wanted to move on. But

Nannie was trapped by a dispute over ownership and so she couldn't sell the property. Her husband was childless and, according to the terms of his father's will, the house should have reverted to Arlie's sister, Mrs Harper Swicegood, in the event of his death. Under state law, Nannie was entitled to take only personal property, but even that had not been properly sorted out. The trouble was Arlie hadn't left any cash.

It was 8am on the beautiful spring morning of 21 April when Nannie appeared on the porch of her home clutching a TV set in her arms. She seemed agitated when neighbours asked her where she was going.

'I've got to go away for a few days and I don't want anybody stealing this,' she said agitatedly.

Three hours later, at 11am, there was an explosion. Neighbours rushed out to see the Lannings' house ablaze. One of them called the fire service but by the time the engines got there it was too late. The firefighters managed to save a few outbuildings but the house and its contents were gone. Everyone, neighbours and fire chiefs alike, were thankful that Nannie hadn't died in the blaze.

The insurance company which covered the house and its contents didn't know what to do because of problems over ownership. So it issued a cheque to 'Mr Arlie Lanning Deceased'. Nannie cashed in the $1,475, as legal administrator of her husband's will – angry that the insurance company had made a deduction over the missing TV set.

Neighbours and relatives had every sympathy in the world for Nannie. Life just wasn't dealing her a fair hand.

Her sister, Dovie Weaver, died in Gadsden on 30 June 1950. The following year her mother-in-law, Mrs Sarah E. Lanning, died, aged eighty-four, from cancer. Nannie nursed her through her illness, right to the end.

The podgy grandmother, however, was still desperately searching for love – and it wasn't long before yet another door opened, thanks to a lonely-hearts club called the Diamond Circle. She sent the club a $15 annual subscripion in June 1952 and before long was receiving scores of letters. This time her chosen prince was Richard L. Morton. The swarthy, sometimes lonely, lovelorn businessman from a small town near Oklahoma was of Indian descent, and that excited Nannie. Within a few months they had met and it wasn't long before Morton was writing to the Diamond Circle telling them to remove his name and Nannie's from the correspondence list because he had 'married the sweetest and most wonderful woman he had ever met'. Morton took his new wife back to his home town of Okmulgee, Kansas, and for a while everything was fine, but Nannie noticed that women did seem to like her husband. He showered money around and they were impressed; they thought he had plenty, just like she had thought. Sadly it just wasn't true. Then one day, as Nannie began to realize the extent of Morton's debts, she discovered that he had bought a woman in the town a gold ring. It wasn't a marriage made in heaven after all. Nannie's mood swings took over. When she wasn't rowing with her husband she retreated into her world of romantic magazines, and she soon found solace with a new penfriend named Samuel Doss. In January 1953

Nannie's mother Louise came to stay. She had obviously picked a bad time. After a couple of days with her daughter she fell ill with chronic stomach pains and died. Four months later Morton was writhing in agony too. He died in May but Nannie didn't have much time to mourn or mope around. As soon as her penfriend Doss sent her the money for her fare she was on a bus to his home town of Tulsa, where she married the fifty-eight-year-old highway department worker and former truck driver on 13 July. Some would say the date was unlucky – it was certainly so for Doss. He was a man set in his ways and he soon irritated Nannie. He hated noise and would continually turn off the radio, even when she was listening to it. He refused to let her put on the fan in blistering heat and insisted they were in bed by 9.30pm. Even Nannie's forays to her neighbour's house to watch TV were banned. It wasn't long therefore before Nannie was on her travels again, leaving Doss for a while because her granddaughter in Lexington had polio. In fact, no one knew where she had gone. There was nothing wrong with the little girl. But Doss obviously missed his wife, for when she returned to Tulsa two weeks later he made her the beneficiary of two small insurance policies. It was a fatal mistake. Nannie was already writing to a new prospective husband, a farmer in North Carolina. A few days later she sprinkled rat poison on her husband's breakfast prunes, smiling as she put the dish before him. Several hours later Doss was violently sick and took to his bed where he stayed for days, losing 16lb in weight. Finally his doctor sent him to hospital, where he stayed for twenty-three days. He returned home fighting fit to a wife who was caring and attentive.

'Drink your coffee, dear,' she said the next morning. She watched it slide down his throat as they sat in the parlour and wondered if he could taste the two heaped teaspoons of rat poison she had stirred into it. Doss died the following day, 6 October 1953, three months after their marriage.

This time, though, Nannie wasn't so clever and she was to bring about her own downfall. The Tulsa doctor who treated her husband was suspicious of his death as he could find no apparent natural cause. He asked for an autopsy and Nannie signed the permit, something she didn't have to do. 'Sure,' she said. 'The same thing that killed him might kill some more of us!' The autopsy revealed that he had enough poison in his stomach to kill eighteen men. Hours later Nannie was arrested.

It was late November 1954. Nannie sat in an interrogation room laughing and joking with detectives, a copy of the magazine *True Romance* on her lap. At first she wouldn't talk much about her husband's death. But after twenty-four hours she was tired and wanted to go to bed, so she suddenly confessed to putting arsenic in his prunes.

'He sure did like prunes,' she told stunned detectives. 'I fixed a whole box and he ate them all.'

The reason was that he never let her watch TV, she said. 'He was a peculiar man. I was not allowed to keep a magazine and he wouldn't let me go to the neighbours to watch television. He wouldn't even let me have an electric fan and always sent me to bed early. Yes, I killed him and now my conscience is clear.'

Looking at her and talking to her, detectives just could not believe that Nannie could be a killer. But now the confessions just poured out. She had killed four husbands, she said. Of husband number two, Harrelson, she admitted: 'He wasn't much of a Christian and he wasn't much of a loss.'

At one stage an officer asked: 'Which one are you going to tell us about next, Nannie?'

She giggled and answered: 'I'm real sorry you boys have had to stay up so late to bother with me. I know you must be tired.'

Slowly, painstakingly, the police began to piece together her background. Agents from several counties, including Page from Tulsa, packed their bags and headed for Lexington. Forensic experts scanned for arsenic in her home but could find no trace. As the days rolled on Nannie would not stop talking. She insisted that she killed for romance. 'Yes, that's about it. I was searching for the perfect mate, the real romance of life,' she explained.

By now the nation was hooked on the story. TV and Press coverage was from coast to coast. Viewers and readers learned that five-times-married Nannie had prospective husband number six lined up before she slipped rat poison to Doss. The plump, forty-nine-year-old grandmother had been writing to dairy farmer John Keel in North Carolina. They had become penpals through a lonely-hearts club. Nannie had even mailed him a cake she had baked, telling him that she was caring for a sick aunt in Tulsa but would love to visit him soon. Reporters tracked Keel down.

'I'm sure proud, mighty proud, that she didn't come to my part of the country,' he said.

The gum-chewing, chain-smoking, giggling grandma was now a household name and a TV news interview was scheduled. That afternoon Nannie kept the cameras waiting as she puffed on one cigarette after another, making herself up behind the scenes. Then, in a freshly pressed blue dress, she told a questioner she believed she was 'all right as much as anybody else'. Merry and cooperative throughout the broadcast, Nannie was urged to take off her glasses and smile.

'You might get another husband if you look nice,' a newsman quipped.

'Ain't that the dying truth,' Nannie giggled back.

It was to be her last public appearance, much to the relief of her lawyers.

Meanwhile Charlie Braggs, the only husband to escape Nannie's murder trail, was counting his blessings. He told reporters: 'Back at that time, I didn't know about poison. The undertakers told me my kids could have been poisoned, but I just couldn't believe such a thing. Some of my folks warned me about Nannie and when she got mad I wouldn't eat anything she fixed or drink anything around the house. She was high-tempered and mean.'

Braggs felt the reason she had not murdered him was the fact that he had no insurance.

On the afternoon of 30 November 1953, Tulsa

Common Pleas Judge Lloyd H. McGuire brought his hammer down on the desk and entered a plea of not guilty for Nannie. She had been led into the court complaining of how cold it was in her cell, then she had stubbornly refused to plead innocent or guilty to the charge of murdering her fifth husband, Doss. The court was in uproar and Nannie's lawyers weren't pleased. They had earlier ordered her to stop talking to investigators and newsmen about the crimes and now they objected to the action of Judge McGuire. They claimed Nannie was insane and had not done anything to help them prepare her defence. They believed she should not be required to plead until after the question of her sanity was resolved. For once Nannie had lost her sense of humour. She stood nervously fumbling with a silver cigarette case as she was held for trial without bond.

Tulsa County Attorney Howard Edmondson, who drew up murder charges against the plump widow, spoke to the Press. 'She killed her husbands because they rubbed her up the wrong way,' he said. 'She gave us a different reason for killing every one of them. She would not have done it for insurance. She didn't get enough to more than pay funeral expenses . . . I never saw anyone like her. She's cool, calm and collected and talks about the murders like they don't amount to anything. She's standing up real well. The only ones who are tired are the investigators.'

Two weeks later Nannie was committed to the state asylum at Vinita, Oklahoma by District Judge W. Lee

Johnson for ninety days of observation to determine whether she was sane enough to stand trial.

On her way to the asylum, reporters clamoured for more words from the giggling grandma and she did not disappoint them. She shouted that she was tricked into confessing to the deaths of her husbands and said she got the idea for the admissions from a magazine story.

'I'm gonna be in prison for a long time,' she shouted.

'Why is that, Nannie?' they shouted back.

'Because they have so much evidence against me.'

Nannie was quickly led away, smiling and waving to the cameras.

All the way through her confessions, however, Nannie was adamant about one thing: she denied any connection with the deaths of her two sisters, her mother and her step-grandson. When detectives confronted her with the toxicologist's report showing that her mother had arsenic in her body, she screamed at them: 'I didn't poison her! I loved my mother more than I loved my own life.'

By now Page was sick of cemeteries. He stood right at the top of the hill in Alabama's windblown and chilly Jacksonville City Cemetery, watching two men shovel out the dirt in the graves of Frank Harrelson, Dovie Weaver and little Robert Lee Higgins. Funny, he thought, Nannie's grandson was buried in the next grave to her late husband Harrelson. The exhumations were being made after Harrelson's brother Ernest had given his approval to investigators.

Assistant State Toxicologist Dr C. D. Brooks had told

the Press, however, that it would be two days or possibly longer before conclusive results could be reached on the autopsies. Detectives already had Nannie down for twelve or more murders. Newswire reports claimed that she was even suspected of murdering her father, Jim Hazel, but Page had already checked that out. Records in the Calhoun County Welfare Department showed that Hazel died in 1953 of senility and other complications associated with old age. Anyone who knew Nannie and had the misfortune to die was a possible murder victim at the moment, thought Page, buttoning up his overcoat. Even Charlie Braggs, Nannie's first husband, had asked detectives to look into the deaths of his other two children by their marriage, and Nannie's brother, furniture worker William, was going back into hospital for tests following a stomach disturbance he had suffered when his sister cooked for him months ago. Page walked down the hillside to the cemetery gates.

That same day, 6 December, an autopsy was being performed over at Lexington, North Carolina, on the body of Nannie's mother-in-law, Sarah E. Lanning, who had died in 1950 at the age of eighty-four, allegedly of cancer.

Two gravediggers chopped at the frozen soil with their spades, as their breath steamed in the cold air. Slowly and quietly the steel casket containing the body of Mrs Lanning was brought up. Dr David Plummer sighed deeply and began his work. At least he would be retiring tomorrow, he thought as he removed vital organs from the body. An hour later the hole was refilled and the group went quietly on its way, after entering their third grave within a week.

The whole investigation, however, was being held up by a tornado that had struck Wellington. More than 100 homes had been damaged, telegraph and power lines were down and railway tracks ripped up. The Red Cross had moved in to help the homeless. All available police forces were being used for the emergency.

Page sat in the back seat of the police car as he was driven to his motel. He was glad of the rest. He just wanted to lie on the bed and drink beer. His mind kept going back to the grave of little Robert. The boy's body was so badly decomposed that they had difficulty finding any organs to test for arsenic, so the pathologist had to scoop up the surrounding soil. Arsenic was an indestructible material and evidence would remain in the earth. The next day Page was woken by an early morning call. The body of Frank Harrelson contained a large amount of arsenic but there was no trace in the body of Nannie's mother-in-law, Sarah Lanning, her sister Dovie or her grandson Robert. The final report on Robert said that the baby 'had not absorbed a toxic amount of poison during life'. It did not make clear, however, that there were no traces of poison. Nannie now stood formally charged with the arsenic poisoning of four husbands and her own mother. She was wanted in Kansas, North Carolina and Alabama if Oklahoma ever turned her loose.

Kansas wanted the giggling grandma for poisoning her fourth husband, Richard Morton. North Carolina wanted to try her for the murder of third husband Arlie Lanning and her mother, Louise. Alabama wanted her to stand trial for the murder of Harrelson and there could be other charges later. But Oklahoma had her now for the murder of fifth husband Samuel Doss.

The following month Page was browsing through the *Dispatch* as he was being driven to the sheriff's office in Lexington. Nannie, who had been sitting in her cell in Tulsa knowing the game was finally up, had mailed a letter to one of her daughters, who in turn had passed it to the newspaper. Page read the letter with interest. It appeared with a cautionary editor's note:

'The following account was written by Mrs Nannie Doss in her cell at the Tulsa, Oklahoma jail during December and mailed to a daughter, Mrs Florine Lanning of this city. Mrs Doss, who earlier had confessed to poisoning four husbands, denies such action in her story, which she asked to be published so that her friends might know the truth.'

Nannie's letter read:

> I married, as my father wished in 1921 to a boy I only knowed about four or five months who had no family, only a mother who was unwed and who had taken over my life completely when we were married. She never see anything wrong with whatever he done but she takes spells. She did not let my own mother stay all night and in 1924 we had a darling little girl born to us but about a year before that my man started running around. He would go off for three or four days at a time and

about three weeks before she was born I left and went to my mother's and stayed till after she was born and he promised to do better and I went back but then it just got worse but I tried to hold my home together. Till in 1926 when we had another darling daughter and after I got to where I had to quit my job in the cotton mill, he ran off to North Carolina and stayed awhile.

I had to keep boarders for a living and after she came along we never tried to live together, although we lived in the same house for about 13 months. Then he brought home a woman with a child to live and when I told him one of us had to go he said it would be me so I left and went back home to my mother on Saturday. On Monday I went to work in a mill in Anniston, Alabama, and my mother was keeping my children and I was trying to make an honest living for us all.

Then in 1929 I remarried to a man by the name of Harrelson, who did try to help me make a living, but he was so bad to drink and get in jail till it taken lots he made to pay out with. Then the depression came on. We picked cotton three hundreds pounds for a dollar and then we saved a little. He would go off and spend it and get drunk. He even taken to making whiskey till he got caught. Then he quit in 41 or 42. He had a cancer taken off his face in 45. He passed on, all from drinking which I accused of poisoning which I never done.

Then I met Mr Lanning. I married him in 47 and he was very much a drunkard and did not work but after five or six months of pleading I got him to go to town and get him a job and after about a year I also got him to go to church and he was a very good husband. Only when I would have to go home (I mean back to Alabama) I had a sister which was a cancer victim and I had to go back and forth and stay with them but I still tried to hold my home till he got sick and passed out in 1952. My father passed out March 1, 1952 and everything I had while I was away keeping house for an honest living.

Then in 1953 I remarried to Mr Morton who was an Indian and in five months he died which I don't know anything about it only I never knowed anything about his affairs. He never told me anything about his work nor his business. No way but when he passed out I became aware of he owed most everybody, so they say, and of course he could not defend his self. I even paid his two wives' burial in 1954.

I met Mr Doss and we was married, not for money because neither one had any, and in four months after three months of being very ill he passed out in hospital. I wanted to know what was wrong with him so I left him for an autopsy which is now pinned on me for killing him and which is the blackest lie I ever told but when you set up all night with about 75 men call you a lie and threatening to hang you and then two or three comes along and tell you that they are your friend and never before been in custody of the law, you feel like doing just anything so they told me if I confessed of poisoning Mr Doss that they would keep me here in Oklahoma so I did but I lied because I was so scared and wore out for I was up Friday night, Saturday and Saturday night till I did confess.

They let me lie down but would come right back and get me up again, so when I pay for this it was not me who done it but Harry L. Stege who talked me into telling a lie because I was afraid, so please see that this is published so all my friends will know the truth about this.

Wrote by Mrs Nannie Doss in County Jail, Tulsa, Oklahoma.

P.S. In 1953 I lost my dear mother, also my husband, Mr Morton, also my dear sister, which was a cancer victim. Also in 1921 my father stabbed me in the hand because I tried to separate him and my father-in-law which was fighting. Also my brother-in-law cut my right arm which I am still carrying scar of today.

Page put the newspaper down on the back seat of the car and looked out at the rain, wondering if Nannie was really insane after all.

Each side in the sanity hearing at the Tulsa District Court presented four psychiatrists and a psychologist to back their claims. County Attorney J. Howard Edmondson called Nannie 'an expert liar' but Public Defender Gordon Patten told the court she was a 'victim of society'. Some experts told the judge that she was 'mentally defective' and a hospital supervisor agreed, along with members of his staff. But one psychiatrist testified that Nannie was in an intelligence area with 30 million Americans, while another labelled her a sociopathic personality – 'someone who was selfish, demanding and never considering the consequences of her actions'. A psychologist asserted that Nannie knew right from wrong and had an intelligence level quotient above that of a person requiring confinement in a mental hospital. Nannie chuckled almost uncontrollably when another psychiatrist testified that she was a shrewd, calculating female trying to escape the electric chair. The defence rested with testimony from Dr Felix Adams, who worked at the hospital where Nannie underwent ninety days of observation. He said that Nannie might soon kill again if she should ever be released. All through the evidence Nannie kept up her rhythmic chewing, biting harder on the gum when a tape recording made on the night she was arrested was played. Edmondson pointed out that the taped interview clearly showed Nannie 'lied and was capable of defending herself'. She laughed loudly at the attorney's remarks that she had an ability 'to lie time after time'. He labelled her 'a master of evasion' and claimed her motive for the killings was to get money from insurance policies ranging from $500 to $1,400 on her late husbands. 'There wasn't much money involved,' he said, 'but looking at her background of poverty, toil and sweat, it looked like a lot to her. Isn't it more than a coincidence that she always had her name put on policies as beneficiary, regardless of how short a time she had been married to the man? I don't see how there could be said any element is missing which would be needed to warrant her death.'

After they had all had their say, it took the jury just two hours to decide that Nannie was mentally competent to stand trial for the murder of Samuel. When the verdict was read, Nannie, still chewing gum, again sounded off to newsmen. She told them she was satisfied with the jury's findings, quipping in her own inimitable style: 'It's OK with me if it's OK with them!' There was no appeal from the jury's decision, and she was sent for trial on 6 June 1955. Defence lawyers left saying they would still plead insanity on her behalf. They didn't have to. For on 17 May Nannie finally pleaded guilty to murdering her last legal husband, reversing her original plea of innocent, so there was to be no trial after all.

She told her daughter Melvina, who visited her in jail: 'Don't worry, dear, because I'm not.'

The prosecution was still seeking the electric chair, and her defence counsel had advised Nannie to enter the plea in the belief she would receive a life term and later be committed to a state mental hospital.

On 2 June Nannie arrived at the Tulsa court to be sentenced, stopping for a few moments to cuddle her two little granddaughters. Moments later she was ordered to spend the rest of her natural life in gaol by District Court Judge Elmer Adams. His decision upheld the Oklahoma tradition of never having sent a woman to the electric chair. But he said it was still possible for three other states to prosecute the widow if she was ever freed. Page watched as Nannie was led away chewing her gum. More than a dozen relatives and acquaintances had been exhumed in her trial. Nannie had gone from husband to husband marrying and burying. Between marriages she had frequently worked as a housekeeper and had nursed sick relatives and friends, several of whom had died. She told those who would listen that she 'didn't like to poison nobody even if he wasn't no good'. But the feeling that a husband was about to pass on seemed to provide her with a morbid delight. Page walked through the swing doors of the courthouse and out on to the steps. The sun was shining and there was no wind. It was a terrific day to be with his family. A new law was passed in Oklahoma following Nannie's conviction. It ruled that autopsies must be performed in all deaths of mysterious circumstances. Today it is nicknamed the Nannie Doss Law. Page and Nannie's paths were to cross again, however. In 1963 the special agent became warden of the Oklahoma State Penitentiary where Nannie was an inmate. One of Page's first tasks was to visit his old adversary.

'It was just like an old friend coming to my home,' said Nannie, who had embraced religion and been baptized. She continued to be an avid reader of romantic magazines and novels. But it wasn't long before her giggling was replaced with despair. In October 1964 she made a surprise appearance before the Oklahoma Pardon and Parole Board to ask for clemency. She claimed she was innocent. 'They said I used rat poison – but they can't prove that because they can't find where I ever bought any,' she said. She was ill and needed medical attention. She had a painful limp and suffered from phlebitis. Asked if she really hoped to be set free, she replied: 'I wouldn't have anything to live for if I didn't. Sometimes I wish the authorities would let me be tried in North Carolina. Maybe they would give me the electric chair. Time passes slowly in prison. Behind my smile is a heavy heart. I have always made people think I was happy, even though I wasn't. My daughter is ill in North Carolina and that worries me. I should be at her side nursing her back to health. I have just lost my desire to live.'

Nannie told reporters that she had suffered two slight heart attacks.

'Maybe the Lord will be kind and take me soon,' she said.

She spent her time at Ray Page's penitentiary attending church services and working in the laundry. When they were short-staffed in the kitchen she always offered to cook and make coffee. They never let her.

Nannie died of leukemia in 1965, aged sixty.

Chapter Three

CHRISTINE FALLING

'The way I look at it is there's some reason God is letting me go through this. If God hadn't wanted me to go through this, he wouldn't have let it happen.'

Blountstown, Florida, 1982

The sun came out behind the clouds and baked the thin roofs of the tumbledown trailers. Everyone in Blountstown, a small town of several thousand people, fifty miles from Tallahassee, was glad to drive around in their air-conditioned cars and listen to the music banging out over their radio system. Everyone this particular day, except two grieving women alone with their thoughts, just half a mile from each other.

Lisa Coleman, seventeen, sat in the cramped, two-bedroom trailer on Canal Street she shared with her mother, sister and stepfather. She stared, vacantly, at the small electric fan as it whirred around and ruffled her hair. Her ten-week-old-son, Travis, had died just when she thought he had won his battle against pneumonia. On the other side of town, Christine Falling, nineteen, dazed and haunted by the ghosts of five children, sat sipping fruit punch and chain-smoking as she watched the TV news in her trailer home. 'Is Christine Falling the victim of a fantastic coincidence, or is she a prime suspect for murder?' asked the reporter on the screen. Falling's face remained expressionless. Nobody knew why five children had died in her care since 1980, and at least three others had fallen ill. Doctors had examined her twelve months earlier, searching for a mysterious, lethal virus, but they had found nothing wrong. State epidemiologists doubted she was reponsible for the illnesses. Now she sat waiting for the autopsy results on little Travis, whom she had been babysitting, just like the others who had died.

Falling, a little under 5 feet 6 inches, stood up and lit another cigarette then looked at herself in the cracked mirror. She had lost four stone in weight over the last year, and now at ten stone she appeared better for it, she thought, patting her stomach. Wearing flip-flops, a white T-shirt and plaid jeans with frayed ends, she straightened the bandana that held her long, dark hair and went outside where a local newspaper reporter had been waiting for an hour to interview her.

'I've been through all this before with five other young 'uns,' she told the young girl who scribbled in a notepad. 'I don't know what's happening. It's enough to get you scared. I just try to keep my mind off it.'

The sun blazed down and she wiped the sweat from her forehead with her arm. The reporter was anxious; she knew that when Falling got too tense, she blacked out and suffered epileptic fits, often ending up in hospital. But the girl pressed on.

'Don't you think about the children who died then? Or think about their familes?' she asked.

'Sure, I care and I wonder. I know what these familes go through, but I can't let it get to me.'

Falling had once vowed to stay away from children, but gradually changed her mind after doctors gave her a clean bill of health.

'The way I look at it,' she said, 'is there's some reason God is letting me go through this. If God hadn't wanted me to go through this he wouldn't have let it happen.'

Falling told how, as an unhappy child, she had tried unsuccessfully to commit suicide by slashing her wrists, or overdosing on pills. 'Now I figure that what's gonna happen is gonna happen, whether I try to do anything about it or not. Sooner or later things have got to get better. I guess it is just my will to go on. It wouldn't do no good to withdraw and go crazy.'

She looked at the mess of beer cans and wine bottles under the trailer. 'I'd clear them up, but two damn rattlesnakes live there,' she mused, mopping her brow again. 'You had better come in, it's too hot out here.' She ushered the reporter into the trailer. The living-room was sparse; a broken window was patched with tin foil and torn bedspreads served as makeshift curtains.

'Do you mind if I cook?' she asked.

'No, please go ahead,' said the reporter.

Falling fried some fish and potatoes for her boyfriend's

lunch. Robert Johnson, who worked with the city paving crew, would be back soon. He had found little Travis dead on a small mattress next to his bed in the trailer at 8.30 on Saturday morning.

'Are people staying clear of you in the town because of what has happened?' the reporter asked.

'Some people, yes, they look at me, especially when I go down to the news-stand to buy my papers. It gives me a spooky feeling. Some of them start whispering. The way they point and look at you, it gives you a weird feeling.'

Falling, one of nine children, took a knife from the drawer and cut some more potatoes. 'It was pretty rough when I was small, mainly because I was always by myself,' she admitted. She used to stutter and people were wary of her because she suffered from blackouts, she said. All she ever wanted was some love.

'When I was growing up, I wanted parents, but when I got to a certain age, I found out it wasn't going to happen.'

When she was fifteen, after three days in the eighth grade, Falling left school to get married. It ended two months later. 'I was sad about that,' she said. 'I always wanted to have children of my own. I was pregnant twice, and I had miscarriages both times. In the end, the doctors told me not to have any kids. That's why I love to babysit.'

Falling walked to the door with the reporter. 'I don't know why those kids died,' she said. 'Maybe I have got some kind of disease – but they just can't discover what it is. Right now, I'm at a standstill. I'm not having an easy life at the moment but it will straighten up one day, you'll see.'

The reporter drove off wondering if she really believed Falling. She stopped at the town's showcase, the nine-year-old Calhoun County Courthouse, a steamlined slab of concrete and brick, with wooden rocking chairs between its front columns. Falling knew the building well. She was currently facing six bad cheque charges to which she had pleaded not guilty.

Calhoun County Sheriff Buddy Smith turned up the air-conditioning and got out a file. 'Falling's juvenile record goes back about six years,' he said. But he always found her honest and cooperative whenever he talked to her. The reporter listened as he painted a bleak portrait of Falling's life. She was impoverished, uneducated, unskilled and was shuffled from one home to another by relatives and social workers. 'Everyone knows about her. Blountstown is the kind of place where everybody knows everybody,' he said. Most everybody worked for timber or paper companies or on surrounding farms. In 1978 Falling was judged delinquent, according to court records. The files revealed that she had no parental supervision, was certain to run away, and was a danger to herself because of a suicide attempt.

'She never had a chance in life, I feel real sorry for her,' said another police officer as the reporter walked back with him to her car.

At Goodman's Café, a twenty-four-hour restaurant in the shopping precinct, owner Mary Goodman leant across the coffee bar. 'It's spooky all right,' she said. 'Might as well tell the truth about it. I'm scared to death of her. Everybody is in shock. It's a terrible thing to happen to a town.' The reporter finished her coffee and drove on to her destination – the two-bedroom trailer on Canal Street, flanked by ramshackle huts and a hog pen, where Lisa Coleman was expecting her.

Lisa sat staring at the stack of plastic containers full of chicken bones on the table as the reporter made some coffee.

'I'd like to move to Alabama now, just to get away, know what I mean,' she said, pointing to the cardboard boxes full of clothes on the sofa.

'Sure, course I do.'

The reporter sat at the table with her and started writing in her notebook. Lisa left tenth grade to have Travis, her first child, 'a sweet child, a nice child'. Now she swore he would be her last. 'I'm not going to have another baby,' she said, choking back tears. 'I couldn't bear to lose another.' Lisa didn't blame Falling for her son's death. 'She was too nice, too kind; she loved him.' Instead she suspected the baby may have been released too soon from Tallahassee Memorial Regional Medical Centre, where he had been hospitalized for pneumonia.

'I thought he was really cured and I decided to celebrate,' she said. 'I'd been worrying about him every night. I just felt like going out and having some fun.' So she asked Falling to keep Travis that fatal Friday night, as she had done once before. Yes, she had heard a little bit about Falling's background, but she just did not believe it. By Saturday morning her son was dead. That afternoon, doctors removed the baby's organs for tests and that evening Lisa's friends buried him in a homemade coffin. Pinched for money, they dug the grave themselves in a rural Calhoun County cemetery. Doctors had found no bruises, no broken bones, no signs of foul play. The autopsy results would be ready in ten days. The reporter drove back to her office remembering the story her colleague had filed the day before.

Although Falling was one of nine children, he wrote, the only family member she saw regularly was an older sister who lived in Perry. Her father and stepmother, Tom and Eva Slaughter, also lived there, in a house off a dirt drive surrounded by boards, rusted pieces of metal and old cars. The two hadn't seen Falling since the year before, when two of Mrs Slaughter's grandchildren, Joseph Spring and Jennifer Daniels, died in Falling's presence. But Slaughter did not think his daughter was to blame for any of the deaths. He said: 'As good as she loves those little ones, I don't know why in the world she has such bad luck.' His wife, however, said: 'If I was Christine and all those young uns died on me, I'd stop babysitting.'

True, thought the reporter as she drove down the highway to Tallahassee. Why didn't she stop babysitting? Did Falling have a mystery virus or had she killed them? One man was busy discovering the answer she was searching for.

*

The coincidence was almost too much to believe. In a sunbaked stretch of farming communities spread across northern Florida, five children had died suddenly of ailments or accidents between February 1980 and July 1982 and three others had been hospitalized. All had been cared for by nineteen-year-old babysitter Christine Falling. If doctors, police and parents suspected foul play, they took no action – until now. For Joseph Sapala had arrived on the scene. The cool, forty-one-year-old son of a Michigan lawyer was a master of forensic pathology and the newly appointed Panama City district medical examiner, responsible for North Florida's Panhandle counties. Nicknamed Dr Quincy because his manner and methods were like the fictional TV character, played by actor Jack Klugman, he told reporters: 'I am trained to think in opposites. If a natural death is presented to me, I automatically look for homicide or some other cause, and vice versa.' Sapala had performed the autopsy on two-month-old Travis Coleman but he had put the laboratory tests on hold. The moustachioed former US Navy surgeon needed to preserve the small quantity of tissue he had taken from the baby's body and frozen, until he decided what microscopic examinations should be done.

Sapala's first suspicions were that Travis had died from cot death, the syndrome where babies died without any apparent medical explanation. Cot death struck more than 200 children in the state of Florida each year – and about 7,000 annually in America.

Sapala was good. Damn good and he knew it. After his wife had died in a tragic car accident, he had remarried and moved to Panama City, where he hoped he would be warmly welcomed and needed. He sacrificed a salary of $167,000 a year as a pathologist and teacher for the new $36,000 examiner's job. When he got to Panama, however, the reception was cool. Slowly he began to build his reputation. His techniques, never seen before in the area, helped switch verdicts on earlier cases in the six Panhandle counties, encompassing 3,879 square miles. In one instance he found gunshot wounds in a supposed accident victim, in another case, an apparent fire casualty turned out to be a victim of murder. Now he had the case of Travis Coleman. Sapala looked up at the picture of TV Quincy star Klugman, hanging in his office. God, he was down. Lately some undiagnosed problems had been threatening his practice. Trying to improve his decaying basement morgue, he had run up heavy financial losses. He had pleaded for funds from county officials and sent them bills for his expenditure, which exceeded his $60,000 budget. They had staunchly refused to pay, accusing him of wasteful practice. True, he had performed 118 autopsies during his first 184 days on the job. But he felt he had to do them.

Sapala snapped himself out of his thoughts and returned to the tests on Travis. What he found was to lead to the end of the trail for Christine Falling. Several weeks later Sapala testified before a grand jury that Travis had been smothered, citing evidence of severe internal ruptures. Falling's friends, neighbours and family could not believe it. She was such a kind person.

The little girl looked like a discarded rag doll as she chased her friend around the old rusting cars and pick-up trucks that lay on their sides rotting in the dirt tracks around their trailer homes. She clambered over an old Ford with no wheels and jumped down the other side.

'Gotcha! Gotcha!' she screamed, clutching Mary's pinafore dress.

'Let go now,' Mary shouted, but the girl held on. 'Let go I said, it's tag, you're supposed to let go!'

Still the little rag doll held on. Mary screamed, kicked and scratched her opponent, who tightened her grip. They both rolled in the mud, kicking and punching until they were exhausted. The rag doll was Christine Falling and in her mind she had won the game. This was her playground, a world of rusting metal objects and house-trailers years past their prime. A town of tarpaulin shacks that were homes along with creaking, timber lean-tos. Old burnt-out cars and empty petrol cans lying among discarded washing-machines and gin bottles that had once given their owners a night's escape from reality.

Christine Laerne Slaughter was born on 12 March 1963, under an unlucky star, Obese, dim-witted and epileptic, she had only ever known poverty and her life was to be a bizarre, rootless and lonely trail. The one thing that could have saved her from self-destruction was love – something she never had. Her mother, Ann, was married to sixty-five-year-old woodsman Tom Slaughter when she was just sixteen. The couple, who lived in a little rundown house in Perry, already had an eighteen-month-old daughter, Carol. Seven more children were to follow, most of them finding their way into foster homes as the years went on. Tom only claimed one child as his, a boy who died in infancy. No one quite knew who the others belonged to as his wife had a habit of disappearing for weeks on end. She used to head for the big towns like Blountstown, 100 miles to the west. Christine and her sisters' lives were miserable and so was the neighbourhood. This was logging country and men counted their blessings if they were lucky enough to land a job at Buckeye, the local paper plant. Women worked as clerks in the company's offices or on supermarket checkouts when they were not busy having babies.

Pipe-smoking Tom was a kind, proud man who tried hard to care for his family. Money was tight, sometimes almost non-existent, but he did his best, especially when his wife felt like taking off. One summer's day, while Ann was away again, Tom went into the woods to cut timber for the evening's cooking. The kids were playing near by and he turned when he heard a scream. At that moment a tree crashed down on him, splitting his head open. Somehow the wiry old timberjack survived, but he suffered internal injuries which would take months of treatment. There was no one to care for the children and he reluctantly agreed to adoption. A few days later a neighbour took the girls to Sunday School at the Calvary

Baptist church. During the lessons and hymn-singing they were uncontrollable, running around, shouting and throwing books at each other. When the school finished they were introduced to carpenter Jesse Falling and his wife Dolly, who eyed them with disapproval.

'Well, Dolly,' Jesse said later that evening by the fire, 'do you really want to adopt them?'

'Someone has to take them, I suppose,' she replied.

Dolly's matter-of-fact answer hid her eagerness. At forty-five, childless and desperate to satisfy her maternal instincts, she was only too pleased to agree. But one thing was for sure, she would see to it that the church and the Bible would be their real parents.

In 1967, Christine and Carol were legally adopted by the Fallings. Another family had already asked for Carol, but Jesse and Dolly agreed to take Christine only if they could have Carol too.

'You ain't never been taught anything right,' Dolly shouted at the sisters. 'But you're sure gonna learn now!' Her words launched the only stable period of Christine's life. Stable but unhappy. For Christine was by now difficult to handle.

One Sunday evening, she and some other friends had sneaked out of church.

'Where are we going, Christine?' one of them asked.

'To see if cats really do have nine lives,' she said.

'The preacher said they do,' one of the other girls replied firmly.

Christine ignored her. 'Here puss, here puss.'

The skinny, unsuspecting black cat trotted over to

Christine's wiggling fingers. She stroked it and it purred. Seconds later she grabbed it by the tail and tossed it as high as she could into the air. Sunday nights were to become cat-stalking nights. Months later she and her friends gave up the game of throwing the animals against walls or wringing their necks. They had learned that cats did not have nine lives. Once they were dead, they were dead to stay. Despite the cruel experiments, Christine insisted to her sister that she loved cats. Just like she insisted she loved the babies who were later to die.

The new family clung together for eight years. Things went well at first. Jesse had a well-paid carpentry job and the family enjoyed boating trips on the St Johns River. Only one thing seemed odd to Dolly. When Christine played tag with neighbouring children, she would grab them and hang on.

Dolly worked hard at making the girls behave, especially Christine, whom she would beat hard with a stick. But the sisters were well dressed and always on time for Sunday School and there were presents at Christmas and Easter. As the sisters grew up, Carol stayed slender but Christine got chubbier.

Christine had beautiful thick hair and got mostly As and Bs in elementary school. But she was living with a personal nightmare – she suffered from stuttering and epileptic fits. Dolly simply gave her an order: 'You'd better not have epilepsy around me – I've gone too many miles for you! You understand me?'

Despite the daily teachings of the church and the disciplinary eye of Dolly, there were violent family fights.

One night, neighbours called the police who took eleven-year-old Carol and Christine, nine, away. They were taken to Great Oaks Village, a children's refuge 200 miles downstate in Orlando, where they stayed for a year.

Dolly said: 'Christine had stared skipping school and staying with rotten, dirty people.'

Her adopted daughter wasn't liked by staff members from the start. They found her to be a compulsive liar and a thief. One report noted that she would do anything for attention, even if she knew her behaviour would lead to punishment. When teachers were asked to file a memo highlighting something special Christine was interested in, they left the page blank. And in reply to a question: 'What would you single out that is good in the child's behaviour?' the answer was 'Nothing'.

In the early 1970s, things started going downhill for the Falling family. Jesse became disabled, due to illness. Seeking lighter work, the family moved to Orlando, in the sun-baked south. Next came Merritt Island, but that didn't work out either and so they returned to the Perry area. Sometimes they all worked on chicken farms in exchange for their living expenses. The girls helped gather eggs, just so they would be given some for breakfast. The Fallings were broke. But the real trouble began in the summer of 1975, when the children began to rebel under their adopted parents' tight discipline. Christine started skipping school and falling in with a bad crowd. She looked for kicks to escape her depressing world. Sex was one of them, and she slept with a stream of boys and men. She became a big, heavy-set and mean girl who pestered doctors for means of birth control. Just before Thanksgiving that year she left the Fallings to live in Blountstown with her natural mother again. She was just twelve years old. Between November 1975 and March 1976 a social worker reported that Christine lived at five different addresses. Relatives drove her to school, but couldn't make her stay. Already the fantasies were taking over and she would constantly tell everyone she was pregnant. All she did was row and fight the other girls.

About the same time, Carol also left the Fallings. By 1977 both girls had married, each around the age of fourteen. For some time Christine had been dating her stepbrother, Bobby Joe Adkins, who was in his early twenties. He was kind and attentive and she felt secure. They married on 19 September 1977 – but just a few days later things began to go wrong. Falling could not control her temper and they rolled from one row to another. On one occasion the podgy teenager picked up a stereo system and hurled it at her husband's head. Six weeks later they parted – and so began a series of bizarre visits to hospital by Falling. Over the following two years she complained of snake bites, red spots, bleeding tonsils, dislocated bones, falls, burns from hot grease and vaginal bleeding. In all, she made fifty visits to the emergency departments of several hospitals.

During this time, Christine was constantly on the move. She turned up in Miami, then Tampa and Marianna. Next came Perry, Blountstown, Lakeland, Steinhatchie and Lake Wales. Soon she was state-hopping across to Georgia, West Virginia, Ohio and Colorado.

There was nothing to hold her in any one place, no sense of home, no sense of belonging. Wherever she went children made fun of her weight, following her down the street and taunting her. But even though she weighed nearly fifteen stone and was scruffy, men found her attractive. There was no shortage of lovers, only of love. Falling went from trailer to motel, motel to trailer. By 1978 she was in trouble with the law and had attempted suicide. Soon she began to appear in court records as a delinquent. In a literacy test she declared that the Russians had bombed Pearl Harbor, Abraham Lincoln was the founder of electricity and she lived in the nineteeth century. Her IQ was 69 – a sexual figure she used to boast about to her lovers.

Falling was always desperate for money. Jobs were hard to come by and she was too dim to work in a store. Babysitting for cash was the answer and after all, she loved kids – except when they cried. Parents liked her. She was good at taking care of their children. She cuddled them, fed them their bottles, gave them candy and cookies, changed their nappies. She liked little girls better than the boys – because their clothes were prettier and she enjoyed dressing them up. She'd never had any pretty clothes, or dressed up when she lived with Pa. But all the time a hatred burned deep in Falling. When mothers showered their children with affection she felt the pangs of loneliness. She wanted them to stop. If not, somehow she would stop the bonding. But that wasn't the only thing Falling hated. She couldn't stand the sound of a child crying. No one had cared when she cried as a child. She didn't know what to do to make it stop. One day she was to find a way. That day came in the hot, muggy Panhandle winter of 1980.

It was February and Falling was living with two families in Blountstown. While everyone was out collecting fishing bait on the river bank, Falling babysat two-year-old Cassidy Marie Johnson at the little wood-framed house tucked in a scrubby pine forest where they all lived.

Cassidy was rowdy and hard to handle. Falling shouted at her to be quiet, but shouting made things worse. Finally, Falling snapped. She took Cassidy into the back bedroom, closed the door and squeezed her windpipe until she lost consciousness. It worked. The child lay silent. When Cassidy's twenty-four-year-old parents, Linda and Billy Johnson, arrived home and found her listless, they were frantic with worry. The three of them rushed her to the local doctor, Falling cradling the child in her arms. At first the doctor diagnosed encephalitis, an inflammation of the brain, but he wasn't completely satisfied. There was a bump on Cassidy's head and some bruising. Was she a child abuse victim? he wondered. Falling, however, visibly distressed, explained that Cassidy had fallen from her crib and hit her head. About two hours later she had lost consciousness. The doctors referred the child to hospital in Tallahassee, giving the parents a sealed note. In it, he suggested the authorities checked out their babysitter. That note mysteriously disappeared.

During the next two days it looked as if Cassidy was improving and regaining consciousness in hospial. But on the morning of 28 February she suffered seizures and died. In his autopsy Dr Jerry Harris discovered no evidence of encephalitis. He found bruised bone and scalp tissue indicating that Cassidy had suffered a blow to the head, but the injury did not appear severe enough to cause a coma and there was no history of serious illness. He was baffled. Everyone comforted heartbroken Falling and she seemed to pick up when emergency workers praised her for wrapping little Cassidy in blankets, holding her close and breathing into her mouth in the race to hospital.

Soon Falling was on the move again, shuttling back and forth between several familes in Perry and Lakeland. But now she seemed quieter, reserved, almost lost in her own thoughts. She never bothered anyone. She would clean dishes, wash the floors and babysit for the people who took her in.

The next baby to die in Falling's care was four-year-old Jeffrey Davis. It was 1981 and Jeffrey's parents, who were distant relatives, asked Falling to babysit for them while they went into the wetlands to collect earthworms to sell to local fishermen. When they returned their son was dead. Falling, again distraught, told them he had been taking his morning nap when she realized he had stopped breathing. Death was put down to myocarditis – heart inflammation.

Three days later Falling babysat the dead toddler's cousin, Joseph Spring, while his parents attended Jeffrey's funeral. They returned home to find him dead too.

'I put him to bed for a nap and he woke with a scream,'

Falling told them. By the time she got to his crib, he had stopped breathing. 'Mainly, it was the same way it happened before but this time Joe Boy shouted before he died!' Like Jeffrey, Joseph's cause of death was put down as myocarditis, possibly caused by a virus transmitted from person to person. Could this be a clue to the series of deaths behind Falling, doctors wondered?

The grieving families consoled the young babysitter, who kept breaking down in tears. Wherever Falling went death seemed to follow, and by this time publicity was catching up with her. But there was no evidence of murder and she seemed as distressed as the victims' parents. She readily agreed when doctors suggested they test her for traces of a mystery lethal virus. After rigorous laboratory examination, however, they discovered nothing. But the clean bill of health did not shield her from public torment. She was turned away from restaurants and motels. She couldn't get a job and passers-by steered clear of her. Mothers snatched their children from her path and the youngsters invented games using her name as a sort of bogeywoman. Falling felt alone and isolated. She told those who would listen that she had decided to stay away from 'young 'uns' for a while and took a job as housekeeper for seventy-seven-year-old William Swindle, who lived in a tiny cottage on a farm near Perry. Was this a new beginning, or another end? Sadly for Swindle it was another tragic end. When she finished her first day in the new job the old man was dead on the kitchen floor. There was no autopsy. Swindle had suffered from heart trouble and cancer. Officers investigating the death noticed discoloration around his neck, but the dark marks must have been due to cancer radiation therapy. Death was put down to natural causes. At the time, his family did not reveal that Falling had been working for the old man. They didn't see any reason to. Falling returned to her 'young 'uns'.

The next baby to be put in her care belonged to her stepsister, Geneva Daniels. Eight-month-old Jennifer Daniels, the half-sister of Joseph Spring, was gurgling with happiness when Falling and Geneva took her for whooping cough and polio vaccines at the Taylor County Health Department offices. But she started crying after an injection and Falling couldn't stop her. They drove home, stopping off at a supermarket so that Geneva could buy some nappies. Falling stayed in the car, cuddling wailing Jennifer in a blanket. When Geneva returned she noticed that her baby wasn't crying any more. As they drove away Falling remarked that Jennifer had stopped breathing. They sped to hospital in Perry, where the emergency room staff worked in vain to revive the child. An autopsy found no apparent cause of death. 'There was just nothing you could put your finger on,' said medical examiner Peter Lipkovic. In fact there was. A finger had been on tiny Jennifer's windpipe.

Some doctors and detectives believed, however, that Falling was the victim of circumstance. Both she and the children she babysat came from poor backgrounds and the probability of disease was always with them. Haunted by the deaths, Falling decided it was time to move on again, telling those who would listen that if she thought about the past it would bring on blackouts and convulsions.

'I have no goals,' she told a bartender. 'I never put my mind to thinking about wishes. I guess that's the kind of life I have always had.'

Sex and drink kept her going, as the Revd James W. Funderburk was to find out. Early in 1982, Falling arrived on his doorstep – the Huntington, West Virginia City Mission. The podgy teenager confided in the minister, telling him that she had became an outcast – that people were calling her a witch. Funderburk found her a troubled and driven girl who always seemed to want to do the right thing. He tried his best with her but it wasn't easy. Falling suffered seizures and was arrested for being drunk and disorderly, fighting and grand larceny.

Funderburk, a kind, avuncular man whose aim was to help those who had fallen on hard times, tried to understand the girl he had given temporary refuge to. But he told police: 'She does things, we know she does, but when we challenge her she denies them adamantly. I really believe, she believes what she says.'

When Falling told him about the babies who had died she denied any responsibility for them. 'I just don't know what happened to those children,' she said. 'Why do people blame me?'

But even the mission was to close its doors on the ungainly wanderer. Funderburk finally asked her to leave because of her drinking and dating. 'Christine isn't that pretty to look at, but men seem to flock to her, if you know what I mean,' he confided in a police officer.

By spring, Falling had found her way back to Florida and had moved into a tumbledown Blountstown trailer with her new boyfriend, Robert Johnson, the uncle of the first child to die in her care, Cassidy Johnson. Soon she was babysitting again.

Lisa Coleman, seventeen, thought her ten-week-old son Travis had won a bout with pneumonia when she dropped him off at Falling's home on the hot afternoon of 2 July.

'At last I can go and have some fun,' she told Falling, showing off her new red dress. Lisa had been sick with worry for weeks as her son battled against pneumonia in hospital. Now he was on the mend and she could go out on the town. Falling cuddled Travis, who was staying the night, and waved her friend goodbye. It was the last time Lisa was to see her baby alive.

That night Falling and Johnson slept in their bed with Travis in a cot on the floor by their side. When Johnson woke the next morning the baby was dead. Distraught once again, Falling told the police that she last saw the boy alive at 4am when she fed him, changed his nappy and put him back to sleep.

Panama City-based medical examiner Dr Joseph Sapala was called in to perform an autopsy. He arranged for the Broward's County medical examiner's officer to perform tests on tissues taken from the Coleman boy, but those tests had not yet begun.

Sapala's preliminary findings indicated that the child was recovering from pneumonia when he died, but the doctor said he was still considering all possibilities, including murder. Later he discovered that Travis had died through lack of oxygen. He told reporters that could be attributed to Sudden Infant Death Syndrome – or to suffocation. Many people, however, including the parents of some of Falling's victims, still believed the fat, vacant-eyed babysitter was innocent. But a few days later she took everyone by surprise when she walked into Tallahassee Hospital's psychiatric unit and admitted herself as a patient. One doctor described her as suicidal.

Many people were filled with sympathy for her. She had been pointed at and called a killer. Had the town gone too far?

While she was in hospital Sapala appeared before a grand jury. During the autopsy on Travis he had discovered severe internal ruptures, indicating that the little boy had been smothered. Now the truth began to come out. The grand jury returned three indictments against Falling for first-degree murder. Weeks of intricate legal manoeuvres followed, but behind the scenes Falling was already blurting out a tape-recorded confession in hospital. Meanwhile, convinced that the teenager was being railroaded, Tallahassee sympathizers formed a support group to raise money for her legal expenses. Baya Harrison, a private Tallahassee lawyer, and two colleagues agreed to take the case free of charge. As five law-enforcement agencies tracked down the leads, the defence team plunged into a marathon of motions and depositions. They convinced a judge to disqualify himself, alleging that his actions favoured the state's case. They fought unsuccessfully to suppress the introduction of Falling's taped confession in court but they obtained gag orders on the case, which were promptly challenged by several newspapers.

In December 1982, exactly five months after the last of five children had died in Falling's care, the nineteen-year-old babysitter, facing the death penalty, shocked the country by plea-bargaining and pleading guilty to strangling Cassidy Johnson, Jennifer Daniels and Travis Coleman.

It had been poverty that had shielded her from detection. Officials had blamed the deaths on diseases that seemed natural in unsanitary and poor conditions – encephalitis, myocarditis and cot death. In exchange the state agreed not to prosecute her for three other deaths under investigation – those of Jeffrey Davis, Joseph Spring and seventy-seven-year-old William Swindle.

'If nothing else, this case indicates how incredibly easy it is to murder a child without trace,' said State Attorney Jerry Blair, prosecuting in the Daniels case. A baby can be killed with slight pressure to a certain artery – and the marks disappear shortly after death, he added.

Blair was later to be involved in the prosecution of serial killers Ted Bundy and Aileen Wuornos.

Falling was sentenced to life in prison with the possibility of parole in twenty-five years – just before her forty-fifth birthday.

'It was her decision to plead guilty,' said defence lawyer Harrison. 'You have to understand that she was facing the possibility of six death sentences!' But Falling pleaded guilty, he said, without his recommendation, one way or the other.

Now, for the first time, the guilty pleas meant that the public could hear the terrifying taped confession from Falling, made while in the psychiatric hospital. In twenty minutes she summed up the entire nineteen years of her life.

'I don't even know why I did none of this,' she said. She killed because she was enraged by the children's misbehaviour. Other times, she said, she just got the urge to kill.

Reporters clustered round the tape recorder as Falling's voice rang out in an office in the Taylor County courthouse.

In the case of Cassidy Johnson, Falling said: 'She got kind of rowdy or something. Anyway, I choked her until she got purple and stopped breathing.'

As for Jeffrey Davis, she said: 'He just made me mad or something.'

Then came Joseph Spring. 'He was asleep. I don't know. I just got the urge and wanted to kill him.'

Jennifer Daniels: 'She was continually crying and crying and crying and it made me mad, so I just stuck my hands around her neck.'

Travis Coleman died because 'I just choked him – no apparent reason, I don't guess.'

Falling had watched a lot of murders on TV and they had obviously profoundly affected her.

'I seen it done on TV shows,' she said. 'I have my own

way though. Simple and easy. No one would hear them scream.'

She called her murder technique 'smotheration'.

She said: 'I did it like, you know, simple, but it weren't simple. I pulled a blanket over the face – jus' the right amount for a little 'un. A voice would say to me "Kill the baby" over and over, very slow and then I would come to and realize what had happened.'

The babysitter admitted she had killed the children by squeezing their necks with her fingers. At nineteen, lonely and loveless, Falling was at last ready to settle down – in a state penitentiary. There she would get an education, a permanent address and three square meals a day – amenities she had gone without for most of her nomadic life. Her confession was not influenced by drugs or pressure, said Calhoun County Sheriff Buddy Smith, who was present with investigator Ronnie Stone when her words were taped.

'I've known her for a number of years,' he told reporters. 'She knows that she did wrong, and she wants to get the problem solved.'

Harrison agreed. 'Falling is remorseful,' he said. 'That's why she confessed to Sheriff Smith. The sheriff did not go to her, she went to the sheriff.'

Only one statement was recorded but Falling also made numerous confessions to nurses, doctors, hospital aides and law officers. Falling's adoptive mother Dolly thought differently. 'She didn't know what she was doing with all that confessing,' she said. 'She was given drugs. I don't think she's guilty. I've seen her play with children on the front porch and in the yard and it worked out beautiful.'

In all, six deaths and three serious illnesses suffered by other children were linked to the infamous babysitter. But she never confessed to the murders of Joseph and Jeffrey. And she never owned up to any responsibility for the death of William Swindle. Her decision to plead guilty to three charges sparked three days of feverish negotiations involving five law enforcement agencies. When agreements were made a series of court appearances and Press conferences were called. Falling appeared calm throughout, whispering only 'Yes sir' to most of the judge's questions. Who would have thought that the dim-witted babysitter could have risen to such prominence with just a thumb on a little windpipe?

Psychologists classified her as a text-book female serial killer – a caretaker killer. Women like her preyed on young children, hospital patients and nursing home residents. Often they got away with it because people didn't realize that people were being killed. The killers themselves could draw sympathy and understanding. Their heartbreak and apparent complete innocence over the deaths couldn't possibly be an act.

One thing was sure, Falling was sane, according to three mental health experts, including two chosen by her defence team.

The families of two of Falling's victims differed in their opinion on the sentence. Linda Faye and Billy Johnson were fuming. Their daughter Cassidy was dead – because of a serial killer. In the parlour of their wood-framed house, as dogs nipped and barked at the dust of a passing pickup truck outside, Billy told a reporter from the *Tallahassee Democrat*: 'Those young 'uns are dead and she's still living. That's not right. Those young 'uns ain't never gonna eat no more and she ought to be put in the same place. As soon as she said she did them murders, they should have buried her.'

If a jury had found Falling not guilty, Johnson said, then she should go free. But since Falling admitted she was guilty, there was only one punishment.

'You can't go get those babies out of the grave and ask them if they would rather be in prison or be dead. Her life should be done the same way.'

Tall and dark-haired, Linda paced around their modest living-room and picked up a colour portrait of Cassidy. 'What if Falling gets out in twenty-five years and starts this again?' she asked. 'She has been here and yonder, here and yonder. No place to go, bumming off everyone. Prison's no big punishment for her. She should get the death penalty.'

The Johnsons were in bed early that Friday morning when Linda's mother rang.

'Falling has made a deal, she won't be going to trial, they're giving her twenty-five years,' she said.

'That can't be true,' Linda answered. 'She can't get twenty-five years for murdering kids. That's about right for armed robbery.'

Linda turned on the radio and there, wedged between country and western music, came the official news. The Johnsons were flabbergasted. But secretly, behind the scenes, state attorneys saw little chance of getting the death penalty for Falling. One of them said: 'You've got to strangle, kick and beat a person and then in his dying gasp he has to look up at you. Then the killer looks down and blows his head off with a shotgun. It has got to be that heinous and cruel to be executed by the state!'

After a full day of court appearances, Falling, sporting a new, curly hairdo and wearing a new pink dress with black high-heeled shoes, smoked a cigarette in the Calhoun County Jail dining-room. Now she looked forward to studying computers at the Broward Correctional Institution, a maximum security jail for 500 of Florida's most dangerous women, near Fort Lauderdale. She sent her adoptive mother Dolly, whom she had not seen for seven years, a card. It simply said: 'I love you.'

Down the hall, Sheriff Buddy Smith leaned back in his chair after five months of intense investigation.

'Falling's relieved to know she's done wrong and she is going to pay,' he said. 'Even though it might not be the price that some people think she ought to pay.'

Three days after she was led away to gaol, Falling gave a radio and newspaper interview in the offices of Sheriff Buddy Smith. Dressed in pants and a T-shirt, she seemed relaxed, calm and relieved it was all over. The one thing she was angry about was the Press. 'They tried to take advantage of me,' she said. 'They asked if I did it. Whether I did or didn't it's none of their business. I pleaded guilty because I decided I had better not take a chance with my life. With three murder charges I could have gotten a lot more.'

When asked if she felt that even after she had served her time there would still be a cloud hanging over her, she replied: 'I'll pay my debt for what I did. After that, there's no need hanging on to it.'

Ten years after the case that shook the Panhandle counties, people were still haunted by the killings.

Defence lawyer Baya Harrison recalled: 'She didn't throw fits or give us a hard time. She wasn't rude or anything like that. But there was just an absence of any feeling of life, of love.'

The father of three doubted he would ever tackle such a case again. 'The thought of choking a child, I just couldn't handle it,' he said.

The most upsetting part, he added, was knowing that so many children could be injured or killed and the attacks go undetected.

State Attorney Jerry Blair, in a statement to the *Tallahassee Democrat*, said: 'I have no doubt that there are children being murdered who are classified as Sudden Infant Death Syndrome. But if a medical examiner has no evidence to suggest a crime, there is very little else he can do.'

Falling was to take centre stage again – in a Cable News Network documentary, broadcast from her jail. The interview offered no conclusive answers to the question of why she took the lives of those who had hardly started life at all. But the producers found she had all the classic components that contributed to the making of a female serial killer – an abusive upbringing, brain disturbance and failure to bond with parents.

'It has been a kind of mystery to me, as much as anyone else, as to why this happened,' said Falling. 'Because I love kids to death!'

She revealed how she envied all the affection lavished on her young charges. She yearned for the same kind of treatment from relatives and employers.

'They wouldn't, um, spend time with me,' she said. 'And it was like the babies took up their time they normally spent with me. I guess I started resenting that.'

While insisting she loved the children, Falling added: 'I guess you could say they were taking up space.'

Looking back, she said: 'The only part I really enjoyed was watching the cops and doctors running around trying to figure out what was going on, what was happening.'

Falling acknowledged blacking out much of her memory.

'I can speculate why I did what I did, but that's all I can do,' she said. 'It could have been because of the jealousy, it could have been anger – um, I don't know. I guess that's something no one will ever know, because apparently I don't want to know.'

Falling will be eligible for parole in the year 2007. She talks about moving to Canada to live with a stepbrother. Sometimes she vows to stay away from children. Sometimes she says she wants to be a babysitter again.

Chapter Four

VELMA BARFIELD

'I just cannot remember a lot. I didn't have a clear day for ten years.'

Rayleigh, North Carolina, 1984

It was midnight. A candle flickered for a moment in the wind, then died. It flared again, along with another, then another. The grassy slope overlooking the prison was suddenly lit by a sea of 300 tiny flames. Slowly, doggedly, three shadowy figures walked up the hill towards the burning candles that had been thrust into empty soft drink cans. As the woman and two men drew near there was a burst of bright television lights. Velma Barfield's sister Faye and her two brothers, John and James Bullard, walked through the crowd as the cameras rolled. They spoke in turn, thanking and blessing the protestors for their support. They were answered by whispers of 'Amen', and 'That's right!' It was like evensong.

Faye turned from one figure to another, shaking hands.

'It hurts. I'm going to miss her so much,' she said, with tears streaming down her face. 'We hadn't planned to come over here, but we wanted all of you to know that we love you.'

'We love you too – and Velma,' the muted voices replied. 'An eye for an eye makes the whole world blind,' someone shouted.

'We're victims as well,' said Velma's brother John, 'double victims because it was our mother she killed and she is our sister. It was hard. But we understand, we forgive.'

James turned to the cameramen: 'When I saw Velma earlier today I told her, I'll see you later – with the Lord. She is not afraid. We went in to lift her up and instead she lifted us up!'

Inside the blue-stone walls of the sprawling Women's Correctional Center, lawyer James D. Little stared into Velma Barfield's eyes. The plump, hazel-eyed grandmother who read the Bible every day and crocheted dolls for her grandchildren could hardly speak.

'It's not fair of you to leave me here with all this misery when you are going to all that glory,' Little said tenderly.

She closed her watery eyes for a moment and squeezed his hand.

'Velma, if I didn't believe and know that when you go from here you will be joining the Lord, I couldn't witness this execution,' he added, closing his eyes too for a moment.

The killer the world had nicknamed Death Row Granny turned to the woman warden.

'I am sorry for all the hurt that I have caused,' she said quietly. 'Please thank everyone who spoke for me.' The warden's eyes watered too. Who would have thought that such a woman would have had this effect? She had poured rat poison into her mother's Coca Cola and poisoned at least three other people, watching them die in agony. But the shy, rosy-cheeked grandmother was huggable and lovable. It wasn't her fault. She had been drugged at the time and she wasn't drugged now. Was it wrong to try and save her? Who knows. In the end, sadly, no one was to have the answer. A few hours later Velma, dressed in her favourite pink pyjamas, was led slowly to the stark, white room where she would go to the glory her lawyer had promised. As she lay in her death chamber under a blue-grey sheet, the former nurse and housekeeper kept her head turned away from the sixteen official witnesses on the other side of a glass viewing panel. She was still wearing her glasses but kept her eyes closed most of the time. When she did open them, she stared straight at the tan plastic curtain that concealed the prison staff who would execute her. Memories of her life were slipping away in her mind. Once she had been happy but that was a long time ago. She was a nice person, most people thought so. She couldn't help her drug addiction, it had just happened. Was she remembering her father throwing her into the deep lake when she was a child so that he could teach her to swim? She had panicked then, like she had panicked so many times in her life. But it had been nothing like the panic she had felt the night he came into her room to beat and rape her. No one had come to her aid then. Screams were commonplace in her home. How often had she lain awake listening to the screams of her brothers and sisters as he beat them?

The warden gave a signal and the tan curtain moved for a moment as Velma's executioners started to pump sodium thiopental into her arms. Velma closed her eyes for the last time, falling into a deep sleep. She licked her lips and seemed to move them as if in prayer. Her colour began to change from a healthy pink to grey, draining away from a spot on her forehead and working down. When they were sure she was in a deep sleep they injected two doses of procuronium bromide into her. The paralytic substance stopped her breathing. A peaceful end for the serial killer who had tapped her nation's conscience. A woman who had sought only love, protection and a standard of life that was never available to her. Men just could not believe that she could murder.

The doctor slowly removed Velma's glasses, checked her pupils and listened to her heart with a stethoscope. He pronounced her dead at 2.15am before drawing a curtain between her and the witnesses. The woman who by her own admission had watched her four poisoned victims, one of them her own mother, die slowly and in agony did not suffer in her own passing. Minutes later, one of the witnesses, Tom Fuldner, a reporter for WWAY-TV, stood before an encampment of lights, cameras and satellite dishes that had grown up outside the gaol and told newsmen: 'I was struck by how peaceful it was.' As he spoke, inmates inside the prison held lighted matches to their sealed windows in tribute to the sweet-faced, plump grandmother who had always looked as if she should be at home baking cookies. Velma had become the first woman executed in the United States for twenty-two years, and the first white woman ever to be put to death in the state. But not everyone had sympathy for the huggable killer. There were hoots and yells of triumph from another grassy bank outside the gaol as the hour of execution passed. Dozens of pro-death-penalty demonstrators waved signs saying: 'The law is the law' and 'God bless the victims'. It was their day, they had won. They went home satisfied in the knowledge that Old Testament justice had been done.

But the last word came from a woman who approached Velma's lawyer James Little in a fried-fish shop. She told him that she was not sure how she felt about the death penalty, but she was definitely against it for Velma Barfield.

'Why is that?' Little asked.

'Because I identify with Velma, I really do. I think: there but for the grace of God go I. She could have been any woman.'

Velma's head rattled as she took a can of beer from the fridge and poured it into a glass. She stopped for a moment and stuffed a piece of tissue into one of the rollers in her hair so that the Valium and Sinequan pills inside did not roll around any more. She wondered what she had done with the Tranxene pills. Had she hidden them in the dishwasher? She would have to check her hiding places later – the rolls of toilet paper, her bra, the bins in the yard. She peeped through the crack in the open door at Stuart, slumped on the sofa watching TV. He wouldn't be disturbing her for a while. Quickly she opened the cupboard and grabbed the can of Terro ant poison she had bought at the drugstore for a dollar, mixed some into the glass of beer, swallowed two purple pills and went into the lounge.

'Dinner will be ready in five minutes,' she said, passing him the beer.

Her fiancé, fifty-six-year-old tobacco farmer Stuart Taylor, grunted and gulped his liquor as Velma looked on. If he fell ill he wouldn't shout at her over the cheques she had forged. She hated being shouted at. Images of her father flashed across her mind.

'What are you staring at?'

'Nothing, I was just thinking,' she answered.

'Thinking 'bout what?'

'About Humbard. Can't we go?'

Evangelist Rex Humbard was appearing at a revival meeting in nearby Fayetteville that night. Over dinner, Stuart reluctantly agreed.

'I'll make us a cup of tea before we go,' said Velma, returning to the arsenic-based ant powder in the kitchen.

It was a wonderful night in the devoutly Baptist Robeson County. But not for Taylor – he was doubled up with stomach cramps, sweaty and weak. He begged her to take him home.

The phone rang at Alice Storms's house.

'Hello, it's Velma.'

'Velma, it's late, something wrong?'

'It's your father, dear, I think he's got flu pretty bad.'

For three days Taylor thrashed around in his bed with cramps and vomiting as Velma stood and watched.

'Please don't worry, I'm taking care of everything,' she told his forty-year-old daughter again and again over the telephone. 'Don't bother to come over, Daddy is resting.'

On the fourth day, Velma took her weak and thin fiancé to hospital. Only the night before she called his daughter to ask if it was all right to give him an aspirin.

Hours later he died as baffled doctors struggled to discover the cause of his illness.

The screams of a new baby rang out in the little unpainted wooden-framed house deep in the pine-tree countryside of Sampson County, North Carolina. It was 29 October 1932. Murphy Bullard smiled and drank another beer. His second child, Margie Velma, had arrived and there would be seven more. He didn't know then, though if he did he probably would not have cared, that eventually most of his nine children would suffer from alcohol or drug abuse. The tough cotton mill worker walked out into the night air and took a deep breath. The little house was his kingdom and those in it were his subjects. He smiled to himself. He would soon teach his children how to survive and respect him.

Inside, his wife Lillie stared at the ceiling thinking about her life. She believed Murphy was a good man. He worked hard and never shirked overtime. The pay was there every week. Love-making between them wasn't what she wanted. He only satisfied himself and not her. He was demanding. But he loved her . . . well, he said he did. She longed for tenderness but had to accept the way it was. After all, where else would she go? What would she do without him? Anyway, the beatings weren't so bad. She looked at her newly-born daughter Velma in the cot and smiled. This was something good in her life. She remembered her own father, who had died when she was just eight. God, how she had missed him, still missed him. She tried to picture his face but couldn't. She remembered rushing home from school every day to make sure her mother was still alive. One day, when she was sixteen, she had come home and her mother was dead. Her unhappiness had started then. She went to live with her sister-in-law and became a kind of Cinderella, working in the fields, coming home to cook all the meals and do the housework. Even when she was ill she was forced to work. But her daughter Velma wouldn't end up like that, she vowed. The midwife put Lillie's new-born daughter in her arms. No, she promised herself, touching Velma's lips, my daughter won't end up like me.

Velma's father, Murphy, was a violent and abusive man who worked at the local Burlington Mills repairing looms and teaching others how to fix them. The family feared his rages, especially when he was drunk. Work came before them, he was a true company man. If the mill needed him to work an extra shift he did, regardless of sickness in the family or their needs at school. Some, of course, believed that was a good quality. He was paranoid about handouts from the state. 'Man is born to work,' he would say. As Velma grew up, she grew to fear him, and sadly her mother's vows at her birth fell by the wayside. Lillie offered no protection as her daughters and sons went from beating to beating. Like so many families the Bullards lived from one pay-day to the next, but there were good times. Christmas was fun and the children always had presents. In the summer Murphy would take them and the neighbourhood kids into the front yard to play baseball. Some Sunday afternoons they would play until it was almost dark and Velma would be the only girl. On other occasions Murphy would take the children down to the old creek his father had gouged into a swimming hole. He would stand on the bank and hurl them into the deep water to teach them to swim. They soon did. But Velma was uneasy. There was something about the way Murphy touched her. It didn't seem right. To the outside world Murphy and Lillie were the perfect couple. If a neighbour was sick or in need they would always be there, and they never missed a funeral. Even if they didn't know the dear departed very well, Murphy would change his shift at the mill to be at the graveside. But behind the doors of the family's little wooden house it was another story.

It was a cold spring day and the sky over Sampson County was low and colourless. Velma wrapped her coat tightly around her as she walked home from school, the sharp, chilly wind snapping at her runny nose. She had no interest in the array of blooming azaleas and fuchsias under the oak trees, her mind was on other things. She had so wanted to stay behind with her classmates and cheer the boys on in the basketball match, but her parents wouldn't allow it. They would never let her do anything after school hours. She had to come home to do the housework and cook. To her mind she was just a slave.

As she walked down the front path to the family's wooden home she could hear her father shouting at her older brother Olive, was was screaming with pain. Velma tiptoed to the kitchen door and saw her mother sobbing as she stared out of the window overlooking the back yard. Velma sneaked off to an upstairs room and peeped down at her father and Olive from behind a curtain. He was killing him, beating her brother so hard that the back of his shirt was soaked in blood. It was a row over the family car; Olive had wanted to use it. Her father was yelling, punching and kicking. For God's sake, why didn't her mother stop him?

That night Velma tossed and turned in her bed wondering if her brother would die. She knew there was nothing her mother could or would have done. She was frightened of Murphy too. Finally she got to sleep, only to be woken a few hours later by the shouts of her father. She crept again to the kitchen door. He was twisting her mother's arm and pressing his hunting gun against her neck. Velma went quietly back to her room and stood staring at her bed in the darkness. It was on that same bed that her life was to change when she was just thirteen.

It was in the early hours of the morning and Murphy had been on the night shift. He was drunk when he came into Velma's bedroom. Instinctively she knew what he wanted; it was useless to scream, no one would come to help her and she would just be beaten. After he had raped her she lay bruised and sobbing, wondering who would believe her. Her mother wouldn't, nor her aunt who lived next door, and the neighbours thought Murphy was a wonderful man. She would be called a liar and he would beat her again. Velma, feeling dirty and filled with guilt, was to live with her secret nearly all her life. Her only answer was to try to hide her father's wine bottles whenever she could.

When she was sixteen the family moved to Parkton, a pretty town of oak-lined avenues and brightly painted houses in the rural, tobacco-growing Robeson County. It was a close-knit community and everybody seemed to know everybody else's business. Velma started to date Thomas Burke, a tall, thin young man with thick, wavy black hair who was a year ahead of her in high school. They would go to movies in Fayetteville and then on to Buddy's Barbeque or Steve's Tower in the Sky for a burger and coke. But Velma never felt at ease. Her father had imposed a strict curfew on her and if she was home late she would be beaten.

'As soon as the movie is over I always know I'll be in for it,' she told a friend. 'It is always past the time I should be home so I just go on to Buddy's and try and have a good time, because I'm being punished anyway. Might as well be three hours late. Trouble is I never really enjoy it, I just keep thinking about the beating I'll get later.'

Thomas was easy to fall in love with. He was a lot more tender than her father had ever been and she couldn't get enough of his loving in the back of the car or in the woods. Then one day he asked her to marry him. Velma, seventeen, was filled with dread.

'I really want to but I'm too frightened,' she told him. 'If I ask my ma and pa they'll only say no.' Thomas agreed, so they didn't ask. They eloped to Dillon, South Carolina, just over the border. No one bothered to ask them for their birth certificates. When Velma told Murphy what she had done, he went wild. She had asked her mother to tell him but she had been too frightened. Murphy threatened to have the marriage annulled. He suspected that Olive had conspired with Velma and Thomas and went after him, threatening to beat him, but her brother managed to get away and stay out of his sight for a few days. Murphy came home, sat in the chair and wept.

The first fifteen years of Velma's marriage was the best time of her life. The couple made a down payment on a little house in Parkton, a town of about 500 people near the county seat, Lumberton. When Velma first crossed the threshold of her own home she vowed: 'I'll never let a man beat me again – and nobody will ever beat my kids like my pa did!' Privately to friends, she admitted that she wasn't old enough really to know what love was but she was happy. 'For two children, we get along pretty good,' she would say.

When she was nineteen Velma gave birth to a son, Ronnie, and two years later along came her daughter Kim. They were an everyday American family. The house was always open to friends and filled with the smells of home baking. Velma would scurry around in a pinafore handing out hot cakes and buns to kids who came in off the street. She, Thomas, Ronnie and Kim did everything together. They went to the mountains, to the beach, to basketball games, and although Velma would come home from work at Burlington Mills around 8.30am, she'd still sometimes stay up all day and go with her children on school trips, remembering how her father never went on class outings with her. Religion wasn't forgotten either. Velma made sure her children went to church twice on Sunday and to Wednesday night prayer meetings.

The house also became a second home for Velma's young sister Faye. She spent most Saturday nights there. Velma never danced but Faye loved to. Velma and Thomas would take her to the Ocean Plaza, where they would sit and watch her dancing the night away before driving her home.

'Did you have a good time?' Velma would ask her sister in the car.

'Yeah, great.'

'Good, because that's all we came for,' Velma would said contentedly.

Life was good. Thomas loved his job driving a van for Pepsi-Cola, and the money Velma brought in from her job in the cotton mill meant they could afford the odd little luxury. By now, Velma was Faye's second mother. They would talk about everything and anything. Almost anything, that is, for there was still one guilty secret

Velma hadn't discussed – the terrifying night her father had come to her bedroom. Faye was to suffer almost the same fate when she was fifteen.

Early one summer's morning Velma opened the door to find her sister distraught on her porch. Their mother Lillie was in Florida and Murphy had made a pass at Faye in the kitchen. Luckily she had managed to push him away and flee to her bedroom, where she locked the door. Velma felt the hatred for her father rise again. She took Faye into her home, where she stayed until their mother came home, but they never told Lillie. 'Thank God those tragic days are over for me, I'm so lucky now,' Velma confided to her husband, who didn't fully understand what she meant.

Sadly, however, things began to change for Velma. When she was twenty-eight she had a hysterectomy and it profoundly affected her. She felt Thomas didn't love her any more, that she wasn't a whole woman. Her husband did his best to reassure her but it was no good, her mind was fixed. Then Thomas was involved in a car accident. It left him with blinding headaches. Later, Velma was injured in a crash too and it left her with severe back problems. She was in constant pain. Thomas started drinking heavily, and at first she thought it was because his father had died and he would get over it. She was wrong, and before long Thomas's misery was ruining their lives. Velma hated alcohol because of her father's drunken rages. She didn't even like the odd can of beer in the house so she began to hide his drink bottles and flee from his abusive attacks.

'It's tearing me apart,' she told a neighbour. 'I guess I've just had so much in the first seventeen years of my life, seeing people beaten and everything. Thomas has been so good to me and the kids, but now it's all different. I just don't think I can deal with it, he is not the man I married now he is drinking. I just can't cope.'

Neighbours and workmates told Velma to leave him, but she still held out hope that things would return to the way they were in the early years of her marriage. Thomas lost his beloved job as a delivery driver for Pepsi-Cola and he began to drink even more. The pressure now was all on Velma, struggling to raise two children by herself while her husband was in a permanent alcoholic daze. Money was short, and she took on two jobs to pay the bills. She worked by day as a sales clerk at the Belk Hensdale department store in Fayetteville and by night as a machine operator in the cotton mill. Then came another turning point.

'You damn bitch!' screamed Thomas, swinging his fist at her. Velma ducked and fled screaming from the kitchen as her husband almost fell over in his drunken rage. It was the first time he had ever tried to hit her and she turned to the two people who would understand, her brother Olive and, strangely, her father Murphy. They came to the house and quietened Thomas. Velma stood watching her father holding her husband down. Life had turned full circle. Her father had changed. He was wonderful with her children, Ronnie and Kim, and they thought the world of him. From that day on, however, Thomas became more abusive. One cold spring morning, clutching an iron bar, he ran screaming after Velma and the children as they sped off in the car. When they returned in the afternoon they found him drunk and comatose on the bed.

Life was again dealing Velma a bad hand. She was weak and confused. She had lost 20lb and couldn't eat. One morning as she was leaving for work the porch spun in front of her eyes and the next thing she knew she was sobbing in a hospital room. The doctor put his hand on her shoulder but she still couldn't stop shaking. After a while they spoke quietly to each other and he handed her a bottle of blue pills.

'Here, you must take these for a while, they're tranquillizers. They'll help you deal with things. It's important that you follow the instructions.' The doctor wasn't to know but he was handing out a death warrant.

Velma went home and put the bottle in the bathroom cabinet. From time to time she would take one, and when things got really bad she would take two. Two were always better than one. The doctor was right, they did help her cope and before long there was a new bottle of pills, then another, then a cupboard full of bottles. As the months went on Velma formed a plan in her mind. She decided to have her husband committed to the state hospital in Raleigh. She mentioned it to Ronnie, who sobbed and begged her not to. She agreed and for a while did nothing. But her chance came when Thomas was jailed for drunk driving. She signed the papers at the police station and he was hospitalized for three days. When he came home the atmosphere was electric. In his eyes she had embarrassed him and he would never forgive her. There was no love between them. Gone were the days of hot cakes and buns and trips to the mountains. Thomas was addicted to booze and Velma was addicted to drugs.

The end came one cold evening in 1968. Thomas was stoned out of his mind. He stumbled up the stairs and fell on to his bed. Then, apparently, he lit a cigarette and lost consciousness. The mattress burned and he suffocated. To this day there are some who believe Velma was behind his death.

In the months and years that followed, Velma deteriorated. She cried alone, squatting in the corner of her bathroom, like a foetus in the womb, afraid of what would happen if the pills ran out. The tranquillizers were her lifeline, and she had managed to set up a string of doctors throughout the county who gave her the medication she so desperately needed, even though her cupboards were already full. She was paranoid about being found out and would do anything to conceal her habit. In her hazy world she didn't realize that her family already knew. She was fighting for survival. But she still had friends.

Faye talked to her brothers.

'I've seen bottles from different doctors in different towns all over her house,' she said. 'She can just pick up the telephone and ask for a new prescription. I found a bottle of medicine, all kinds, stuck down her bra. She was out of this world, sometimes she doesn't even know what day it is, what time even. She has pills of all colours in a paper towel in her pocket, there are more in her purse.

She has changed so much. She doesn't seem loving any more.'

Wherever Velma went, her family and friends hid their own medicine bottles, fearing that she would steal to feed her craving. Her two children, Ronnie and Kim, would search her house for pills and throw them out when they found them. Like an alcoholic, Velma's hiding places for her fix grew even more complex.

'She takes enough at one time to knock her out completely,' said Ronnie. 'I just don't understand how someone can stay so groggy for three days at a time. Then she suddenly seems to come out of it, and I think she's OK.'

Velma didn't see it that way. 'I can't live without my pills!' she would scream at him. 'Why don't you bloody understand? Do you want me to die? This is my life, what right have you got to stop me living? For God's sake leave me alone!'

They were taking away her strength, why didn't they understand, she thought. But not to worry, she would find a way to survive.

In August 1970 Velma married retired civil servant Jennings Barfield. She had met him through his son, who worked with her at the Belk department store. Barfield was in his late fifties, a widower and devout Baptist. He suffered from emphysema and heart disease. To begin with, he didn't realize that Velma was addicted to drugs or that she didn't love him. But she felt sympathy for him and he seemed to like her. Through her haze of medication, she dreamed that perhaps she would again find the happiness she enjoyed in the early years of her first marriage. She needed an anchor, a tender relationship. Barfield was a good man, even her daughter Kim agreed. She didn't know that in the beginning Kim had been so worried about the relationship that she had tried to warn Barfield about her mother's drug-taking, but he had just felt she was against the marriage and put the thought from his mind. When the penny did drop it was too late. One night he turned up at Velma's parents' house and said: 'Take her in, I can't do anything with her.' Dazed Velma stayed just a few days with Murphy and Lillie before returning to his side.

In March 1971 Barfield died, apparently of a heart attack, and so began a new chapter in Velma's tragic life. Her pills consumption grew, and early in January the following year she was in the back of an ambulance on her way to Southeastern General Hospital in Lumberton, suffering from an overdose. She returned home only to be readmitted days later to have her stomach pumped out following a suicide attempt. Kim told the doctors how her mother was constantly unsteady on her feet and her left eye was badly bruised due to a fall. The only way to treat her was with more drugs.

In April that same year Velma's father Murphy died of cancer. 'I had learned to love him as much as I had hated him,' she told Faye. 'He turned out so good to my kids. I guess he tried to do with them what he wished he had done with us.'

Five months after his death, Velma again attempted suicide and spent twenty-one days in Southeastern

General Hospital. Again the only way to treat her was with more drugs, but the dosages were gradually reduced and by the time she left she was off librium completely. Back in the real world Velma tried hard to adjust. She threw herself into her job at Belk's and for a time all went well. She was one of the store's most dependable employees. But after a while her dependency on drugs returned and the store manager began to notice a change in her personality. She would ignore customers or became impatient with them. Sometimes she failed to show up for work at all. The final straw came when her manager discovered she was getting pharmacies to deliver her prescriptions directly to the store. Velma was fired, and once again she believed that life had dealt her a huge blow. Luckily, she managed to get a job at Burlington Mills in the town of Raeford. Again everything was fine, until she overdosed one morning after coming home from work.

'I really don't care if I live or die,' she told doctors.

Velma never returned to the mill. What followed was a string of other jobs and overdoses. She was treated for chronic drug abuse, endogenous depression and a fracture of the left shoulder following a fall at her son's trailer home. She would often leave hospital with as much medication as she went in with, but every time she left she was optimistic about her life. Next came a job at Moore's department store in Red Springs, but in March 1973 she was arrested for passing worthless cheques and put on probation. The following month she was arrested again – for obtaining drugs on false pretences. Velma was now living with her sixty-four-year-old mother, Lillie, and in need of money to support her drug habit. She took out a $1,048 loan from a finance company, using her mother's name. By now Lillie was beside herself with fear of her daughter and she began to tell the rest of the family that Velma was forging her cheques. One winter's morning, after Velma had given her mother a glass of Coca Cola, Lillie had a pain in her stomach. That afternoon she went down with a severe attack of flu. A few days later she was dead. Velma went to the toilet and flushed away the can of rat poison she had bought at the local drugstore.

By now she could hardly bring herself to speak to Faye. If something bad happened they had always hugged and cried together. After their mother's death Velma just stared into space. Eight months later she was taken into hospital for thirty days, suffering from drug dependence and abuse.

In early 1975 money was again short and Velma was convicted of writing worthless cheques, serving six months in the North Carolina Correctional Facility for Women.

'I stayed on medication the whole time,' she admitted to her son after being freed, 'but nothing heavy.' She told him how she had felt safer in prison. There was a structure there and she was looked after. Outside she felt like a lost fish swimming in a huge pool. On her release, Velma quickly went back to her old habits, shopping from doctor to doctor for sedatives, even forging prescriptions herself. But she did manage to hold down a job as a nurse's aide and that is how she met tobacco farmer Stuart Taylor.

It was September 1976 and Velma was working as a live-in nurse at the Lumberton home of his eighty-five-year-old aunt, Dollie Edwards. Taylor, well-built with dark black hair, was ten years older than Velma and had an alcohol problem. He was a Jekyll and Hyde character. When he was sober, he was kind, tender and understanding. When he was drunk he was violent and abusive. But most of all he was lonely just like Velma. They became friends, then lovers. They went to church together and enjoyed dining out at Jimmy's seafood restaurant or the local Western Sizzler. Taylor even invited Velma and her family to dinner, cooked by him and his mother at his farm. The tough-faced tobacco farmer, who was separated from his wife, finally got a divorce, but he secretly kept seeing his ex-wife and Velma became distressed when she found out. Days later Taylor's aunt Dolly died, twisting and turning in agony with gastric pains.

Velma and Taylor's relationship had rocky patches right from the start. One cold winter's night Taylor showed up at Kim's house where Velma was staying and banged violently on the glass doors, demanding to see her. She had forged a $100 cheque on his account. Unless she repaid the money, Taylor threatened to call the police. Her children paid him back.

Velma's need for money to feed her drug habit was endless. But then she had some luck. A local pastor suggested to Margie Lee Pittman from Lumberton that Velma could be just the person to care for her elderly parents. After all, Velma was a twice-weekly Baptist churchgoer. Margie thought it was a good idea, and kindly housekeeper Velma was soon ensconced at their home. In June that year Margie's father, John Henry Lee, discovered that Velma had forged a $50 cheque on his account. Velma had to stop him telling everyone. The morning he found out, she sprinkled rat poison on his cereal. He was sick for nearly a month, twisting and turning in his bed with torturous vomiting, diarrhoea and convulsions. His weight plummeted from twelve stone to just over eight. Doctors diagnosed gastro-enteritis and chronic intestinal inflammation. Velma was with him throughout his suffering and sent an ornate wreath to his funeral, which she attended.

Velma's family were by now doing all they could to help her out. Everyone loved her, but they had their own lives and their patience was wearing thin. Velma would arrive at her daughter's home every night spaced out on drugs.

'Mum, you're going to have to get yourself out of this, we can't help you,' Kim would tell her.

Kim and Ronnie had their own problems, as people do. How much longer could they go on trying to help a mother who would not help herself, as much as they loved her? One afternoon Velma turned up at her son Ronnie's trailer home.

'Please let me stay, Ronnie,' she begged.,

Ronnie could hardly look his mother in the eye. He hurt so bad inside. But he had to be firm and told her she couldn't.

'Please, Ronnie, please. I promise I won't take anything.'

'Mother, I can't trust you.' They were the hardest words he ever said in his life.

By the time Velma and Taylor became engaged, Velma was working as an aide at the United Care Nursing Home in Lumberton, earning $2.60 an hour. Some weeks she spent as much as $100 on drugs and payments to doctors who prescribed them to her. She and Taylor planned to marry in the summer of 1978. But on 3 February of that year Taylor died – the victim of a mystery virus.

Taylor's daughter Alice couldn't get over how kind her father's fiancée was. She had rung her every day during his illness. Along with the rest of her family, Alice felt great sympathy for Velma. She even raised $400 to help Velma out of her bad patch. After Taylor's funeral, to which Velma sent an identical wreath to the one she had sent John Henry Lee, Velma asked for and received Taylor's wedding ring. Slowly, however, doubts began to form in Alice's mind. Her father had always been a strong man, hardly ever showing signs of illness. She asked for tests beyond the standard autopsy and arsenic was discovered in some tissue samples taken from Taylor's body.

Detective Al Parnell, of the County Sheriff's department, checked the death certificates of four other local people close to Velma. Three out of the four had shown gastro-intestinal symptoms associated with arsenic poisoning, prior to death.

Parnell questioned Velma for three hours. Sometimes she cried, sometimes she got angry, as she denied killing her fiancé. Even for the tough, no-nonsense cop it was a harrowing experience. He had known Velma for years, sat next to her at dances, chatted with her as his twin boys played in her backyard.

The next day Velma called her son, Ronnie, who was in Red Springs visiting his in-laws.

'They are saying I killed Stuart,' she sobbed down the telephone.

'Who are *they*, Mum?'

Velma could hardly speak through the haze of drugs and emotion.

'The . . . detectives.'

'Did you though, Mum? Did you do it?'

'You know, son, you know I wouldn't do that.'

Ronnie put the telephone down convinced of his mother's innocence.

Rumours travelled fast in the small, close-knit town of Parkston, and Ronnie soon discovered that his mother was going to be arrested. It was a cold, grey day as he left work early and hurried across town to the Sheriff's department. An hour later he stood listening in disbelief to a recital of the damning evidence. He told the officer where he was going and left, his mind racing. Making his way over to the Rowan Trailer Park, where his mother was staying, he remembered that she had been on the midnight to 8am shift at the nursing home and would now be asleep. He quietly opened the door of her trailer, went in and sat on her bed. Velma stirred, looked dreamily up at him, and clutched his arm.

'I've spoken to the detectives, Mum, and I believe them, not you.'

Velma started crying. Ronnie leant over and opened

her hand. She had been gripping a Kleenex, packed with ten different types of medication. His mother tried to go to the bathroom but he stopped her, scared that she would kill herself.

'Come on, Mum, I'll take you down to the police station.'

Confronted again by Detective Parnell, Velma finally confessed to having killed Taylor with ant poison, an arsenic compound available in drugstores. She had not meant to kill him, she said. She had only meant to make him sick and then nurse him back to health so he wouldn't be angry with her for forging cheques on his account. When questioned further, she admitted poisoning Taylor's eighty-five-year-old aunt, Dollie Edwards, and John Henry Lee because he had discovered that she had forged a $50 cheque on his account. And yes, she had poisoned her mother, Lillie. The words from her own mouth echoed around her. It was like a whole part of her life had come undone.

'Velma, it is time you had real help,' Parnell said quietly. That day in his office, Velma had already taken two Sinequans, two Elavils, three Valiums, two Tylenol 111s and two Tranxenes. The bodies of Dollie Edwards, John Henry Lee, her own mother Lillie and Jennings Barfield were exhumed. Arsenic was found in all of them. Now her life would change yet again. While awaiting trial she told all who would listen that she had had 'an experience with the Lord'. Whatever it was, it did profoundly affect her and there was an inward change. 'I know there isn't anything the Lord doesn't forgive us for, except rejecting him,' she said. 'We lead our own selves astray by listening to the lies of Satan.'

Velma's trial began on 27 November 1978 and lasted only six days, including jury selection. It was the first time Velma's court-appointed attorney, Robert Jacobson, forty-two, had tried a capital case. The tanned, blond defender filed a motion for assistance but it was denied. The state's lawyer, Joe Freeman Britt, was listed in the *Guinness Book of Records* as the world's deadliest prosecutor. He had obtained twenty-three death verdicts in twenty-eight months to mid 1976, when he had thirteen defendants simultaneously on Death Row.

Jacobson argued that Velma was not guilty by reason of insanity – then called to the stand a psychiatrist who maintained that she was sane. In her defence Velma testified that she had intended to keep her victims ill until she could repay the money she had stolen and earn their gratitude by nursing them back to health. She needed the money, she said, to pay for tranquillizers, anti-depressants and amphetamines. But Jacobson couldn't make Velma show remorse on the stand. Instead Britt, with his tough style, so angered her that she argued with him and, after his summing up, sarcastically applauded.

Said Jacobson: 'I begged her to get up there and cry. Women can turn on the tears when they want to, and she sure needed to then. Instead she did just what Britt wanted her to do, she tried to fight back. I hate to say it but it is all a big game and she just couldn't or wouldn't play it.'

On 2 December 1978, Velma was convicted of the

first degree murder of Stuart Taylor. It took the jury less than sixty minutes to reach their verdict. She was sentenced, that same day, to death. Evidence of other deaths had been introduced in extensive detail during the trial by prosecutor Britt.

As Velma's lawyers started a lengthy series of appeals that took them all the way to the US Supreme Court, she was already on the harrowing road to beating drug addiction at Robeson County Jail. Along the way the plump, hazel-eyed grandmother had become a born-again Christian. Her lawyers now claimed that the judge did not clearly inform the jurors as to how they could consider the effects of drugs on Velma at the time of the crime. But later, Superior Court Judge E. Maurice Braswell, in denying her post-conviction motions for a new hearing, ruled that while there may have been errors in her trial, there were no perfect trials. He underlined his point by describing a recent football game between the Pittsburg Steelers and the Cleveland Browns. Velma's lawyers were angry. 'We sat listening to him in disbelief,' said one. 'He was talking about a football game. Her life was riding on a football analogy.' Time was running out for Velma. The appeals were exhausted. After six years her case had been reviewed by eight courts and twenty-one judges, with five postponements of execution.

It was a cold spring day just before Easter 1984. Velma's brothers Olive and John Bullard drove south from Parkton for nearly two hours, picking up an old family friend, retired teacher Wade Holder, in Fayetteville. Velma's thirty-year-old daughter Kim picked up her two girls, Stacie, eight and Wendy, four, in Lumberton. Faye Bullard came with her daughters, Angela and Dahlia, from Charleston, South Carolina, along with Velma's son, Ronnie. They were paying one of their last visits to their mother, grandmother, sister and friend, who was sitting on Death Row.

Faye hoped the orange orchid she had bought for her sister would not be taken away by the guard at the electrically operated iron gates of the North Carolina Correctional Center. It wasn't, even though presents weren't allowed. Kim's little daughters danced and skipped in their new yellow Easter dresses but no one smiled. Slowly the small party walked across the courtyard lined with flourishing azaleas to the single, sixty-feet-square cell in the red-brick maximum security building where Velma lived. Gates groaned open and closed, one uniformed escort was replaced by another and there were bits of paper to sign. Finally they stood before her. The little girls ran to their grandmother, who swept them off their feet and hugged them. No one would let go. Velma had crocheted some Easter bunnies with big fluffy tails for them. As the girls picked them up, there were hugs and tears with the rest of the family. Life for Velma now was a commode, a shelf packed with religious cards and a radio blaring out sermons from the Bible station. There were boxes of letters too. She received around fifty a week from well-wishers in places as far away as Nashville and New York. Among her supporters was Ruth Graham, wife of evangelist Billy Graham. They all felt that she had served as a source of counsel and inspiration for other prisoners. 'They'd come in ready to kill themselves and here she was with a death sentence, mothering and helping them,' said Sister Mary Teresa Floyd, fifty-three, a nun who had resigned as a volunteer co-ordinator at the North Carolina Correctional Center to devote more time to the thirty-member Velma Barfield support committee. Velma herself echoed her supporters' thoughts. 'The majority of us have put our own selves here in this prison. When we learn to accept that, we begin to make some progress,' she told a world eager to listen. Several of Velma's most devoted correspondents were young inmates of the jail, some only fifteen years old. 'That's just a baby placed in prison, you know,' said Velma. 'I call them my adopted kids. It's hard when you see their hurt. I can relate to them because I have hurt too – I know that feeling of not wanting the daylight to come.' Velma had picked up some bad habits in jail. She started smoking as a substitute for drug-taking and she was over-eating.

'Lord, it's terrible,' she told her warders. 'When I came in here I was only about 125 pounds, and now, oh golly, I must be up around 168.' Everyone laughed. No one hated her.

But there were other views. 'She may have religion now, so they say. Well, she had religion before, so we all thought,' said Margie Lee Pittman, who had hired Velma to look after her father before he died of arsenic poisoning. Prosecutor Britt found little that was persuasive in Velma's tale. 'Just how many people do you know with difficult childhoods who go around killing people?' he said. 'If she gets out, she will kill again. They're trying to get sympathy by making her out to be some sweet little old grandmother.' His statement caught the imagination of middle America, struggling to protect their families against muggings and murder. 'Hell,' he added, 'we would probably discover she poisoned half the county if we only had the resources to exhume all the bodies for autopsies.' And Alice Storms said: 'We don't want revenge, we want justice. The credibility of our system depends on the laws being carried out and a jury of her peers said she should die. If anybody had told me ten years ago that I would be passing around petitions and making picket signs for somebody to be executed, I would have said they were crazy. I never even used to believe in capital punishment. But – and God help me if I'm wrong – every time I even think about what that woman did to my daddy, I want to see her dead! She took one of the most precious things in life anyone can have – a father. She stood over my daddy and watched him writhe and twist in pain and she said nothing!' But Velma's lawyer James D. Little countered: 'Her drug-taking is not an excuse but an explanation. No one is saying she should go free.'

Velma said quietly: 'I have known all the time that the appeals could be exhausted and that we could come to right where we are today. I have lived with that all this time. I know that a date is going to be set.'

The family talked quietly to their champion, forty-year-old attorney Little, who had resigned his position as chief counsel for the Public Staff of the North Carolina

Utilities Commission so that he could devote most of his time to trying to save Velma's life. He claimed that the jury was never presented with the full breadth and depth of Velma's addiction and her background. If evidence available at that time had been brought out, they might never had sentenced her to death.

In pamphlets, newspaper interviews and talk show appearances, Velma's supporters revealed all of the gruesome detail from the beatings and rape by her father to the inadequacy of her mother to handle his temper. Velma only revealed the rape to her minister and her sister after the trial. 'I've just kept things bottled up inside,' she said.

Little had expected that the US Supreme Court would not grant Velma's appeal for a new trial and that the execution date could be as early as July. He was to be wrong on only one count: the execution would be in November. One evening, staring out of the window of his home as the rain beat down on the trees along the drive, he realized that his only recourse would be the clemency proceedings. From that moment on he urged all the family to speak to Governor James B. Hunt Jr personally.

Little paced up and down his lounge. He was desperate to show the Governor that Velma had turned her life around and that any compassion he could show would not be misplaced. He had to convince him that if she spent the rest of her life in jail he could expect her to have a positive influence on her fellow inmates. The Governor also had to be convinced that the Velma her friends and family loved now was the Velma they knew and loved before the killings happened. Little, however, was worried that Velma's image could work against her, given that capital punishment was disproportionately imposed on black males. 'Velma's statistically OK to kill,' he had grimly told colleagues. 'She is white, she is middle-aged, she is a woman. Executing her would even the score.' The Press clamoured for words from Velma, and they got them. She told reporters: 'Even if I have to live in jail I would like to see my family as much as possible – and see my grandchildren brought up. I would also hope I could contribute something to the other ladies who are here in prison. I want to help them cope with their own situations because I know what it is to hurt.' Velma was reflective about her mother whom she had poisoned. 'Hardly a day passes that I don't wish I could sit down and talk to her,' she said. 'Things come to mind that a girl should share with her mother sometimes. I came from a family of nine children. My father was high-tempered and very abusive to us kids – and to Ma. I grew up being afraid. If only I could have talked to someone about the hurt and pain that was going on inside.'

It was Little's last chance. But the hardest part for him came the next day. Velma's relatives were aware that family members could be present at her execution. Little explained to them that the witness room at Central Prison was small and that there had to be public witnesses as well as four members of the Press.

'I know Velma would like some of you to be near her if this happens,' he said. 'But you all ought to talk about this amongst yourselves. I want to deal with it only when it is necessary.'

Faye broke down in tears and her daughter Angela hugged her. Little could not look at them. His jaw was set so hard that a muscle in his cheek was pulsating.

The family did their best with North Carolina Governor James B. Hunt. He listened to them all – and he also heard pleas from relatives of Velma's victims. But in the end it was to no avail.

Minutes after he rejected Velma's plea for clemency, exhausting her last hope of appeal, an affidavit was filed by Little expressing her wish to be spared further delays. Hunt told reporters: 'Death by arsenic poisoning is slow and agonizing. Victims are literally tortured to death. It has been a tragedy for an entire community as well as our state.' Of nearly 4,800 letters on Velma's case received from people throughout the country, more than 2,900 favoured the death penalty. Among 3,600 letters sent from North Carolina, more than 77 per cent argued that Velma should be put to death.

Little felt crushed, but he had to think of the woman he now believed had suffered enough. He turned down thirty pleas from death penalty opponents urging him to delay the execution with paperwork. He said sadly: 'At some point, it is necessary to face reality.'

As Velma's children began making funeral arrangements, their mother's case was inflaming passions across America and the western world. She was a serial killer but there was more sympathy for her than her male counterparts. Was she cunning to the end like Mary Ann Cotton and Nannie Doss? No one will ever know. But one thing was certain, all of them had shown mercy to their victims. For friends and relatives of both Velma and her victims, the case was a test of the judicial system. Just how many people she actually murdered will remain a source of speculation throughout time. Even Little admitted that she could have also poisoned Jennings Barfield, her second husband. When his body was exhumed it contained a lethal dose of arsenic. Velma's daughter Kim said: 'It has always been a question in the back of my mind, whether Mummy had anything to do with Daddy's death too . . . but I never asked her.' Two of her brothers, both proud men with a strong code of loyalty to their kin, claimed the incest story about their father was a lie.

Days before her execution Velma sat serenely in her cell, oddly detached from her past and seemingly unconcerned about the next day. But wouldn't any killer facing execution? A killer's only hope is public sympathy. All she would say was: 'I just can't remember a lot. I didn't have a clear day for ten years.' One of her last acts was to donate her organs for transplant. But officials later reported that only the skin, bone and cornea were saved for the living.

Little had the last word: 'I'm going to live with Velma Barfield for the rest of my life, always wondering if there was anything else I could have done,' he said.

Chapter Five

TERRI RACHALS

'There is a real war inside of me because I do not know whether I committed these acts or not.'

Albany, Georgia, 1986

The man and woman walked solemnly along the corridor leading to the psychiatric wing. Neither of them could really believe that they were doing this. They had known her for so long; they liked her, admired her even, everyone did. Head nurse Diana Hall and nursing director Lou Raines, walking side by side, thought of Terri Rachals as a professional, a registered nurse who loved her family and her patients too. Lou glanced behind at the woman police officer checking Terri's handcuffs. Surely it couldn't be true – or could it? Had she really killed patients in the hospital? Now she wanted to kill herself, he knew that. At this moment in time, how could they help her?

Later, they all stood in hospital administrator Duncan Moore's office. Twenty-four-year-old Rachals, standing handcuffed and silent next to a lawyer; Dougherty County Sheriff's investigator Ed Taylor; Moore; Raines and Hall. Others too.

'Terri Eden Maples Rachals of 3100 Dunaway Drive?'

'Yes.'

'You stand charged with the murder of Andrew Daniels by administering potassium chloride to him intravenously,' said Taylor quietly.

Rachals's eyes showed no emotion. There was no trembling of the hands, no anger, no surprise. She was just respectful to all around her. In reality she couldn't remember anything about the crime she was alleged to have committed. A sobbing in the background broke the silence. The medical staff were in tears as she was led quietly away, facing investigations into two other suspicious deaths and up to nine assaults at the 432-bed Phoebe Putney Hospital in Albany, Georgia, where she was believed to be a loving and caring nurse. Moore stood in silence as the door closed on his office. What the hell was her motive, if it was all true? It couldn't have been euthanasia. It was unlikely that a patient would have made that kind of communication to only one nurse. There were lots of doctors and nurses on the unit, someone would have told him about it. There was no pattern to the suspected assaults, no apparent link with age, race or sex. The only common denominator was that they were all very, very sick. Moore turned and looked out of the window, tears in his eyes too.

What he didn't know was that the Phoebe angel had been suffering from a passive, aggressive personality, severe depression and histrionic traits, a combination of disorders that had made her a risk on the wards.

That same afternoon the Press clamoured for details

about the arrested nurse. Inspector Johnny McGlamery, Chief of Operations for the Georgia Bureau of Investigations, sat pole-faced before the cameras, as police officers do. He sipped water from a glass and refused to comment on whether other charges were pending. But he added: 'I won't comment on my idea of the motive, I can't at the moment.'

Rachals's hospital friends and colleagues, however, were only too anxious to provide the Press with details. Meanwhile many of the medical staff were already receiving calls from former patients and their worried relatives, anxious to know if potassium chloride remained in the body.

'She never seemed strange,' one nurse told a reporter, refusing to be identified. 'Her husband is handicapped and she had a lot to be responsible for, especially with their two-year-old child. It is hard to believe, I have known her for years. We all loved her, we still do.'

Another hospital official said: 'There has been genuine grief among the nurses. It must tell you something about what kind of person she is if we are all in tears. We are all destroyed. We thought this kind of thing only happened in the big cities. We just keep asking each other what we can do for Terri. We are praying for her.'

Moore acted to calm the fears of former patients and their families. 'If I were a relative or a loved one of a patient who had been in the intensive care unit, I would have a question or two myself,' he said. 'But everybody can stop worrying. Potassium compound is commonly used in intravenous solutions. There is no residual damage to patients who were in our intensive care unit. They're not going to wake up dead!'

He had the last word as he sat at his desk facing a barrage of questions from reporters. 'If you put a portrait of Terri Rachals on paper you wouldn't expect this arrest to happen.' Prevention was impossible. 'We don't feel there is any way you can prevent something like this happening. Obviously we don't, or we would have! But there is no reason to believe this could happen again here. It was a person problem, not a hospital problem. It was highly regrettable but it should not reflect on the hospital. We are definitely going to go forward. We have a fine record. Records are to build on, not to stand on.' The reporters hurried to the telephones. They were fighting for space. The big story of the day was President Reagan's announcement that the United States would detonate an underground atomic bomb the following month, regardless of Soviet leader Mikhail Gorbachev's plea for a test ban.

The emotion following the arrest of Rachals had led to counselling sessions for Moore's staff. One tearful nurse who rang the hospital from home was told by a team set up to calm their fears: 'We'll all get through it somehow, by supporting each other as we do already; you are not the only person to feel like this.'

As the tears flowed, the true story of the evil that had crept into the seventy-five-year-old Phoebe Putney Hospital during the winter months of 1985 began to unfold. But was Terri Rachals a female serial killer or not? Books and newspapers in America and Britain branded her as one. Her friends, family, lawyers and some of the jury who judged her remain uncertain. This is her story.

George Pete Donaldson dropped the cigarette end into the soft-drink bottle on his desk and watched it fizzle out in the last dregs of orange squash. Damn it, he would give up smoking tomorrow; he needed a hit of nicotine right now. He sat back and rubbed his eyes, then gazed around at the curtainless, uncarpeted room that was his office on North Jackson Street. Three chairs, two tables, file trays with 100lb of documents, a desk covered with books and medical notes and no telephone. On the door he had pinned a notice saying: War Room.

This was Donaldson's bunker. From here he would be defending his client Terri Rachals, indicted on six counts of murder and twenty counts of assault. The odds were stacked against him – and against her.

'Telephone, Mr Donaldson!'

The woman's voice shouting up the stairs broke his thoughts. He knew it would be his client on the telephone. She called frequently, collect, from a pay phone at Georgia Regional Hospital in Augusta, where she was undergoing psychiatric evaluation while awaiting her trial, which started the next day.

Donaldson walked down the stairs to take the call. He had seen Terri a few days earlier and they had spent their time walking around the perimeter of the campus-like hospital grounds. It was a good place for her, Donaldson thought. There was initially no room at Central State

Hospital in Milledgeville, where she was held before being transferred to Augusta, and she had been forced to sleep in the hall. Now she worked in the hospital greenhouse and spent most of her free time in the library, where she read the Bible and spiritual books that friends had sent her. She was also reading publications on the effects of alcoholism on families, maybe because her adoptive father was a self-avowed alcoholic who had taken the cure. Donaldson's client was on anti-depressants because of fears that she might try to commit suicide. But that afternoon in his office he wasn't too worried about her. There was no place that she went in hospital where she was not observed. She was escorted from building to building and was only allowed to move around the grounds without guards if she was with an appropriate visitor like himself. He picked up the telephone.

'Hello, Mr Donaldson.'

'Hi, Terri, how are you doing?'

'I'm missing my family.'

Terri saw her husband Roger and her two-year-son, Chad, two out of three weekends. The cost of travelling and hotel accommodation was prohibitive. The family had no money. The couple had sold their home to help pay legal costs, but the cash didn't provide enough to pay Donaldson's fee. At 400 hours he had stopped counting the time he had spent on the case. Now it was more like 700 hours and that was without the trial. Some of the costs he was paying from his own pocket because he believed his client was a woman who desperately needed help, even though she was being branded as a serial killer.

'They'll be praying for you,' he said. Her husband, her son and Donaldson prayed together each time they visited her.

'I'm scared about tomorrow.'

'Don't be. We'll all be with you.'

Donaldson planned to introduce the testimony of fifteen witnesses who would give an insight into the mind of his client. But his best hope was Terri Rachals herself. He was going for a not guilty verdict. He knew that a 'not guilty by reason of insanity' finding would mean at least five years in a mental hospital. But a straight 'not guilty' would release her. In that event he hoped that she would go into a psychiatric hospital for long-term treatment. She had mental problems, he knew that.

After ten minutes of reassuring his client, Donaldson put down the telephone and climbed the stairs.

He was worried. It was the first time he had tried a murder case. He needed another cigarette.

The quiet, diligent nurse with layered brunette hair bustled about the intensive care unit, joking with her colleagues and checking the medical notes of patients in her charge. She was well thought of by the other nurses and admired by doctors, who considered her a well-trained professional. In every respect twenty-four-year-old Terri Rachals appeared to be a normal young woman. She attended Weight Watchers classes, played with her two-year-old son, cross-stitched and kidded around with patients' families at the Phoebe Putney Hospital. But beneath the surface, this quiet, unassuming angel nursed a burning secret. She was haunted by the memory of seeing her much loved adoptive mother die in an intensive care unit when she was just eleven years old. Always at the back of her mind was the whiteness of her mother's face, as white as the sheets around her frail body, and the tubes, all those tubes sticking out of her skin. What happened to Terri Rachals that day as a child somehow profoundly affected her for ever. So too did the events that came after.

Things were not easy from the start.

Rachals was two years old when her mother suffered a nervous breakdown and she was adoptive by Louise Maples and her husband Jim. For nine years they lived as a normal family, but when her adoptive mother died things changed dramatically. Rachals adored her father and he was all she had but after the death of Louise he began to drink heavily and allegedly dragged his adopted daughter into the murky world of sexual abuse. A jury would later hear allegations of how in the summer between her junior and senior years in High School he would lock her in a room, hit her and rape her at gunpoint. The drinking and molestation finally drove her from their home when she was sixteen and she moved in with relatives in Albany, attending Westover High School. The one thing that kept Rachals going during this time was her burning desire to help others. She dreamed of becoming a nurse one day. Was it a real deep caring within her – or the deep desire to have control over others weaker than herself? Perhaps it was simply a way of doing things to make up for her guilt feelings of being sexually abused a a child. No one will ever really know.

Rachals was a strong believer in God and went to the Byne Memorial Baptist church, where she sang in the choir and was a regular visitor to Sunday School. It was there that she met her future husband, Roger, a printer at an Albany supply company who suffered from cerebral palsy. They began dating as Rachals went on to nursing college to fulfil her ambitions.

At last there seemed to be some order in her life. A nursing career she always dreamed of and a man who was besotted with her. Marriage had to be the next step and they agreed to tie the knot. For a while everything was fine. They seemed the perfect couple as they settled down to a life in a middle-class suburban Albany neighbourhood. They were thought of as 'nice and average'. But the die was cast on Rachals' life and things began to go wrong for her again. Within a year she and Roger were having sexual problems. When he touched her she would pull away. She loved him, but she kept seeing her father's drunken face staring down at her. In the end, the long silences, the hurt, proved too much for her and she confessed to Roger that her father had molested her. The kind, caring cerebral palsy victim was understanding as always, and for a while their marital situation improved. He learned how to handle his fragile young wife and their relationship grew stronger, especially after their son, Chad, was born. But the haunting problems in Rachals's mind would not go away, and before long the sexual problems returned. Her mother's tiny face buried deep in the white sheets of the intensive care bed, her father's drunken stare, both were imprints on her mind that returned like camera images without warning.

She later told a court: 'Roger would get angry with me about my problems and tell me to leave him alone. But I found that very difficult to do. I wanted to make everything OK, talk to him and sort it out.' When she pestered him verbally, he would hit her out of frustration, she claimed.

Things went from bad to worse as the months went by. Her personality seemed to change. She began discovering hundreds of dollars in her purse that she could not account for. All she could remember was that her father claimed he had lent it to her. She also began to gain weight, even though she believed she was on a strict diet. When her husband found hamburger wrappers in her car, she knew they had to be hers – but she didn't remember eating hamburgers or buying them. Clothes that she had never seen before appeared in her wardrobe and on many occasions she could not account for the long, lost hours between leaving work and arriving home. When she checked her car afterwards, large amounts of petrol would be missing.

This was the backcloth to the life of registered nurse Terri Rachals during the months that led up to November 1985. No one on the wards of Phoebe Putney hospital knew the terrifying secret world behind her warm smile and unending kindness.

Tuesday, 13 November was a day like any other. Rachals laughed and joked with the other nurses, attended patients, made coffee and checked medical notes in the eight-bed intensive care unit. No one noticed her fussing around seventy-three-year-old Moultrie truck driver and former construction worker Andrew Daniels. Daniels had undergone surgery to treat an abdominal abscess the previous day and appeared on the mend. He was on an intravenous drip and responding well to treatment. Then, for no apparent reason he suffered a massive cardiac arrest. He died twenty-four hours later. There was no suspicion of foul play, why should there be? Death was part of hospital life, so no autopsy was called for. His death certificate filed in the Dougherty Probate Court revealed that he was a diabetic and the cause of his death was listed as kidney failure. But hospital officials were puzzled. The number of deaths in the unit had risen sharply. At first they thought the equipment was at fault. They had not long finished replacing it and now they wondered if the machinery was too sensitive. Or had they received a rogue batch of drugs? One clue was that Daniels appeared to have an extraordinarily high level of potassium chloride in his body, 20 milliequivalents. The colourless chemical was used in small, diluted amounts in the treatments of nearly all surgery patients. Potassium was also found in many foods, including bananas, coffee, oranges, salmon, sardines, tomatoes, canned tuna and turkey. The recommended daily allowance was 2-6 grammes, with the normal American adult averaging 4.5 grammes. Taken in small doses over a day, it passed quickly through the human system. But if taken all at once, especially if someone was ill, it could prove fatal –

and did. Daniels appeared to have had 1.5 grammes in his body in one quick hit. In fact, straight into his veins, a method used by some states for execution by injection. The hospital management couldn't believe they had a killer in their midst. Everyone on the intensive care unit had worked there for so long. Rachals herself was a three-year woman, dedicated to 'one-to-one' care. She had never had a single reprimand in her career. But when administrators checked the records and found that nine people had died of cardiac arrest in the unit that November, they were suspicious. The normal number over a month was three to four. Very few patients who suffered cardiac arrest died. Normally a buzzer would go off and the team would resuscitate them. The managers had no alternative. On 25 November they implemented Code Nine Protocol, a security measure involving cameras, extra surveillance of patients, checks on drug supplies, tests on used intravenous tubing and probes into the health of recovered patients. Potassium chloride was made available only under a 'sign-out' system. Even a state epidemiologist was called in to investigate, just in case there was a deadly virus at work. The careful monitoring went on for two months, during which time only three more cardiac arrests occurred, well within the normal average of three to four a month. Managers breathed a sigh of relief. The November tragedies were obviously a statistical aberration. It happens.

On 31 January 1986, Code Nine was lifted and things got back to normal. The New Year had brought new hope. Overnight the tension in the intensive care unit disappeared. Nurses laughed and joked freely again, doctors breathed sighs of relief and Rachals was able to concentrate on her 'one-to-one' work.

Four days later however, another patient on the unit suffered a heart attack. Luckily, he was revived. But again doctors were baffled – for the patient had a high level of potassium in the body. Staff checked the diet, the drugs and the equipment. They weren't looking for somebody, they were looking for something. The next day the hospital laboratory discovered high levels of potassium in the patient's intravenous tubing. Code Nine was reinstated and the potassium supply put under lock and key. As a safeguard, all medications were required to be checked out by two nurses. It was possible that someone had inserted the mineral into the IV line. On 11 February the same thing happened again. Special Intensive Care Unit patient Samuel Bentley suffered a massive cardiac arrest. Happily he was resuscitated, but the next day the hospital laboratory reported that intravenous tubing used to inject blood by-product into his body had a high level of potassium. The administrators had no choice: they called in the police and the Georgia Bureau of Investigations took over, but even that move did not bring the answer. Doctors soon found they weren't the only ones to be baffled, detectives were baffled too. There were over 1,200 staff in the hospital to check on. Back came the cameras to see if anyone was slipping in and out of the ward. Relatives were checked out along with the staff, but surely there couldn't be a killer among the medical team, they were so close-knit – a long-serving bunch of trusted doctors and nurses who dedicated their lives to saving others. One person, though, would bring a breakthrough in the case.

It was a rainy, windswept afternoon. Ann Rambusch took off her wet overcoat and shook it before spreading it out to dry on the radiator in her office. For several days Phoebe's worried director of critical care had been checking the chart of shifts during the unusual period of cardiac arrests in the intensive care unit. The 3pm to 11pm nursing shift was a disaster, and what she had discovered didn't please her at all. There were just a few more checks to be made and so she logged on to her computer. An hour later she was certain. In almost every case Terri Rachals was on duty.

On Thursday, 13 March Rachals was questioned by detectives and hospital officials. She sat facing Georgia Bureau of Investigations agent Lee Sweat in a room furnished with only a few tables and chairs. Slowly, respectfully, she began to answer his questions as detectives began to piece together her story. After forty-five minutes the polite, fragile-looking young nurse suddenly admitted injecting deadly doses of potassium chloride into five patients, three of whom had died. The officers were dumbfounded as they switched on a tape cassette to record her confessions. Rachals also told how she removed labels attached to potassium chloride bottles and placed them on the charts of patients who were not supposed to receive the chemical. Then she spoke about elderly patient Samuel Bentley.

Bentley was an eighty-three-year-old retired textile mill

foreman. He had been admitted to Phoebe Putney Hospital in February for treatment of gangrene in his left leg, and also had stomach problems. But his heart was healthy and strong. While in intensive care, however, he had suffered several heart attacks, the first on 11 February. When he died, on 22 February, the cause of death was put down to acute renal failure. But the death certificate also noted 'respiratory distress syndrome' as another significant condition leading to his demise. Doctors diagnosed an abnormal amount of potassium in his body.

'So you injected potassium chloride into the intravenous lines used to treat five patients,' said Sweat, taking notes.

'No, with Samuel Bentley I injected the potassium into the plasma bag instead,' Rachals answered firmly.

That taped statement was later to seal her fate. She went on to reveal that after the plasma bag was attached to Bentley's IV line, she began watching his electrocardiograph strip 'because I knew something was going to happen'.

Sweat looked at the hospital records. They showed that as soon as the strip displayed signs of potassium poisoning, she called for the doctor.

Rachals looked sad for a moment, then leant over and stared agent Sweat in the eye.

'Do you think I have done these things?' she asked.

Sweat stared hard at her.

'Yes, ma'am, I do.'

The questioning was over. Nurse Diane Hall, Rachals's supervisor, helped her from the chair.

'I'm so sorry, I really didn't hurt some of these people. I helped them,' Rachals said softly. 'They promised me they would help me, and now I may have to go to gaol.'

At 7pm that evening Terri Rachals put on her coat and walked slowly down the corridor leading to the hospital's psychiatric unit. Within an hour she had been admitted suffering from chronic depression, after telling doctors that she desperately wanted to kill herself.

Rachals's distressed husband, Roger, arrived at the white-walled special unit where doctors had put his wife in a private room.

'Why did you say you did this?' he said, barely choking out the words.

'I did do it, Roger. I need help and you've got to get it for me,' she replied.

Hours later his wife was sedated and put in a private room. The next morning she was taken to administrator Moore's office and charged. A few days later, her face hidden in her bound hands, she was whisked away to a psychiatric hospital.

On 25 March, a Dougherty Grand Jury indicted Rachals on six counts of murder and twenty counts of aggravated assault involving patients at Phoebe Putney Hospital. Listed as murder victims were: Daniels; Milton Lucas, sixty-eight, of Sylvester, who died on 19 October 1985; Minnie Houck, fifty-eight, of Moultrie, who died on 7 November; Joe Irvin, thirty-six, of Albany, 10 November; Roger Parker, thirty-six, of Sumner, 15 November and Norris Morgan, three, of Albany, 26 November. Rachals also faced aggravated assault charges involving Bentley, Daniels, Houck, Lucas and Parker. Other alleged assault victims were Lee Correctional Institute inmate Frankie Creech (six counts), George Whiting and Jack Delma Stephens (two counts), and Frances Freeman of Albany. Creech later died of brain damage at an Augusta hospital. It was alleged that some patients who didn't die after being injected with the potassium compound were injected with it again after they recovered. They only recovered because they received immediate resuscitation treatment by medical staff.

Rachals and her husband Roger had no money but she desperately needed a good attorney to defend her. They put their house up for sale and hired a man who was to dedicate himself to the case, George 'Pete' Donaldson from Albany. One of Donaldson's first task was jury selection. He was anxious to identify potential jurors who had been prejudiced by the pre-trial publicity, so he hired a jury selection expert. It was to be the cause of his first clash with the prosecution and firebrand District Attorney Hobart Hind.

Hind was angry. He complained when Judge Asa D. Kelley Jr postponed the hearing from 9 to 15 September so that Donaldson's jury selection expert could vet the men and women who were to sit in judgement. Hind claimed Donaldson had disrupted the prosecution's schedule of witnesses and had created extra pressure on his already overworked and understaffed office. He also questioned the motives of the jury selection expert, whom he described as 'a volunteer'.

'It's my opinion as DA that his sole interest in the trip

to Albany, like a number of lawyers who have unquestionably contacted the defence counsel, is to get his name registered in a lurid case through which Dougherty County must suffer,' he told reporters. 'It is none of his business, whoever he is! This volunteer will be working at his own expense, since the defendant is poor and has exhausted her drain on the taxpaper's money for medical help.'

Hind warned he was planning to challenge Rachals's claim of indigency.

Donaldson retorted: 'He's welcome to challenge it. But obviously my client has not worked since 13 March and has had to sell what assets she had to pay a portion of the attorney's fee.'

He added that the Gainesville consultant, whose identity he refused to disclose, was a woman who did not volunteer her help and was being paid by money raised from the sale of Rachals's house.

'My client has not paid all my charges,' he said. 'She sold her house and got what she could to pay some of my fee, which is not high.' He had set aside the sum raised to cover expenses and a portion of that money had been used to hire the jury selection consultant.

Donaldson, with his jacket off and shirt sleeves rolled up, sat behind his desk covered with documents and told pressmen: 'I'm not in this for money or glory, I'm in it to represent a lady who needs help.' He added that he had discussed with Rachals's husband Roger the possibility that they might never be able to pay off their attorney's fees, and he also hit out at Hind's contentions that publicity-hungry attorneys had offered their services for free.

'I've not been contacted by any other lawyers wanting their name in the case,' he said. 'I've been working alone. The consultant didn't contact me, I contacted her.'

If either of them enjoyed an 'unfair advantage', Donaldson contended, it was Hind, who had mustered the forces of the Georgia Bureau of Investigations, the assistant district attorney, the assistant felony co-ordinator and himself. Not only that but Hind had been allowed to set up an office at Phoebe Putney Hospital and had been given 'free access to all employees', while Donaldson had his interviews coordinated by hospital attorneys who remained present.

'I have no grudge against Hind,' said Donaldson. But he contended that the District Attorney had misjudged his motives for hiring the jury selection expert.

'No lawyer tricks,' Donaldson said. 'It is a reasonable request. Usually defence lawyers are screaming for a change of venues. If we are to avoid moving this case to another county, which we don't want to, we have to engage in additional safeguards. This is not a typical case.'

The jury selection process he proposed to use would finally save taxpayers money, he said, by avoiding the need to change venue.

Donaldson had filed a formal plea of not guilty to all charges on Rachals's behalf. He also gave notice that he would be raising the issue of insanity or mental incompetence. Rachals's nursing licence had been suspended by the state Board of Nursing and she was undergoing psychiatric evaluation to see if she was mentally fit to stand trial.

Neighbours in the quiet middle-class street where she lived refused to believe she was capable of such evil. 'If you believe your mother could do it, then you'd believe that she could do it,' said one. 'She's not a murderer. That's the craziest thing I've ever heard!'

The Press and the media were awash with motives for the alleged crimes and most of the so-called experts seemed to agree that she was driven by a desire to end the suffering of terminal patients. The debate raged on.

A month later, Rachals's psychiatric evaluation was completed. The DA's office announced that she would face a jury after all. Doctor Thomas Hall, the medical director of Central State Hospital's forensic services division, in Milledgeville, Georgia, had notified officials of Dougherty Superior Court that Rachals was 'fully competent to intelligently assist her attorney in the preparation of her defence and was competent to stand trial'. Hall's evaluation also addressed the debate surrounding Rachals's possible motives. 'It could be considered that there was a mitigating circumstance in that she feels the patients she allegedly terminated were asking to die and she felt she had to do something to relieve their discomfort and misery,' he said in a letter. 'At no time have we been able to find evidence that these feelings were directed by delusions of any nature, however.'

And so Donaldson began his jury selection process. He sat in a small hearing room with his controversial consultant and told each of the thirty-eight prospective jurors during individual questioning that his client suffered from a mental disorder or illness that caused periods of time when she couldn't remember what took place and during which she did unusual things. Rachals, he added, had undergone 'some fairly substantial abuse' from the age of eleven until she was sixteen.

'Do you believe abuse can shape or mould personality?' he asked one prospective juror. And he asked them all if they were familiar with *Sybil* and *The Three Faces of Eve* . . . films about women with multiple personalities.

'Do you believe a person can have a mental disease or disorder that affects them to the point they don't know what they are doing?' he probed.

The prosecution was swift to counter his line of questioning. Assistant District Attorney John Hogg waded in. He asked the prospective jurors if they believed a person could fake mental illness to avoid being held accountable for their actions. Donaldson responded with a question of his own: 'Do you think people might fake being sane to keep people from thinking they are crazy?' he shouted.

'Do you know anybody who is a hundred per cent sane?' Hogg replied.

Hind knew damn well that Donaldson was going to raise the issue of Rachals's sanity. He countered: 'The other side of the coin is, have you ever met somebody who is meaner than sin? They want power and control so much they will do horrible things to people. I'm not just trying anybody. I'm trying a registered nurse. That's one of the finest callings on earth. She has disgraced her cap.'

And so the argument went on. Finally, the result was that twenty-one potential jurors were disqualified after saying they had already formed opinions concerning Donaldson's client.

It was noon on 16 September 1986 when Terri Rachals, dressed in a peach-coloured skirt and a peach-and-cream striped blouse, was led, head bowed, into the Dougherty Supreme Court. She nodded to her attorney Donaldson and quietly sat down beside him. Her husband Roger, looking pale and shaken, rested his head on his arm with his face hidden from pressmen.

Fifteen minutes later, DA Hind, who had subpoenaed eighty-nine of the 100 witnesses, stood up and cleared his throat before making his opening statement to the jury of seven blacks and five whites.

Nurse Terri Rachals, he said, 'felt like a second-class citizen all her life'. And because she wanted power and control she sought it on the dark side of the street by murdering patients at Phoebe Putney Hospital.

Rachals showed no emotion as he went on. 'Some folks are just criminals – not insane. You are not trying an average everyday person. You are trying a registered nurse. When this individual graduated from nurses' training, she was given the Florence Nightingale pledge in a small Bible. That pledge says: I will never inject someone with a harmful drug. What you will now realize in the next few days is that these are torture killings. These people were surgically wounded.'

For the first time, Rachals lost her composure. She was visibly distressed, with tears in her eyes. Donaldson comforted her. Hind paused for a moment and walked up and down as if lost in thought. Rachals, he went on, had accomplished what she had set out to do, experience power and control by throwing the hospital into chaos.

'She set out to manipulate everything at the hospital and right now she is nationally important. She has achieved her aims.'

Hind also contended that mercy killing was not her motive.

One of her alleged victims, Lucas, a sixty-eight-year-old truck driver, was joking with his doctor about going to watch a ball game. Hind said: 'He was on his way out of the unit. She hit him on the way out of the unit. His heart failed. It was in no way associated with what was wrong with him.'

The prognosis of another alleged victim, three-year-old Norris Morgan, was poor, Hind acknowledged. 'The doctors said he didn't have a chance. His head was crushed but his strong little heart wouldn't let him die. Perhaps God had plans for him. We'll never know. She took his life.'

Rachals sat with her head bowed and eyes closed.

Donaldson sat shaking his head. He had declined to make an opening statement.

The state's first witness, Phoebe's director of critical care Ann Rambusch, took the stand. A murmur went round the court and the judge banged his hammer, bringing silence. Slowly, painstakingly, she told jurors that Rachals was either the attending nurse or on duty when eleven patients named in the charges suffered cardiac arrests.

Suddenly her voice choked with emotion and she wept as she described how fifty-eight-year-old brain cancer victim Minnie Houck died.

Donaldson approached the stand as Rachals sat with her head in her hands.

'You showed emotion over the death of Mrs Houck,' he said. 'Well, Terri showed a great deal of emotion over the death too, didn't she?'

Mrs Rambusch nodded in agreement. 'Yes.'

Donaldson pushed on. 'Mrs Houck expressed several times after surgery that she wanted to die, didn't she?'

'Yes.'

Mrs Rambusch told how three or four cardiac arrests each month were normal in the hospital's intensive care unit, but in November hospital officials had noticed an abnormally high number. 'Patients seemed to be sicker. We had disaster on the three to eleven shift,' she said.

Under searching cross-examination from Donaldson she agreed, however, that open heart surgery patients were generally brought into intensive care during that shift.

'So the three to eleven shift is the most critical time for those patients. If they are going to have problems it is likely to be in that time span after surgery.'

Mrs Rambusch agreed.

Donaldson returned to his seat, leant over and whispered something into Rachals's ear. Murmurs broke out in the room again.

A few days later the court sat in silence as Rachals choked back the tears and blurted out the story of her early years. She had been just eleven years old when her adoptive mother Mrs Maples died, she told the jury.

'My dad was very lovable. I adored him. He was the one I went to when I wanted something,' she said. But after her mother died he began to drink heavily.

'It was the night before Thanksgiving and he was drunk. He called me to his room and told me to lie down beside him on his bed. I did. I didn't think anything of it – but then he began to kiss me all over.' Rachals stopped for a moment, trying to compose herself through the tears. Donaldson nodded to her to try and go on. 'I began to cry as he molested me, I felt sick to my stomach.'

The next day, when the family gathered for Thanksgiving dinner, she did not tell anyone about the incident because she feared being taken away from her father.

'Don't you see, he was all I had left,' she told the jury.

Maples had denied sexually abusing his adopted daughter, but admitted that sometimes he drank so much that he did not remember what he did.

At 3.10pm on Tuesday, 13 September, the jury, Judge Kelley, Hind, Donaldson, court officials, Rachals and a handful of reporters filed into a room for a Jackson-Denno hearing where GBI agent Lee Sweat was waiting to play the twenty-minute confession he had taped.

Jackson-Denno hearings allowed defence lawyers to object to confessions they claimed were not factual and believed were not given voluntarily.

Donaldson argued that Rachals's mental state was

unbalanced at the time the recording was made. They sat quietly as Sweat turned on the machine. Rachals, who had seen transcripts of the tape but not heard it played back before, broke down and wept.

'I just couldn't stand to see them suffering any more,' she said emotionally in the taped interview. 'I wanted to stop doing it, but I didn't know how.'

As he left the hearing Donaldson was surrounded by reporters.

'In her mental state she would have confessed to the sinking of the *Titanic*!' he clipped. He needed a break and went out into the sunshine to a light a cigarette.

An hour later, he approached the dock where Rachals was sitting. She had testified that she did not remember injecting the patients named in her taped confession, and now did not believe that she had done so.

'You heard the confession tape-recorded by the Georgia Bureau of Investigations agents?' Donaldson asked.

'Yes,' she answered quietly, looking at him with trust in her eyes.

'Did you think you were telling the truth?'

'I was real confused. They told me they thought I had done it. I started thinking about such crimes very seriously, and I thought maybe I did do it. I had so many strange things happen to me I could not explain.'

Rachals vaguely remembered the names of some of the patients whose heart attacks it was claimed she caused, but she did not remember injecting any of them with potassium.

'I wanted to talk to the Georgia Bureau because I

wanted to clear my name,' she said. 'At the time I didn't think I needed a lawyer.'

After the agents told her she was in the unit during 98 to 100 per cent of the heart attacks, she began to visualize injecting the mineral into the plasma bag used to treat Samuel Bentley.

She told how the agents who taped her statement couldn't have been nicer. 'They seemed to know what they were talking about and I have a real high respect for authority,' she said.

Hind rose to his feet and walked across to Rachals.

'Have you ever justified mercy killing?' he asked.

'No, sir. I have very strong feelings about the right to die with dignity, but I do not believe in mercy killing.'

Rachals stepped down and her close friend, nurse Laura Cook, took the stand. She testified that the accused Phoebe nurse was present when the heart of patient Frankie Lee Creech inexplicably stopped beating on 13 November.

'She asked to watch him when I went to lunch,' Laura said. 'I was walking out of the intensive care unit doors, and before I hit the elevator, I heard the alarm bells.'

Laura hurried back to the unit and found Rachals performing resuscitation on Creech, a twenty-six-year-old Lee Correctional Institute inmate who had been in a coma since suffering a head injury.

Laura added: 'Terri said . . . "He did it again." He had suffered several cardiac arrests before. When I asked her if anyone else had been in the unit she said: "No, just me."

Creech survived that arrest, but on 24 November he was rocked by six more. His primary care nurse, Kelley Bruner, said he had appeared 'very stable' all morning but at 11.30am, when she stepped out of his room, the alarm went off.

She rushed back with other nurses and he was successfully resuscitated. 'Throughout the series of cardiac arrests, Rachals was watching monitors at the nursing station while we were in the room,' she said.

Hogg later asked Bruner: 'How long would it take someone to inject 10ccs of a drug into an intravenous line?'

'A matter of seconds,' she replied.

Donaldson approached the stand. 'If someone came in and injected a patient five times, and each time he had a cardiac arrest, do you think you would remember?' he asked.

'Yes,' she said.

'Do you remember that happening?'

'No.'

Soon it was the turn of the psychiatrists. Doctor Everett Kuglar, the superintendent of Georgia Regional Hospital in Augusta, took the stand.

Kuglar, ordered by the court to provide a psychiatric evaluation of Rachals for the defence, told the jury that the defendant suffered from chronic depression, 'a long-standing' hysteric personality and a dissociative disorder. It caused her to slip into 'fugue states' during which she was capable of carrying out purposeful activities but was not aware of her environment. Kuglar claimed that while in a fugue state Rachals was incapable of distinguishing right from wrong.

'I think this girl can believe things that she has not done and cannot believe things that she has done,' he said.

The court heard of the long, unexplained lost hours between the time Rachals left work and arrived home, of the missing petrol, and of the unexplained hamburger wrappers in the car. Juryman Darrel Corhen, a Pizza Hut restaurant manager, fidgeted in his seat. He wondered why she never got lost on her way to work for a couple of hours? There would have been a record of it. Or why she never wandered around the hospital for hours? His thoughts came back to the courtroom as Kuglar went on to tell how victims of such a rare disorder had histories that were almost always consistent.

'They have been badly sexually abused and are torn between guilt and the need to please Father,' he said. 'They put themselves into a fantasy world where they can cope.'

And because of their disorder, he added, they were extremely susceptible to suggestion, particularly from authority figures.

'I don't know whether she did these things or not,' he said. 'But people like her can confess to things they did not do. I do not think she is a normal person, period. She is a very sick person who needs to be in a hospital. The disorder is treatable. These people need three to six years of rather intensive psychiatric treatment.'

Hind drew a sharp response from Kuglar when he suggested the psychiatrist had coached Rachals before she testified.

'I haven't taught her anything, I have no reason to,' Kuglar retorted. 'I'm paid by the state. This was a court-ordered evaluation.'

He said Rachals had experienced fugue states since being under his care.

'She would run around, writing on the walls: "Leave me alone, damn it!" I don't think it is very normal to write on walls for a person as passive as Terri.'

Three other psychiatrists were called to give evidence: Dr James B. Craig of Central State Hospital, who evaluated Rachals for the prosecution, Dr Omer Wagoner of Americus, who evaluated her for the court, and Dr Mansell Pattison of the Georgia Medical College, who was hired as a consultant by Kuglar.

'I feel she did know right from wrong at the time the alleged crimes occurred,' Craig maintained. But he added: 'I think she is very suggestible, especially to authority figures.' But Pattison agreed with Kuglar that Rachals was incapable of distinguishing right from wrong. It wasn't just the mind of Rachals that was split, the psychiatrists were in two minds too.

Donaldson approached Wagoner on the stand. Hind in his opening statement had described Rachals as 'a tigress stalking her prey'. A witness for the defence had described her as 'a puppy looking for love'.

'Which description would you use?' Donaldson asked Wagoner.

'She is a hurt puppy,' he replied.

After nine days of evidence it was time for the prosecution to make its closing statements. Hind stood and cleared his throat, staring hard at the jury.

'Ladies and gentlemen, Terri Eden Maples Rachals had the ability to be the nurse of the year, but was the murderer of the century,' he said. He paused for a moment before adding that her own father, Jim Maples, had become the twelfth victim in the case through her claims on the stand that he sexually abused her as a child. Maples was 'tried for incest and child molestation and convicted without a jury', he said, claiming that the defence did this nationally and had sentenced him to a life of disgrace and ignominy.

Then Hind turned on the foundation of Rachals's defence – her mental competence. He echoed his assistant's contention that she was not mentally incompetent. He told jurors that a confession freely given was 'the highest form of evidence', reminding them of the statement taped by agents on 13 March in which she admitted injecting five patients with a potassium chloride solution. In her confession she acknowledged injecting some patients but denied doing so to others. Such discrimination, Hind said, was the act of a rational person.

Next came Hogg. He walked towards the jury. 'Terri Rachals knew what was going on last October, November and February,' he said. When hospital officials implemented a surveillance system called Protocol Nine, it made it more difficult to obtain potassium chloride. 'That's when she stopped injecting patients.'

Rachals was cunning, he added. 'When they stopped Code Nine, she started in another way.' Since a new hospital policy required two nurses to witness any injections, Rachals injected a bag in the elevator, when she was alone. Hogg picked up a frozen plasma bag used in the treatment of alleged victim Samuel Bentley and displayed it to the jury. Shortly after receiving a transfusion from this bag, he said, Bentley suffered a heart attack. A former Phoebe technician had testified that she found thirty times the usual amount of potassium in the plasma bag. At first, the potassium content of the bag was so high it could not register on the machine. Finally a microanalyst for the Georgia Crime Laboratory in Atlanta testified that the potassium level in the bag's tubing was eleven times higher than normal.

In the 13 March taped confession, Rachals said she had injected Bentley's plasma bag and the IV lines of four other patients with potassium chloride. Three of them died.

The prosecution rested its case.

On Thursday, 25 September, Judge Kelley, in his fifty-minute summing up, told jurors that since the mental capacity of the defendant was an issue, they had to consider four verdicts: guilty; not guilty by reason of insanity; guilty but mentally ill; or not guilty.

'The defendant shall be found not guilty if such person did not have the mental capacity to distinguish between right and wrong during the commission of the alleged crime,' he said.

At 10.42am the jury retired to consider its verdict. In

the jury room the seven men and five women wandered around in silence for a few minutes. Then they sat down at a long, oval table and said a little prayer before beginning their deliberations. An hour later they sent a note to Judge Kelley asking to listen again to Rachals's taped confession, and they wanted to review reports from the State Crime Laboratory concerning punctures in Bentley's intravenous solution bag. Kelley refused their request, saying that since the evidence had been closed it could not be provided to the jury. Then they asked for an easel, which was sent in.

After nine and a half hours' deliberation the jury returned. They found Rachals guilty but mentally ill of the 11 February assault on Phoebe patient Samuel Bentley. They acquitted her on six counts of murder and nineteen other counts of aggravated assault involving patients in the hospital's surgical care unit. Judge Kelley deferred sentence until 1 October.

The court was in uproar. Reporters ran for their telephones.

Hind was furious. 'Justice has been thwarted!' he said.

On the morning of sentence, Donaldson asked Judge Kelley for his permission to read a statement to the court, written by Rachals. The judge agreed, as the former Phoebe nurse sat expressionless beside the attorney who had fought so hard for her. She didn't even glance at her former colleagues, dressed in their intensive care uniforms, sitting in the front row of the court.

Donaldson rose to his feet and loosened his tie. He then read the letter.

'As a Christian I know that to hurt or take another life is wrong,' he said. 'There is a real war inside of me because I do not know whether I committed these acts or not. I honestly don't think I did – but if I did, I know I could never have done it with hurt as the intention. I would also like to apologize to the state for all the time and expense this case has taken. And lastly, I would like to say that I know my sentence will be fair – so all I can ask is that I be allowed to have the mental counselling necessary to once again be a productive member of society.'

A hush fell over the court as Donaldson sat down. He put his arm around Rachals, dressed in a white blouse, blue skirt and maroon sweater, as Ann Rambusch, director of Phoebe's critical care, stood to make an emotional appeal that 'no mercy' be shown.

Rambusch cleared her throat and began. 'As Terri Rachals gave no mercy, she should receive none in return,' she said. 'For the victims, for the families, for the nurses and for the patients past and present, I ask for the maximum sentence.'

She said she had never seen patients' rights 'violated in such an obscene and brutal way'. And she added: 'She knew the difference between right and wrong. She was in control then and she remains in control now. Rachals is more dangerous than a tigress – she is more like a lean and hungry wolf. She has written a sorry chapter in nursing history.'

Chattering broke out in the court as she sat down. Moments later Judge Kelley passed sentence. He sent Rachals to gaol for seventeen years with three years' probation. He also ruled that on her release from prison or any other institution, she must be tested on a psychological stress evaluator every two months for five years to determine if she was engaging in any illegal activity.

Donaldson was crestfallen. He had claimed that his client had been imprisoned in her mind for fourteen years, since the day her mother died when she was eleven. He had not anticipated such a severe sentence and planned to appeal. He wanted Rachals to be returned to Georgia Regional Hospital, where she had been undergoing psychiatric evaluation for several months.

The sun came out behind the clouds as he walked down the steps from the courthouse, clutching his briefcase. He stood for a moment and buttoned up his shirt collar as reporters clustered around him.

'My client is holding up well,' he said.

'Mr Donaldson, you have expressed concern that Terri Rachals might become suicidal if sentenced to a long jail term. What do you think now?'

'She's very emotional at the moment but philosophical. I'm sure they'll take whatever precautions are needed to ensure her wellbeing while incarcerated,' he said.

Donaldson walked into the sunset with the jury, the Press and the public in disarray.

'The general consensus of the jury was that Rachals was guilty!' Pizza Hut manager Corhen later told the *Albany Sunday Herald*.

The juryman added: 'She could have been found guilty on other counts but we had no evidence. The prosecution blew it! People are telling me: you let her go. I tell them: if you want to blame someone, blame your prosecutor because he had to prove it and that was something he failed to do.'

Jury foreman Warren Butler, a manufacturer's representative, said: 'In a few cases she might have been guilty of other charges. But we don't think we got evidence from the prosecution to support beyond a reasonable doubt that she was.'

Prosecutors should have provided proof that potassium chloride was missing and could have been used in the alleged assaults, other jurors said.

'When Rachals revealed in her taped statement that she removed labels attached to potassium chloride bottles and stuck them on the charts of patients who were not to receive the chemical, the District Attorney should have brought those charts to court,' added Willie Davis. 'But he didn't. The DA failed to bring strong enough evidence. I'm not going to convict her because somebody thinks she did it.'

A woman juror, who did not want to be identified, asked: 'Where was the missing potassium? Without evidence to show some was missing, I couldn't find her guilty. Anyway, just because she was the nurse on duty doesn't mean she did it. Other nurses were on duty too. Why point the finger at the sick girl?'

Rachals said in her taped confession that she had injected potassium chloride into the intravenous lines used to treat four patients, but that in the case of Bentley she had injected the mineral directly into the plasma bag instead.

'She definitely remembered doing that one,' commented Davis.

In a newspaper poll, the jurors said they were convinced that Rachals suffered from a mental disorder that caused her to confess to crimes she did not commit. But they did not believe that she would have corrected the GBI agent over the injection of potassium chloride into the plasma bag if she were not guilty.

'We think it was done in a state of poor mental health,' said Butler.

Davis was sceptical about Rachals's various states of mind. 'Once you commit a crime you can always say you did it while suffering from insanity,' he said. But he added that the psychiatric testimony convinced him that Rachals's mental problems could have led her to make a false confession.

'I know of people who have been accused of crimes they didn't do but have confessed,' he said. 'I'm forty-eight years old and I was raised in the South. I know of black people who were beaten into a confession or promised something if they confessed. It can happen.'

Corhen also wondered why Rachals was charged with inducing heart attacks at some times and not at other times when she was present at the unit and serving as the primary nurse for the patient who suffered the cardiac arrest. 'That raised a lot of questions,' he said. He contended that Rachals could have been found guilty of causing the five heart attacks she originally admitted to if the prosecution had backed up the confessions with solid evidence. 'The prosecution was taking it for granted that she was automatically guilty – and didn't do its homework!'

The jurors also said they believed some of the heart attacks could have been the result of natural causes.

'There was a feeling among us that the high potassium levels could have been caused by other factors,' said Butler.

'Some patients were the victims of God, not victims of her,' said the unnamed woman juror.

'It boils down to a lack of evidence by the District Attorney's office,' said Joyce Day, another juror.

'You can't say a person did it unless you have evidence,' echoed juror Winfred Knight, a truck driver.

Hind, however, said the verdict represented 'a permissive approach to crime'. He claimed that prosecutors 'couldn't have presented a better case than they did under the atmosphere and the conditions they had to work'.

The defence counsel received as much praise from jurors as the prosecution received criticism.

'The defence did a spectacular job,' Davis said.

'Donaldson was ready for the case, he asked the right questions,' echoed Corhen. He said jurors noted early in the trial that Donaldson was building his client's defence around the issue of her mental competency. 'But the deeper he got into it, it looked like he was saying: since the prosecutors are practically giving it away, I'll go with it!' he said. 'Donaldson just kept hammering at the lack of evidence linking her to the alleged crimes. Everybody went in thinking: we'll find her guilty! But the last two days of the trial went from there to . . . maybe she did it, maybe she didn't, based on the witnesses and the evidence. This case could have been proven beyond a reasonable doubt.'

Corhen felt that Hind had 'tried to come on too strong' by describing Rachals as 'a tigress stalking her prey'.

He added that the prosecutors should also have taken up the offer of a defence witness, Dr Mansell Pattison of University of Georgia Medical School, who testified that he could induce susceptibility to suggestion in someone within five minutes.

'I wanted to raise my hand and have him prove it,' said Corhen. 'If someone could do it to me, I'd believe it. If the prosecutors had asked for it I would have volunteered, because I don't believe he could have done it. The prosecution fell down, big time!'

On one thing the jury were united. They all agreed Rachals needed psychiatric treatment. 'We were all very concerned,' said the anonymous juror. 'We said a prayer before and after our deliberations. I pray we did the right thing!'

Corhen had the last word. 'It hurts,' he said.

In October 1986, a court-appointed psychiatric team decided that Terri Eden Maples Rachals should be admitted to prison and treated on an out-patient basis rather than serve her seventeen-year sentence in a mental hospital. She was taken to the Women's Correctional Institute in Hardwick, Georgia.

Relatives of her alleged victims filed eight lawsuits in the Dougherty County Superior Court, claiming that she caused death or serious injury to her patients. Also named as a defendant in the suits was Phoebe Putney Hospital.

Chapter Six

DOROTHEA PUENTE

'Did you know I used to be a very good person once?'

Sacramento, November 1988

The crowd outside the quaint, tree-lined Victorian house at 1426 F Street had waited ten hours in the drizzle to see another body. Police officers pushed neighbours and out-of-town sightseers back as another bulldozer moved in. Twenty men with hammers and crowbars were knocking holes in the floors, smashing up concrete patios and tearing down the garden gazebo. Paving slabs were being ripped up and the brick wall bordering the front yard was already a pile of rubble. Forensic scientists stood huddled over lumps of soil on a table in the kitchen.

It was all a devastating blow for Ricardo Ordorica. The overweight, 4ft 5in tall Mexican immigrant stood mopping his brow with a grimy white handkerchief as the home he had rented for $600 a month to his dear family friend Dorothea Puente two years earlier was being destroyed before him. When white-haired, softly-spoken Dorothea had told him she wanted to turn the two-storey house into a rest home for poor and elderly people, Ordorica, then forty-eight, believed he had finally stepped up a rung on the American ladder to success. He was a good man, who had worked eight years as a night janitor to earn the down payment for the imposing little house set behind a wrought-iron fence and brick pillars in downtown Sacramento, and his first and only tenant meant that he could afford to move his family, whom he loved so dearly, to a better neighbourhood. Things were going well. He had also been promoted to chief gardener at the hotel where he worked. But in less than two years his dream had turned into a nightmare. Now he faced ruin. Surely the police would pay for the damage they were doing? he told himself. But even if they did, who would live there now, what with the bodies and all? He would never get another tenant. His mind was working overtime.

Using hoes and steel rods to probe the rain-soaked earth, detectives had found one body buried under a metal utility shed and, a few hours later, a second in the meticulously maintained front yard under a shrine of St Francis of Assisi. One of them was an elderly woman, wrapped in a tablecloth like an Egyptian mummy. The sex of the other was unknown – it was just a collection of bones.

'We won't stop digging until we have turned over every square inch of earth in this goddam garden!' vowed police Sergeant Bob Burns to his men. Ordorica heard him and more panic set in.

'I can't understand it,' the Mexican reasoned with an officer. 'Dorothea wouldn't have done this. She wouldn't have murdered anyone. We love her. She loves my kids like they are her nieces and nephews.'

His jumbled mind slipped back to the day he had met Dorothea fifteen years earlier. He was at a local bar where they had both gone with their respective partners to hear a group of Mexican singers. She smiled at him across the smoke-filled room and he put his thumbs up as a sign he liked the music. She sent him a beer. She was like a movie star, draped in fur and pearls. She was with her husband. There was a bodyguard and a chauffeur. They became friends in drink that very first night, and talked about the singers, about Mexico, about life. They vowed to stay in touch through the haze of alcohol – and they did.

Puente became a close friend. She was so caring. She adopted Ordorica's wife Veronica as her own sister and helped his family to overcome the language barrier with the Americans on the block. Then Dorothea's husband divorced her and she needed help. Ordorica was there for her and she moved into the top floor of his little palace in downtown Sacramento. Within months she became so attached to their four children that she called herself their aunt.

Ordorica looked on as another piece of his precious brick wall came under the pickaxe. The letters, yes, the letters, didn't these people destroying his home know about them? The letters from the King of Jordan, the Shah of Iran and the Pope. She had shown them to him. Where the hell were they? The police should see them, then they would know she couldn't possibly have done this. He remembered how she had told him the Shah had proposed marriage to her and she turned him down because she knew in her heart that he needed to marry someone who could give him an heir, and she couldn't.

The crowd was noisy. Ordorica walked to the gate and stared out at them. Goddam ghouls, one nutter was already wearing a T-shirt with the words: 'I dig Sacramento!' For God's sake, it was the fourth day the police had been here. They had better put his house back together, there must be at least $10,000 worth of damage by now. Where the hell was Dorothea?

Police had quizzed the fifty-nine-year-old landlady after finding the first body. They quite liked her – after all, how many people in the world dedicated their lives to helping down-and-outs? Not an easy task, and they knew better than most, dealing with the losers on the streets. More importantly, there was no evidence against her. They told her she could come and go as she pleased. And go she did. Wearing purple high-heeled shoes, a pink dress and a red overcoat, she had simply vanished into thin air with $3,000 cash in her handbag. As police continued digging, she got a cab to the bus station and a Greyhound bus to Los Angeles. Within hours the police department realized they had messed up and issued an arrest warrant. But was it too late? The Mayor was already asking questions. Burns was irritated that detectives had let Puente go. They should at least have put her under surveillance. They had been called to the eight-bed-roomed house after receiving reports from neighbours that an elderly tenant had been missing for three months and there were strange smells coming from the back yard. On their first visit, Detective John Cabrera had tugged at a root just under the soil at the rear of the wood-panelled sanctuary for down-and-outs. When it came free in his hand he realized it was a leg bone. Minutes later he had dug up a shoe with a skeletonized foot in it. But there just wasn't enough evidence to charge Puente. The bones could have been there for years.

Burns stood reading statements from neighbours. Puente, they said, used to garden at odd hours, around four or five in the morning, and would often leave six-foot long depressions in the ground. The tough police sergeant tried to create a picture of her in his mind. She was a strange woman, no doubt about it. Some described her as a kind, grandmotherly person; others said she was a cold-blooded crook who drugged and abused old people and was prone to fantasies. Local bartenders had told him she regularly tipped them $10 each month and bought Giorgio perfume and makeup for her favourite waitresses.

'She was a classy lady, a kind of Elizabeth Taylor with white hair,' one recalled. Some weren't quite so kind. 'She's crazy, she's nuts,' they said. Puente had apparently told them tales of having been a prisoner-of-war in Europe. A book about her war experiences was soon to be published, she boasted. In another bar she had bragged that she was a wealthy surgeon who owned homes in Lake Tahoe and Mexico but was forced to retire early because she was losing her hand-to-eye coordination. More recently she had confided to one barman that she had been diagnosed as having cancer and was undergoing chemotherapy. The cancer had been caused by exposure to radioactivity in Hiroshima, where she had served as an American war nurse after the bomb was dropped. Funny, Burns thought, she did have skin cancer once. It had been cured following surgery.

'Bob, over here!' The voice from the garden broke his thoughts and he hurried over to the hastily dug hole in the ground.

As he looked down at the body wrapped in rotting bedsheets, he wondered how one woman could have dug the grave by herself.

Former tenant Homer Myers, seventy-four, had the answer. He said: 'She asked me to dig several holes in the back yard, one of them for an apricot tree. She said she had contacted a nursery and they told her she needed a hole that was four feet by four feet and five feet deep. I thought that was big. Now I know why.'

By the end of that wet and windy weekend, the number of bodies stood at five. Four of them had been buried in the feotal position. Days later police found two more. The final death toll linked to Puente was to be nine.

*

Charles Willeagues was suspicious. She was friendly all right and quite classy. But there was something about her. He couldn't put his finger on it.

'Let's have another,' he said, and the barman poured her a third Martini.

She was a widow from San Francisco who had lost her luggage when a taxi drove off with it.

'I need my shoe fixed,' she told him, taking it off and twiddling with the high heel. 'I don't know Los Angeles very well, can you recommend a place near by? I'm staying at the Royal Viking Motel on Third Street.'

Willeagues, sixty-seven, a disabled pensioner, gave her the address of a good shoemaker.

'He's cheap too,' he said, glancing at her long leg as she put the shoe back on.

'You on social security benefits then?' she asked.

'Yep, it's a struggle.'

'Know the feeling; perhaps we should live together then – two can live as cheaply as one,' she said with a twinkle in her eye, adjusting her stocking around her ankle.

Willeagues looked at her hard. He had seen her face before but couldn't think where. He promised to give her a call. When she left he remembered. He had seen a picture of her on a Channel 2 news broadcast earlier that day. Suddenly he felt sick. The woman he had been talking to was Dorothea Montalvo Puente, who was suspected of murdering seven tenants at her Sacramento boarding-house. The announcer said she had disappeared four days ago and was still cashing their social security cheques. Was that why she wanted to know if he was on the social too? Willeagues called the TV station and then the LA police.

At 10.40pm on the windy winter's evening of Wednesday, 17 November, six police cars sealed off the Royal Viking Motel. Police Sergeant Paul von Lutzow waited until his men were in position, then knocked at the apartment door.

'Who's there?'

'Police, open up.'

Lutzow was about to knock again when the door opened on the chain and a white-haired, elderly lady in a pink dress peered into the night. He showed his police card and she let him in.

'Can I see some ID?' he asked. 'Driver's licence or any other documents.' There was hardly any reaction and he was surprised. Usually when the police went into someone's motel room people got upset, but she showed no emotion. It was almost as if she expected him. She walked slowly to her purse and didn't say anything, just gave him the documents.

'Dorothea Montalvo Puente, you are under arrest. Do you know your rights?'

There was no curse, no struggle, she just picked up her red coat from the bed and went with him. They drove to Burbank Airport in handcuffs and boarded a charter jet bound for Sacramento.

'I've not killed anyone,' she told police. 'I just cashed the cheques. Did you know I used to be a very good person once?'

What followed was the most sensational murder trial in Sacramento history. Puente was found guilty, but the battle to save her life developed into a courtroom debate that delved into the mind of a female serial killer and held America spellbound. It was to have a profound effect on the jury and their lives would never be the same again.

'This woman is like a birch tree, bowed but not broken by the ravages of the weather,' Vlautin told the jury, who sat listening intently. The defence lawyer slowly brushed back his thinning black hair with his hand. Fifty-year-old juror Ruby Hewlett-Ratcliff glanced across at frail, white-haired Dorothea Puente sitting in silence next to her attorneys and wondered how such a sweet little old lady could have carried out a string of horrific murders. Ruby shivered, as if someone had stepped over her grave.

'Sadly, she was bent at a very early age and she never overcame it,' Peter Vlautin went on.

It was a bright sunny morning in October 1993. Judge Michael J. Virga scribbled some notes as the lawyer walked slowly up and down the stuffy, windowless Monterey County Superior Court. Vlautin told how Puente was the victim of abusive and neglectful parents whose lives disintegrated and who were gone from the world before her seventh birthday.

Nine weeks earlier the landlady from 1426 F Street, Sacramento, had been found guilty of murdering three bad-tempered and difficult boarders who had crossed her threshold: Dorothy Miller, sixty-four, Benjamin Fink, fifty-five, and seventy-eight-year-old Leona Carpenter. The jury had been deadlocked on six other counts. The verdicts, returned after twenty days of deliberation, meant that Puente would spend the rest of her days in custody, but the question of her death by natural causes in gaol without parole or by execution was now being put to the court under the American system of Penalty Phase. This allowed jurors to show mercy, compassion and sympathy to a convicted killer. It was the job of the defending lawyers to tap those emotions among the eight men and four women in that small Monterey courtroom. The trial had moved from Sacremento to Monterey nine months earlier, after the judge felt Puente would not get a fair hearing in her home town because of the publicity surrounding the case.

That October morning Vlautin was pleading for the life of the serial killer who had taken some of Sacramento's most difficult men and women into her web on F Street – drug addicts, alcoholics, even the mentally ill. All were unsuitable for shelter at government facilities because they were hard to handle.

Vlautin paused and stared hard at the jury. Would they sentence Puente to die – just like she had sent her victims to early graves in her garden?

Ruby and the other jurors had already heard the tragic story.

Puente was born Dorothea Helen Gray on 9 January 1929 in Redlands, San Bernardino County, California. Her Baptist parents, cotton picker Jesse Gray and Trudy Yates, were drunks who continually verbally abused her.

Money was scarce, and what little the family had went mostly on cheap alcohol. Even at the age of three, Dorothea was kept busy clearing up vomit or climbing trees to pick fruit for food. Jesse died when she was four and her mother was dead before she was six. Puente, one of seven children, was placed in an orphanage but later went to live with relatives in Fresno, California. Later in life she was to create a whole new fantasy childhood, telling people she was one of eighteen children born to Mexican parents in Mexico City.

'That little girl standing out in front of the orphanage is still in Dorothea Puente today,' Vlautin said, showing the jury a photograph of his client as a sad-looking child. He urged them to recognize Puente's humanity. 'There is life, there is hope, please don't give up on her . . . you don't have to kill her.' He returned to his seat, and his colleague, attorney Kevin Clymo, leading the defence team, stood to echo Vlautin's thoughts.

'We're not trying to excuse Dorothea's conduct,' he pleaded. 'We're not trying to convince you that you have made the wrong decision by finding her guilty. There is no excusing crimes of the magnitude for which she stands convicted. But I tell you, men and women of the jury, I have spent the last year close to Dorothea and I have discovered that within her there is still a child of a tender age. Please believe me, I have seen it.'

The jury had heard how Puente was married four times, the first when she was just seventeen, to a man named Fred McFall, who died of a heart attack two years later. A widow at nineteen, she desperately needed money and so began to forge cheques for a living. But these were early days in her life of crime and she was soon caught. A judge sentenced her to a year in jail and she served half of it before being paroled. It was her first time behind bars but it would not be the last.

Months before she was released, she had formed a plan in her mind. Nursing and caring for the less fortunate in society was to be her way of making money. But she liked her men and the physical contact she desperately needed came first. A year after being released Puente had a baby girl, whom she immediately gave away for adoption. She was to wipe her daughter from her mind, claiming in later years that she had always been unable to have children after losing several through miscarriages and stillbirths.

In 1952 Dorothea married a rough, tough Swede named Axel Johanson. It was an often violent relationship that managed to last for fourteen years. But Puente, who did in fact suffer several miscarriages, was no push-over, as time would tell.

In 1960 she served ninety days in Sacramento County Jail after being arrested at a brothel. She claimed she was just visiting a girlfriend but the judge didn't believe her. She was released only to be picked up on the streets and given another ninety days suspended for vagrancy. Johanson, still her husband, apparently wasn't bothered. He was too busy doing his own thing. For Puente, however, a string of brushes with the law followed, each one more serious than the last. Yet she was able repeatedly to place herself into positions of trust despite her growing criminal record. She became a private, in-home nurse's aide, looking after the elderly and disabled and managing room-and-board homes in downtown Sacramento. Puente divorced Johanson in 1966 and married Roberto Puente in Mexico City that same year. But the fact that Roberto was nineteen years younger than her began to play on her mind. She knew damn well he was sleeping around. Soon the marriage was doomed, but not before she took over the largest care home she would operate in her lifetime – a three-storey sixteen-bedroom house, built at the turn of the century at 2100 F Street. When she moved in with Roberto in 1968 she boasted that it had once been a brothel. Portly Puente, who at fourteen stone had trouble controlling her weight, did her best to stay attractive for her young husband. She covered her bulges by wearing flowing lavender and pink chiffon dresses and kept her bleached-blonde hair piled high in curls on top of her head. She was an actress through and through and she desperately needed to be the centre of attraction. She acted the generous hostess, throwing open her home to down-and-outs on festive occasions like Easter and Christmas, always making sure that social workers were invited as well, so they could see for themselves the hospitality on offer. After all, who else in the neighbourhood provided a colour TV in every bedroom? The gushing hostess, who employed a full-time cook, would serve up cuisine with an international flavour, from Italian pastas to Polish stews.

'It does so make my multinational guests feel at home,' she would say.

Before long Puente was alone again. Her marriage to

her wayward Latin lover Roberto ended the moment her fist found his nose. When he came round, he picked himself up off the floor and stormed out of the house, driving off in her new Pontiac Monte Carlo, never to be seen again.

One man who did seem to be close to her was known only as Chief. He had lived with the Puentes for years and Dorothea used him as her groundskeeper. The portly alcoholic was often seen mysteriously digging in the house's dirt basement, removing the debris in a wheelbarrow. Then one day Puente had it covered with a concrete floor. Soon Chief was busy again, pulling down a small garage in the backyard and building a large concrete patio. One morning Chief vanished without saying goodbye to anyone.

In 1976 Puente married Pedro Montalvo in Reno, Nevada. She soon found him to be a physically abusive man who got aggressive in whisky. But she was used to handling alcoholics and she turned a blind eye to his aggression, concentrating on her tenants, at least for a while. They were old, sick or mentally ill and her home was a palace compared with what they had been used to – a side alley, a night by a hot air grate outside a restaurant, a cardboard box on wasteland. To them, Puente was fairy godmother and Florence Nightingale rolled into one. She was obviously kind, she took in almost every stray cat in the neighbourhood. But apart from the colour TVs, the gushing landlady kept the services to the bare essentials – bath facilities, clean sheets and hot meals. By not offering specific, individual medical care she avoided the need to go through licensing procedures.

Before long Montalvo had walked out and Puente kept the top level of the house as her own apartment. By now the money was rolling in. She was generous and therefore always in need of ready cash. Older men were to provide it. Over the years the classily dressed lady about town walked from one vulnerable unsuspecting victim to another until she was convicted in a federal court for fraudulently cashing thirty-four Treasury benefit cheques. While she was on probation, she forged even more. The pattern was set. She could not help taking money from those with little ability to resist her will. They were without love – and so was she. What the hell.

One bright, chilly morning in April 1982, sixty-one-year-old Ruth Monroe arrived at Puente's Victorian boarding house on F Street. To her it was like heaven. She was met by kind, grandmotherly Puente, who showed her around and immediately made her feel at home.

'How much do you charge?' asked Ruth.

'Well, dear, normally it's $350 a month for a room and two meals but I'm sure I can sort something out for around $300. You are receiving social security, aren't you?'

It was like a mom and pop guest-house, only without pop. Ruth readily agreed. Seventeen days later she was dead from a Tylenol and codeine overdose.

'She was so terribly upset about her husband, who was terminally ill,' Puente told police, who put Ruth's death down to suicide. But the following month detectives were back again.

They had evidence that Puente had been slipping knock-out drugs into the drinks of elderly men she met at bars before robbing them of cash, cheques and jewellery. She would introduce herself to victims as a registered nurse or official representative of the fictitious Sacramento Medical Association.

One of them was seventy-four-year-old pensioner Malcolm McKenzie.

It was early one morning as he sat with his friends as usual, sipping a beer in the Zebra Club, the downtown Sacramento bar he felt at home in. He liked Dorothea from the moment she set foot in the door. This was no hooker. This was a lady – he could tell. The neatly-styled, elegant hairstyle, the flowing pink dress and expensive jewellery. This was someone special. Within minutes she was laughing and joking with the men around the bar. Her eyes seemed to sparkle at McKenzie and he kept smiling at her before joining the conversation. Somehow, he couldn't remember how, they talked about real estate, and then his apartment. He offered to show it to her and she accepted his invitation.

When they arrived at his small, one-bedroomed home he sat down in his favourite armchair and asked her to get a beer from the fridge. Instead, she just stood watching him. McKenzie began to feel dizzy, then he couldn't move, but he was conscious. Damn it, she had put something in his drink at the Zebra. He could do nothing but watch, slumped in the chair, as she ransacked his drawers for valuables, including a rare penny collection, which she packed in his red suitcase. On the way out she wrenched the diamond ring off his finger.

On 18 August 1882 Judge Roger Warren jailed Puente for five years after she pleaded guilty to three theft charges on the understanding that the District Attorney would not prosecute her on 'any other charges known'. She had been arrested with an airline ticket to Mexico in her handbag. This was the turning point. It was a devastating blow for the woman who yearned for prestige and affection.

William P. Wood, the deputy district attorney who prosecuted Puente, described her as cold-blooded – but admitted: 'She looks kind of like a Mrs Butterworth, you know, the honey figure on the pancake syrup bottle labels.'

A Sacramento County probation officer said: 'She is known for her generosity and hospitality to those in need but she is a danger to the elderly.' His report told how Puente had suffered a troubled upbringing and had a seriously disturbed personality.

Life in prison didn't bother Dorothea – she lost herself in a world of gardening magazines and told fellow inmates stories of her fantasy life. But it was her passion for talking that was to land her in trouble. One day another woman prisoner was beaten up. Puente, ever popular with her gaolers, told them who was behind the attack. Days later, as she went into the toilet, five women jumped on her screaming that she was a grass. One held her from behind while another threw a blanket over her head. She was kicked, punched and stabbed with a pair of scissors. Prison officials isolated her, putting her in a lone cell for her own safety. But wherever Puente went the door of opportunity seemed to open – and it opened again one morning when the warden passed her a letter. It was from a man named Everson Gillmouth. The seventy-seven-year-old retiree from Oregon liked to write to women in prison, and he had been given Puente's name. The letters between them grew more intimate. But little did Everson know that when he was signing his letters he was signing his death warrant.

On the morning of 9 September 1985, after serving just three years, Puente was released. There to meet her at the gates of the half-way house in Fresno were Everson in his 1980 red Ford pick-up truck and her friend Ricardo Ordorica, who owned 1426 F Street. Everson was smitten by Puente's film-star style and he liked what Ordorica had told him about her. Ordorica noticed that Puente had lost weight during her time in jail. He had to agree she looked good. Within days Puente and Everson announced their intention to marry. To her he was just another rung on the ladder to survival. He had money and she needed that. Sleeping with him was easy. He was tired, fat and undemanding. In a perilous move, Everson had opened a joint bank account in their names.

In September 1985 Puente paid Ordorica $200 for the first month's rent of a small room in his house on F Street. She had plans to take over an old hotel and run it as a boarding-house for the less fortunate in society but she did not have enough money. All the time she was meeting social workers and telling them of her plans. Many knew she had been away for some time – but not that she had been in gaol, and of course, she never told them. What she did tell them was that she could speak Swedish, Norwegian, Danish, Italian, Spanish, Portuguese and Greek. It was an impressive vocabulary and would stand her in good stead for taking on an assortment of multinational down-and-outs. In fact, the only language she spoke was limited Spanish. Then one day she found the answer to her ambitions. She offered Ordorica $600 a month to rent his whole house. Ordorica was rich at last and went off to find a new home in the suburbs.

It was a cold November day when handyman Ismael C. Florez put down his hammer and stood back to admire the wood panelling on the wall. Not bad, she would be pleased, he thought. She was.

It was a good deal all round. Puente had offered Florez a red 1980 Ford pick-up truck for $800 and the installation of some panelling in her home. The truck belonged to her boyfriend who was in Los Angeles, she said, as she signed over the ownership papers in his name. There was just one last job, though. She needed a box for storage. Florez agreed to make one for her. He bought some plywood sheets, nails and two-by-four supports and constructed it to Puente's required measurements – 6 feet long, 3 feet wide and 2 feet deep. He returned the next day to see if any more work was wanted and discovered that the crate had been moved into an upstairs kitchen, filled and nailed shut.

Puente asked him to take it to a storage depot and with the help of a neighbour he loaded it on to his new acquisition, the red Ford pick-up truck. Puente and Florez laughed and joked and listened to the radio as they sped down the highway to the depot. Suddenly Puente turned the music off and told him to pull over to a spot near Joe's Wharf in Sutter County.

'Let's drop it here,' she said.

'But don't you want it stored?'

'Nuh, it's just books and junk really.'

With Puente pulling and Florez pushing from behind they slid the crate off the back of the truck and left it on the river bank.

'Come on, let's go, I've got something for you back home,' she said.

When they returned she gave him a twelve-pack of beer, then helped him drink it.

Two months later, on the cold, bleak New Year's day of 1986, fishermen stumbled on the foul-smelling, damp box west of the Garden Highway. When police prised it open on the river bank they found Gillmouth's decomposed body, wrapped in a white sheet and bound with black electrical tape. He was wearing only jockey shorts, a T-shirt and an expandable watch. There were no signs of gunshot or stab wounds but his body was unrecognizable and detectives didn't know where to begin their investigations. They added him to their files of unsolved murders and it was to be nearly three years before he was identified. Meanwhile Dorothea was busy collecting Gillmouth's pension and sending letters.

She wrote to Gillmouth's sister in Oregon, telling her: 'Gill has been poorly recently, he has lost about fifteen pounds but he feels much better today.'

In another she told how Gill hated writing but sent his love and asked her not to worry about him.

The trail of terror was gathering pace.

In March, against the conditions of her parole, Puente began to open her home to tenants in a big way. Everything was going well, and Ordorica and his family were pleased with their rental income. Puente was in the money – but it was still not enough. The forty or so drug addicts, down-and-outs and alcoholics who screamed and vomited day and night brought back memories of her childhood. She was pleased to escape to the local bars and create a fantasy world with her new-found barman friends. Yes, she needed money, but not for furs or flashy cars, the jury heard. She needed to buy friendship and affection.

Puente had two layers in her mind: the fantasy world she created in a bid to be seen as a soft, caring, sexual woman and the cold calculating world of murder.

Handling her heavy-drinking boarders came naturally. She used them to aid her cash flow. It was so easy. Each month when their social security cheques arrived on the doormat she would collect them. It was the house rule that only she opened the mail. Then she would cash them and play banker. Those guests who drank heavily were given 15 or 20 dollars to have a haircut, or buy a new frock. As soon as they left the house they would head for the local bar, as always. Then they would get picked up by police following an anonymous tip as they staggered home incapable. They would get thirty days in jail and Puente would pocket the rest of their money. Puente liked her drink too, but it was a vice she couldn't handle. When she exceeded a certain limit she would become violent, hitting tenants or throwing things at them. Even a small fridge was to become a missile in one of her battles.

On 19 August, one of Puente's residents, seventy-seven-year-old Betty Palmer, went to see her doctor. It was the last time she was seen by anyone outside F Street. Less than two months later, Puente received a California ID card in Betty's name but it bore the wily landlady's photograph, enabling her to collect her tenant's social security payments.

On 23 February the following year, Leona Carpenter, seventy-eight, was discharged from hospital and placed in Puente's care. She vanished into thin air after spending a few weeks on the boarding-house couch. For twenty months after her disappearance, her bank account received deposits from the Social Security Department which were cashed.

On 21 July, James Gallop, sixty-two, was last seen by his doctor after months of hospitalization for a benign brain tumour and other ailments. He told the doctor he had just moved into Puente's wonderful boarding-house.

On 2 October, Vera Martin, sixty-two, and Dorothy Miller arrived at 1426 F Street. Martin vanished within a day or two and Miller was last seen alive on 23 October at a nearby clinic.

The following February Alvaro Bert Montoya, a fifty-one-year-old mentally impaired homeless man, was referred to Puente by a Volunteers of America street counsellor. When other tenants later asked what had become of him, Puente said she had put him in a cab to catch a bus to Mexico so that he could visit relatives.

On 9 March, Benjamin Fink, fifty-five, who had a long police record of alcoholism and violence, checked in with Puente. He was a troublesome tenant. Puente hated the sight of him falling down drunk all the time. Her mind flashed back to her parents and the horrors of her early years. One night Fink, unable to pass an open bar, was bought home almost unconscious. Later, in the early hours of the morning, he woke in a rage, throwing chairs around his room and breaking the window. Out in the hallway he pounded on the walls until the whole house was awake. It was the last straw for Puente. Tenant John Sharp, sixty-six, watched her help him up the stairs to her apartment. 'I'm going to make you feel better,' she said. He was never seen again. Four days later Sharp complained about a strange smell in the house. Puente explained that it was the sewer, but hours later was seen scrubbing the carpets in her rooms. Ben Fink, she told everyone, had gone north.

Puente had a reputation of being tough with her tenants. One morning an elderly down-and-out guest arrived for breakfast unshaven. Puente pestered him about his appearance and within ten minutes there was a heated argument.

'Get out of my house and stay out!' Puente screamed. She meant it. The man became a gibbering wreck, begging her to let him stay. No chance. He had to pack his bag and leave. Weeks later he leapt to his death from an eighth-floor hotel window.

In April, as the F Street landlady fussed around her garden, digging over the soil blooming with daffodils, the first piece of the jigsaw that was eventually to lead to her downfall was already in place.

Brenda Trujillo, who had once shared a cell with Puente and sometimes lived with her when she had nowhere else to go, was picked up by detectives in the town's red light area as a suspect in a murder investigation totally unrelated to F Street. Police quizzed her for several days, and at her lowest ebb she told them that she had a friend named Dorothea who killed people and kept their dead bodies. The police wrote it off as a ploy to divert attention from herself and decided not to investigate the claims.

But already behind the scenes there were investigations going on. A warning about Puente and her downtown boarding-house had been sounded by the Sacramento County Adult Protective Services Office. It complained to the Department of Social Services that Puente was running an unlicensed board-and-care facility and that she had once been jailed for misuse of client funds. Again the cool, friendly landlady was able to lie her way out of trouble. She persuaded a state licensing inspector, who arrived unannounced on her doorstep, that only a cousin lived in the house but she occasionally offered free temporary shelter to homeless people. The inspector liked her. She was totally believable and he filed a report saying the claims against her were unfounded. At the time of his visit on 30 June, Alberto Montoya was a tenant in an upstairs room.

Things were still going Puente's way. In August, Vera Smith, a caseworker for the Catholic School Services, arrived at F Street to see John Sharp, whom she had placed in Puente's care the previous January. Everything seemed fine and they strolled in the garden together.

'What wonderful tomato plants, they are so big and healthy-looking. I'm tempted to pick one,' she said, little knowing what the fertilizer that made them so healthy could be.

Meanwhile, Puente's fame and good work was spreading. Another social worker, Peggy Nickerson, referred up to thirteen people to the rooming-house because the matronly-looking Puente accepted those who were the hardest to place.

'She is the best the system has to offer. She is a widow with a big house who feels it is time to give something back to others,' she confidently told colleagues. But after a while Peggy did become suspicious because she never again saw the people she sent to Puente. Whenever she tried to visit a client, Puente would say he was ill, not at home or gone away. At first, as her clients were transient, Peggy put her suspicions to the back of her mind. After all, the people she sent Puente were noted for just packing up and going away. No one questioned their leaving. They were people of the streets. But Peggy decided to stop referring clients to F Street that summer because she had heard rumours that Puente was verbally abusing some of the residents.

Then, on 7 November, social worker Judy Moise filed a missing persons report with the police, complaining that Puente had not been able to come up with a reasonable explanation for Bert Montoya's disappearance. Judy knew Montoya well. She liked him and cared about him. He wouldn't just run away. When a uniformed officer questioned residents in the boarding-house, one of them slipped him a note saying that Puente had asked him to lie. Four days later police were digging up her garden.

Over the gruesome days that followed the remains of Carpenter, Miller, Montoya, Fink, Gallop, Martin and Palmer were dug up. All were wrapped in plastic and fabric but only the torso of Palmer was found. Her head, hands and lower legs had been chopped off. Detectives immediately launched an investigation into the 1982 death of Ruth Munroe and the 1985 disappearance of Gillmouth. Days later a comparison of skeletal features from his hospital X-rays proved that Gillmouth was the man found by the river in a wooden box on New Year's Day, 1986. The cause of death, however, could not be determined.

Department of Justice crime lab technicians worked day and night on the case. Their findings were overwhelming. Traces of flurazepam or Dalmane were found in all seven bodies buried in Puente's garden. Pharmacy records showed that she had filled in dozens of prescriptions for the drugs. Meanwhile detectives discovered that

Puente had forged sixty government benefit cheques sent to the victims after their deaths.

On 31 March that year Puente pleaded not guilty to an amended nine-count murder charge and denied the multiple death allegations. The case produced testimony from 156 witnesses, more than 3,100 exhibits and 22,000 pages of manuscript. Puente's lawyers claimed that eight of the victims had died of natural causes and were disposed of secretly because she was frightened of going back to jail.

Vlautin and Clymo summoned a stream of psychiatrists and Puente's friends to try and save her from execution.

The jury heard that an overwhelming and desperate need for attention was the basic, motivating factor in Puente's life. That need, said Doctor Mindy Rosenberg, looking across at Puente sitting motionless in the court, had its roots in her chaotic and tragic childhood, which was marked by emotional deprivation and neglect.

Rosenberg had been called as a witness by the defence to explain the elements of Puente's personality that allowed her to steal, cheat and lie while at the same time committing acts of genuine kindness and generosity.

'It is her upbringing that contributed to the traits that have made her one of life's compulsive caretakers,' the psychiatrist told the jury. 'As a very young child she was often called upon to clean up after her drunken mother and sick father. But she quickly learned that feigning illness and concocting fantasies were ways of getting the attention she so desperately needed and couldn't get from them. Her lies became so fanciful that school officials once sent her home and said she needed counselling. Sadly, no one followed up on the signs that she was suffering from severe emotional problems, and they carried over into adulthood.' Some of the women in the jury nodded in agreement.

Later, many in the court were close to tears as social worker Rose Arroyo took the stand and described the positive impact Puente had made on her life. Rose, choking back sobs as her eyes came into contact with those of weeping Puente, described how the F Street landlady had become her adopted stepmother, instilling in her the values and goals that guided her into a productive adulthood. When Puente took Rose's mother and her family under her wing, they were very poor, six kids and one adult trying to get along on $235 a month.

'Dorothea helped my mother provide food and clothing for us all,' she said. 'I didn't know there was a Father Christmas until Dorothea arranged for us all to go to the Memorial Auditorium when I was eleven and I saw this man in a fluffy white beard and red hood.'

Puente had taught her other things too.

'Like not to depend on men all the time,' said Rose, staring at the jury. 'If you want something out of life, you have to go to school. That's what she said. That's what she taught me. I loved to go into her bedroom, it was the prettiest room in the house. I used to lie in her bed and think I was Cinderella.'

There were whispers in the court as Rose unfolded a letter she had written just days before to Puente, thanking her for all the wonderful things she had done for her family. 'It ends with the words . . . all my love and affection, you are in my mind and my heart,' she said, as Puente burst into tears again.

The following day another letter was read to the court. It was dated 10 April 1978 and came from psychiatrist Dr Carl E. Drake, who had warned that Puente was ill-equipped to run a boarding-house for the down-and-out. 'She ought to retire from this work,' he wrote. 'It is more than she can tolerate and I think the fact that she undergoes so many different problems and so many stresses, causes her to react in a manner that leads me to question whether she is capable of exercising good judgement.'

The letter, written to Puente's lawyers during her trouble with the law more than a decade earlier, documented her contribution to the community. It suggested that she had been handed the short end of the stick by those who were in a position to help her.

'I have seen Puente take in people who have had no resources and nowhere to go,' Drake wrote. 'Some of those were my patients and although they had no way of financially reimbursing her, that never stopped her. She never questioned the fact that they could not pay. She always opened her home and her heart and took in the homeless, the poor, the tired, the weak, the hungry and those who were financially unable to take care of themselves.'

Drake took the stand to urge the jury to spare Puente's life. He testified he was a little past eighty and still working in psychiatry four hours a day, four days a week. Although he believed in the death penalty in some cases because it was the best thing that could be done, he did not see it as a solution for Puente. 'I still believe this lady can be useful and of some help to other people,' he said.

In other testimony attorney Donald P. Dorfman, who had represented Puente in 1978, described her as a lonely person. Even though she was not Latino, she established herself as a highly respected and affluent member of the Mexican-American community in Sacramento, he said.

Dorfman revealed that Puente had purchased an entire table at a $100-a-plate fund-raising event and was greeted warmly by then Governor Jerry Brown and other high-ranking government officials.

'They came over to her, spoke warmly to her, gave her a kiss on the cheek and said: "Hello, Dorothea, how are you?"' Dorfman recalled. 'She was thought of very highly.' As it turned out however, her affluence was an illusion.

Meanwhile Doctor William Vicary told the jury that Puente was a very sick lady who had one foot on a banana peel and the other in the gas chamber. 'She is a very fragile, mentally precarious woman whose desperate attempts to be somebody have led to tragedy,' he said.

'The murders she committed could be traced to the pain, resentment, anger and hatred that ate at her because of years of neglect and maltreatment dating back to childhood.'

But by maintaining her innocence, Puente could still

act like a godmother, an aunt, a friend to those around her, he added. 'In that way she feels she has still got some position in life. If she confessed, she would be treated as a pariah!'

Vicary, hired by the defence, had quizzed Puente five times and reviewed interviews with her family and friends, juvenile court reports and school documents, the jury heard. He had found one of the saddest, most tragic, pathetic family situations he had ever had to deal with.

Puente, he said, grew up without a shred of self-esteem, repeatedly entered destructive and unsound marriages, and tried to run a business that, in its beginning, offered shelter and sustenance to alcoholic and mentally ill men and women. Her frustration and resentment grew as her clients became more and more difficult. 'It had to come out somewhere,' he added, 'and it came out with all those missing people. That was the bridge between her traumatic past and her horrible crimes.'

The jury listened as Vicary told how Puente began fabricating elaborate stories about herself and her situation in childhood as a way of gaining attention and bestowing a sense of worth.

'Fantasies and lies are a symptom of a very sad person who suffers a lot of pain inside,' he said.

Despite her early problems, Puente never got the psychiatric treatment she so desperately needed. When she got older she tried helping others who could not get help either.

'Mother once made me promise to feel sorry for alcoholics and to take care of drunks,' she had told him.

'I want everyone here in this court room to know,' said Vicary, 'that Dorothea actually accomplished many good things, but the stress was wearing on her. Yes, she started to divert cheques intended for her clients. But her arrests in 1978 and 1982 were doubly embarrassing for a woman who wanted people to like and respect her. Her position in the community was compromised and she was devastated. That's when we start to find people missing.'

In his conversations with Puente, she maintained her innocence in all nine homicides. 'Why?' he asked the jury. 'I will tell you why. She cannot handle owning up to any kind of behaviour like that. It is just too shameful.'

The next day Vicary, who many felt had somehow already swung the jury into its verdict, appeared again. The men and women who had spent so long together trying the case listened intently as he told them that Puente did know right from wrong and had the ability to make choices when she was murdering tenants at her boarding house.

The judge then heard how the landlady had hoodwinked other mental health experts into diagnosing her as schizophrenic so that she could obtain Supplementary Security Income benefits in the 1980s. But, said Vicary, she was not and never had been suffering from a psychiatric disability.

'She perpetrated a fraud, with the help of some very friendly doctors, to gain tax-free money from the government, that's all,' he said.

Prosecutor John O'Mara, seeking the death penalty for Puente, stood to cross-examine the psychiatrist. Vicary accepted the lawyer's assessment that Puente was a very manipulative person who sought mental aid when the law was at her back.

'In 1978, after the federal government started a criminal forgery case against her, Puente invented a history of mental illness in an effort to evoke sympathy,' O'Mara said. He elaborated on Vicary's story about her feigning schizophrenia. He revealed how she had told one psychiatrist she had been having hallucinations and hearing animal voices. She even claimed she had been committed to a state mental hospital and received electroshock therapy for eleven years.

Vicary agreed that it was all a lie and said it should have been recognized as one by a competent and honest psychiatrist. He pointed out that the 1978 psychiatric report said Puente had told her doctor that the voices were very frightening but she knew they were not real. 'That should have been a tip-off,' Vicary said. 'Dorothea didn't know the right answers to give. To someone mentally ill, such visual and auditory hallucinations are very real.'

Vicary also told the jury that Puente had a history of denying responsibility for wrongdoing and would admit to something only when there was irrefutable evidence.

'My assumption is that she is responsible for murdering all these people,' he testified. 'I attempted to get some kind of admission from her, but I didn't. She has always maintained that she didn't know anything about the murders or the burials. What she told me is: "I never hurt anybody. I never killed anyone. They're trying to blame me for these things. I didn't do it."'

Vicary admitted that he tried to push her at times but it was counterproductive to challenge her denials. She would withdraw and not talk to him. The psychiatrist had interviewed Puente for 122 hours over five visits since 1988.

The next morning the jury heard again how deep feelings of hatred and resentment, harboured for many years by a sick and disturbed Puente, led to the murders on F Street. But now Vicary explained that she actually wanted to be caught and was glad it was all over. When he visited her after the three guilty verdicts were returned, he thought she would be indignant, outraged and angry. 'Instead she seemed very content, almost happy. A bit like – thank God, I have been stopped. It's over. I have been convicted,' he said.

'We've got a woman here who likes money, I mean, lots of money,' he added. But her need for cash stemmed from a quest for acceptance, respect and appreciation, even love of those around her more than worldly goods. She became prominent in the community because she gave scholarships and loaned money to people who were down on their luck. In her own little world she was a celebrity. To maintain her prominence and her importance she began stealing. "She had this house, this big mansion with forty alcoholics in it, and the Government paid her $300 or $400 apiece to take care of them. That's a lot of money. If you steal a little bit here and there, you get a lot of money. Now she gets arrested. Her position in the community is compromised. She loses this big palace. She is a felon and doesn't have easy access to the money of her clients. That's when she starts drugging and stealing from people she picks up in bars.

'Another arrest, imprisonment and parole bring her back to Sacramento – but this thing that's going on inside her, is it getting better? No. It is getting worse. This woman is very sick. She is very disturbed. Inside of her is a lot of pain, a lot of resentment and a lot of anger. All of her life she has taken care of other people, and these other people are all very destructive like her parents were. They are alcoholics. They are drug addicts. They've got medical problems that they are not taking care of. They are demanding. They vomit. They are not supposed to drink and they go out and get drunk and pass out.'

Puente appeared disturbed and agitated by Vicary's explanation and began scribbling notes to her lawyers.

Vicary looked at her for a moment, then continued. 'There is something brewing inside this woman,' he said. 'It is not necessary for her to kill people and bury them in the yard in order to have enough money to survive, in order to have enough money to donate to people in the Hispanic community or to buy clothing and food for the little girls she wants to help because they remind her of the pain she had when she was their age. This is hate, where is this hate going to come out? That's the undercurrent that explains the killings. Why all these people wound up in the yard.'

Puente's lawyers had skilfully shown that a 'flame of

humanity' still burned in the serial killer. But O'Mara told the court it had to be extinguished.

'How high does the body count have to get?' he asked the jury. He reminded them that the weighing process that marked the guilt phase of the trial was over. 'Now it becomes a moral decision, a moral judgement,' he said.

Only two options were available: life imprisonment without the possibility of parole – or death.

'Either verdict will protect society,' he declared. 'Either penalty qualifies as punishment.'

So the question became one of accountability, responsibility, and justice. 'Aren't all the victims entitled to some measure of justice? All they had were their lives and their little Social Security cheques. She took their cheques and then she took their lives. I want you to remember them as human beings. They had a right to live. Can we dismiss these three murders with the explanation she suffered from an abused childhood?'

Quoting Robert Louis Stevenson, O'Mara said: 'Eventually everyone sits down to a banquet of consequences . . . it is time to tell Dorothea Puente: you have to sit down at the banquet.'

The tough, no-nonsense prosecutor characterized the trial as 'the mother of all circumstantial evidence cases'.

But he told the jurors that reason, common sense and logic would convince them that Puente was a 'cold and calculating killer', whose grandmotherly looks belied the reality that was experienced by victims at her Sacramento boarding-house. He scoffed at the defence contention that all eight died of natural causes and were disposed of secretly so that Puente would not be sent back to jail. 'That is not a rational explanation,' he said, and urged the jury to recognize the humanity of the victims, most of whom were people of the shadows who were afflicted by alcoholism, mental illness, drug addiction or physical ailments.

'How did they get from their rooms in the house to those little holes in the side yard with all that dirt on top of them?' he asked. 'Our common sense, our logic tells us there was a lot going on, and those are the tools that, under the framework of the law, will allow you to solve the puzzles here.'

O'Mara's voice grew louder as he accused Puente of targeting the most vulnerable and least noticed members of society. 'She wanted people who had no relatives, no friends, no family,' he said. 'People who, when they were gone, wouldn't have others coming around and asking questions.'

The victims planted in her garden fitted that profile. 'All were alcoholics and most had either mental or substance-abuse problems,' he added. 'They never did anything except collect money every month and cause trouble for themselves. They had survived many years of violence and deprivation on the streets of America. They got beat up. They got raped. They were taking drugs and doing all kinds of terrible things, and they survived. Then, they go to this island of peace, this wonderful, warm woman who takes in alcoholics and other homeless people and gives them a new life. They get to this nice, quiet place – and they are history.'

O'Mara sat down.

The jurors seemed perplexed as Judge Michael J. Virga sent them out. Four hours later they sent him a message. They were deadlocked. Both sets of lawyers looked disappointed.

'In view of the length and complexity of this case, I believe it is appropriate for you to continue your deliberations for at least one more day,' the judge replied in a note. He reminded them that they had declared a deadlock after eleven days of deliberation in the original Guilt Phase of the trial, but were finally able to arrive at verdicts on three counts. A few minutes after receiving his message, the jurors broke for the evening, announcing that they would return to court at 9.30 the next morning. Puente's life still hung in the balance. If the jurors remained deadlocked Virga could declare a mistrial and it would be up to the district attorney in Sacramento to decide whether the Penalty Phase should be retried.

Defenders Clymo and Vlautin objected to the judge's directive. Clymo claimed it was inappropriate to instruct the jury to continue to arrive at a verdict. 'I think it is pretty clear they must know what their status is,' he said.

Vlautin expressed the opinion that it was an attempt by Judge Virga to coerce the jury. 'They've been together now so long, they must have their minds made up one way or the other,' he said.

The next day the jurors returned. They had voted 7–5 for life imprisonment. Puente had been spared a date with the executioner. Prosecutor O'Mara agreed he would not contest the issue and Virga transferred the proceedings back to Sacramento, where he would sentence Puente to life in jail. As he spoke, the quiet landlady maintained the cool demeanour that had been her main characteristic throughout the trial. Minutes later her lawyers told reporters she was relieved that the long and arduous hearing was over. Clymo took a deep breath and said, 'For the first time in five years, I feel a sense of relief.' Vlautin added, 'I'm ecstatic, and looking forward to getting home to my wife and kids.'

It was finally over, or was it? For now what had been going on behind the scenes in the jury room throughout the original trial was gradually becoming clear. Jurors began to reveal that eleven of them were convinced Puente had killed at least seven of the nine dead. But one juror, thirty-three-year-old technical engineer Jesse Sanchez, had held out against them for twenty days. He told his colleagues he did not have the information he needed to make the decision he was being asked to make. 'He wanted some other jury to decide,' said forty-three-year-old mechanic Michael B. Esplin, who acted as foreman.

For the jurors who spent much of the last nine months sitting in the windowless court room with a serial killer and four attorneys, life after the Puente trial would never be the same. Friendships were forged, lifestyles altered, losses suffered and sacrifices made. Convictions were held in the heart, if not in the courtroom.

'I feel strongly that Puente murdered all nine of those people,' said juror Joyce McGreevy, thirty-seven, a freelance editor. 'I feel a lot of pain, especially for the families of Vera Martin and Ruth Munroe. I feel personally as if I let them down.'

Marjorie Simpson, at sixty-five the eldest member of the panel, had similar regrets. 'I'm heartbroken that we couldn't have come up with nine verdicts. In fact, I'm embarrassed,' she said.

The man at the centre of the controversy, Jesse Sanchez, had saved Puente from at least four more first-degree murder convictions. He had approached Judge Virga after the Guilt Phase of the trial and told him that he was concerned about the verdicts and what had occurred during deliberations.

Now many of the jurors vented their frustrations on Sanchez. Joseph Martin, forty-four, a postman, accused him of holding the whole system hostage. Gregory Miller, thirty-five, a phone company technician, said: 'Sanchez didn't want to participate. He didn't want to be part of it. He was very difficult to communicate with. The man is very intelligent but it was impossible to get him to explain himself.'

Simpson felt that Sanchez wanted a hung jury and Stockton said: 'Jesse told us several times, "Let's send it back to the judge and get somebody else to decide."'

Pump maintenance mechanic Stephen Hinds, forty-four, said: 'I tried to figure out why he couldn't see the same things everyone else was seeing. It is a shame that he couldn't decipher the information as well as we could.'

Jurors told how they took turns confronting Sanchez. It was only on the twentieth day of deliberations that he finally relented and voted for a first degree murder conviction on the Dorothy Miller count. Guilty verdicts on Leona Carpenter and Benjamin Fink followed in short order. 'But when we started to go for Bert Montoya, Jesse stopped us and said he wouldn't go any further, it was all over,' said David Bigham Jr, thirty-one.

Hinds explained: 'Jesse told us, look, every time I agree to something, you want more, and I'm telling you right now, you are not getting more.'

Sanchez, however, kept his silence on the issue which was his right – and after all, juries are supposed to disagree.

The case would forever be imprinted on the minds of everyone involved in it. While some jurors admitted that they kept thinking about the photographs of decomposed bodies unwrapped on the coroner's slab, Stockton was more bothered by pictures of the victims in life. 'Especially Bert Montoya,' she said. 'Seeing him on videotape brought a lot of it home. He was a real person.'

McGreevy took issue with the witnesses who testified that Puente's boarding-house was a warm environment. 'These people wouldn't know the difference between Conrad Hilton and Norman Bates in Hitchcock's *Psycho*,' she said.

Attitudes towards Puente had varied among the jurors as the trial wore on.

'I tried to be as cold-blooded as I could,' Martin said. 'I tried not to look upon her as a poor old lady. I didn't want my personal feelings to influence my decision.'

Simpson said she watched the serial killer closely throughout the first few months of the trial. 'I realized she was not going to show any kind of emotion, so I forgot about her as a person and concentrated on the evidence,' she said.

Ruby Hewlett-Ratcliff, fifty, said her feelings about Puente changed constantly. 'One minute it was like she was this sweet little grandmother, and the next she was like something out of your worst nightmare.'

The Puente trial ran for almost a year from the start of jury selection. The jurors and their stand-ins began hearing evidence in early February. During deliberations, which set a California murder trial record of twenty-four days, they found it difficult to handle the court's order not to discuss any aspect of the case with anyone.

'Some days were really bad days,' recalled Martin. 'It was very frustrating for me and my wife Pat. I wasn't able to sit down and tell her what was bothering me. I lost a lot of sleep.'

Stockton agreed: 'It was like living in a bubble. We seemed to be separated from the rest of the world.'

McGreevy said she was the kind of person who thrived on solitude. 'But I was bothered by not being able to share with my husband the little ironies, the subtleties, the epiphanies of the trial,' she admitted.

The end of the trial brought profound changes to the lives of Bigham, Hewlett-Ratcliff and two US Army soldiers stationed at Fort Ord: Gary Frost and Earl Jimerson.

Bigham quit his job as a sales representative for a major wine producer to go into teaching. 'I wanted to do something that would have a positive effect on people,' he explained. He decided to change careers after hearing about Puente's traumatic childhood and her lack of a role model, someone she could lean on who could have pointed her in the right direction.

Hewlett-Ratcliff returned from jury duty to find her position as a bank vault teller gone.

Frost, forty-three, found that his army unit had been transferred from Fort Ord to Fort Lewis in Washington. Jimerson, twenty-eight, an infantry squad leader, had been reassigned to Washington.

Sacrifice was common among the jurors.

Martin put on hold legal efforts to adopt his fifteen-year-old stepson. Miller and Hinds each had to drive about seventy miles from their homes in King City to the courthouse in Monterey. Miller said he logged 17,750 miles to and from court. Personal losses were suffered by Hinds and stand-in jurors Linda Quintero, thirty-five, and Tina Humphrey, thirty, during the trial. Hinds's grandmother died, so did Quintero's brother. Humphrey suffered a miscarriage during the early part of the proceedings.

About half the jurors said they doubted there would be a conviction at the close of testimony.

'I kept waiting for the one witness who was going to come in and explain this thing to me,' Miller recalled. 'When the prosecutor rested his case, my hair stood up. I couldn't believe that was all he had.'

Martin agreed: 'Honestly, until the judge read the rules we had to go by, I thought it was going to be very difficult to convict her,' he said. 'It wasn't until the jurors began trading views and studying the evidence bit by bit that a clear picture of Puente's crime emerged, at least to the eleven who believed firmly in her guilt.'

Esplin said he voted for the death penalty and felt peace with the Lord pour all over him the moment he made the decision. A statement by Clymo in his closing argument helped him turn the corner.

'When Clymo said we save the death penalty for the worst of the worst, to me this was one of those.'

On 11 December 1993, a surprisingly upbeat Dorothea Puente, wearing jail-issue sweats and sneakers, was ordered to state prison for life, without the possibility of parole.

Sacramento Superior Court judge Michael Virga formalized the sentence. In the court to see the last appearance of the F Street killer were three of the jurors, Simpson, McGreevy and Martin. Sitting with them was Sacramento police detective John Cabrera, who had pulled the leg bone from the mud in Puente's garden.

Although the sentencing brought to a close the lengthy and costly prosecution, many questions remained unanswered.

The cause of death in eight of the killings was never determined, and the whereabouts of Betty Palmer's head, hands and feet remain unknown. Puente had elected not to testify on her own behalf and refused to be interviewed by the Probation Department which prepared a presentence report.

She was locked up for life echoing those fantasy words to her lawyers: 'I never killed anyone.'

Chapter Seven

BEVERLY ALLITT

'I am not competent, far from it. I know I'm not competent. I am one of the bloodiest, crappiest nurses out. I think I am the lowest of the low!'

Grantham, Lincs, 1991

The podgy, round-faced girl in the neatly pressed nurse's uniform strode through Children's Ward Four, her shoes squeaking on the polished linoleum floor as she picked up discarded toy cars and building bricks and placed them back on the table. She checked her watch, dangling on the end of a silver chain. Time to take the temperatures of her little patients.

Beverly Allitt, twenty-four, looked every bit the trained, caring children's nurse. Spick and span, always on the move, tucking in her tiny charges asleep in their cots, or playing with them in the cheerfully decorated games and TV room. No one from outside the hospital would have guessed she had been on the ward only two days. She dispensed comfort to the babies in her care as if she was born for the job. But she was just hours away from dispensing death.

If only medical staff had known, that winter's afternoon, that this temperamental, volatile young woman had been seriously disturbed since the start of her teenage years and that in the five years prior to her employment there she had visited the casualty department of the hospital she now worked in twenty-four times, complaining of fantasy or self-inflicted conditions. Her list of ailments included gall bladder pains, ulcers, vomiting, urinary infections and blockages, injuries to feet, legs, hands, wrists, ankles, fingers, thumbs and toes. She suffered headaches, blurred vision, swollen breasts, back strains and troubles with her appendix. The truth was that the only real illness Allitt suffered was a mental one and she was already notorious in the casebooks of a dozen doctors. But by the end of spring 1991, she and Grantham and Kesteven General Hospital were to become famous in doctor's casebooks worldwide. For the newly-qualified state enrolled nurse on Children's Ward Four was a victim of Munchausen's Syndrome and Munchausen's Syndrome by Proxy, conditions where sufferers repeatedly draw attention to themselves through the creation of injury or drama. The disorder was introduced in 1951 by a doctor to describe hospital addiction. The fictional character Baron Von Munchausen travelled widely and told stories of exploits beyond credibility. To many people who visited Ward Four and its staff, however, Allitt was an angel. That spring, tragically for the parents of some of the children in her care, she was to be an angel of death. Within two months she would murder four youngsters and attack nine others.

The area served by Grantham and Kesteven General had a population of just under 100,000. Among them were 30,000 children. Some 2,250 more were born every year, 60 per cent of them at the hospital where Allitt worked.

As Allitt's shoes squeaked on the shiny linoleum that afternoon of 21 February, an air of calm hung over her ward. There were no emergencies, no seriously ill babies. The half a dozen doctors and nurses felt at ease. They joked and made coffee, played with the kids, taking care to keep medical equipment locked away in cupboards adorned with bright cartoon posters, for it was a policy of the hospital not to frighten the children with medical equipment on show. One person that day wasn't joking, however; Allitt had too much on her mind. She was under a cloud. In a year she had taken ninety-three days off with unexplained illnesses, then she had failed her recent exams and was due to leave the hospital. She was the only nurse on her training course who had failed to get a full-time job, and resentment burned deep inside her. At the last moment, however, understaffed Grantham General decided to grant her a six-month contract and a final chance to learn about caring for sick children, a post she had been turned down for by Lincolnshire's Boston Hospital, thirty miles away, only five days before. Boston had told her she did not have enough experience in dealing with the young. It was simple rejection that triggered the deadly evil within her. She desperately needed to show how competent she could be in the few months available to her. Allitt had always wanted to be a nurse – that's why she had loved to babysit during her schooldays. Secretly, in her own warped mind, however, she knew she just didn't have what it took.

Allitt was spotlessly turned out, the sisters couldn't fault her. Her big nurse's silver watch dangled from its chain and her thermometer pack jutted neatly from her top pocket. But there was something different about her. Her eagerness to please irritated the other nurses. She reported every incident, however minor, to them. Whenever a child needed attention Allitt magically appeared at the side of the ward sister, even though her presence had not been requested.

The calm reigning over Ward Four that afternoon was not to last. As Allitt was washing some cups, a worried mother, clutching her baby, rushed through the doors. Seven-week-old Liam Taylor's lungs were congested due to a severe chest infection, and her GP had told his mother Joanne to take him to hospital. Doctors were sent for and Liam was made comfortable in Cubicle Four, nicknamed Mr Happy's room after a character from a book. X-rays showed signs of pneumonia. Joanne's husband, Chris, raced to the ward too when he got the message about his son after returning home from his job as a ceiling fitter. He arrived at around 4pm. For a while he stood around waiting for news, but the only person who had time to speak to him was the neatly-turned out nurse with the smiling, sympathetic face. She was everywhere that day.

'Don't worry, your baby will be fine, we're going to take good care of him,' Allitt told him. She led him to Mr

Happy's room and he watched with his wife as the nurses tenderly worked on his little son in the glass-sided incubator. Liam, nicknamed Pudding Pants by his parents because he was so chubby, was obviously ill and distressed but Chris and Jo sighed with relief when they heard him cry loudly. Allitt was smiling too, and encouraged the worried parents to go home and have something to eat. 'Everything is under control,' she said. 'He's fine now.' The couple felt relieved and left for their semi-detached home in Grantham, returning at around 6pm. Again the first person they saw was Allitt.

'Liam has had a collapse,' she told them calmly. 'We've been trying to get in touch with you. He was really sick and it shot across the room, a canary yellow colour. I had to go and change my overalls.'

The distraught couple could not check her story if they had wanted to, for there was nobody else around who could have contradicted the nurse's claim. And why should they disbelieve her? But Allitt had lied. The ward sister had been on duty throughout the afternoon and the new nurse was still wearing the same uniform. What happened to Liam was equally inexplicable. Little Pudding Pants had been sleeping peacefully when Allitt had gone to check on him, emerging seconds later to announce he had collapsed. The baby was rushed up the corridor to the treatment room, where doctors connected him to resuscitation equipment, forcing oxygen into his lungs. Within a few hours he had revived.

On seeing their son, covered in wires and with a drip attached to his arm, the Taylors refused to leave the hospital and slept that night in the small parents' room next to the line of cubicles, each with their funny Mr Men posters on the doors. The following day Liam was well enough to be moved back to Mr Happy. This cheered his anxious parents and that afternoon Chris and Jo smiled with relief when they saw their son open his eyes and reach for his teddy bear. Allitt came into the room, put her arm around Chris and told him she had volunteered for extra duty that night.

'I've been specialled to look after him,' she smiled, referring to a system where a nurse is assigned to one specific patient. The couple decided to return later that evening to sleep near their son again.

Shortly before midnight Chris popped his head round the door of Mr Happy and saw Allitt and another nurse propping Liam up and administering a nebulizer to clear his nasal passages. The couple, exhausted but convinced the crisis was over, went to bed just twenty feet away. The staff paediatrician too was satisfied the crisis was over. Tragically, it was really about to begin. In the hours that followed Allitt spent most of her time alone in the cubicle with Liam, her mind racing with resentment that she was struggling to keep her job. She wanted to be noticed, be the centre of attraction. She hardly understood her own thoughts. Early in the morning, with the ward in silence, she began giving orders to the only two other nurses on duty. Being in charge, Allitt had discovered, was easy. Staffing was at its lowest ebb – there simply weren't enough people to run things properly. First she asked nursing auxiliary Alison Clegg to get nasal catheters, then, on her return, sent her to get fresh sheets. At the same time she asked the other nurse to fetch some more pieces of equipment. Both nurses were never more than a few yards away from Mr Happy but they were out of sight. Clegg was the first to return. When she entered the small cubicle she saw Allitt standing rigid by the bed. Below her Liam had turned chalky white, with penny-sized, vivid red blotches beginning to appear on his face. Allitt, visibly shaking, screamed: 'Crash team, call the crash team!'

The other two nurses were astonished to see that Liam was lying at the end of the resuscitation machine, 'crumpled in a ball at the bottom'. They had left the child lying normally. Neither of the alarms connected to go off if Liam stopped breathing or lacked oxygen had sounded. At 4.13am Liam suffered cardiac arrest and for the following two hours the cubicle was swarming with emergency medical staff who fought to save him. Finally, despairing doctors conceded their battle was in vain. Liam had suffered severe brain damage, caused by a lack of oxygen when he had stopped breathing. At 6am there were minimal signs of life. Consultant Charith Nanayakkara, a Tamil known to the children as Doctor Nana, was exhausted and mystified by the first cardiac arrest he had ever seen in such a young baby. He turned away, visibly upset, then went to tell Chris and Jo the tragic news. For a while they sat alone before taking the heartbreaking decision to switch off the mechanical support that was keeping their son alive. Allitt had stood watching the entire drama in silence. At 7.30am the neat and tidy nurse washed her hands, put on her coat and went calmly home to her digs in Grantham. She was not questioned about what had happened to Liam; no one bothered to ask her. She returned at 4pm that day, immaculately dressed, to start the night shift. Liam, who for a time had been able to breathe on his own, had passed on two hours earlier. He was christened shortly before he died. The reason diagnosed for his death was that part of the muscle around his heart had died, a condition almost unheard of in children. But it was strange because the bonny little boy had no history of heart disease. No one ever discovered the real reason why Liam died. Despite pathological tests on his brain, heart and other organs the mystery remains to this day. He was murdered by the nurse charged with his care but still no one knows how. It could have been a chemical like potassium chloride, which causes instant heart failure if injected into the muscles. It could have been a massive dose of insulin, or simply a hand squeezing his nostrils and covering his mouth. However it happened, the nightmare on Ward Four had begun.

As Allitt started her new shift, she realized that she had managed to commit the perfect murder. At last she had become the centre of attention, a leading player in a drama. That realization pushed the physical part of the killing to the back of her thoughts. From that day on a mind that was already dangerously diseased became totally unhinged – and the cosy little world of Children's Ward Four became her very own killing field. It would only be stopped by a combination of science and good, old-fashioned, routine detective work.

Like all female serial killers, Allitt stayed silent about

her crimes to the end, drawing great public doubt and sometimes sympathy. In her case, medical experts and the law argued whether the trail of death was coincidental or part of an unexplained medical condition known as 'cluster', an unidentified virus passed on from carriers.

In the end, however, Allitt was to fight for her own life in a battle against something that wasn't a fantasy – the wasting disease anorexia nervosa.

Friday, 11 February 1994. It was a cold, bleak morning. Cameramen blew into their hands to warm their fingers and the conference room was a sea of raincoats, anoraks and notebooks.

Sir Cecil Clothier, QC, cleared his throat, stood up and addressed the Press.

'The dreadful lesson we have learned is that no matter how numerous and skilful the staff of a hospital may be, a malevolent, cunning and deranged person can nevertheless continue to commit his or her crimes,' he said.

He cleared his throat again and stared solemnly at the assembled reporters.

'It takes only two minutes alone with a helpless patient to kill or injure. Nurses are bound to be alone with their patients sometimes. But from now on we must be prepared to think the unthinkable – whenever a patient's condition cannot be accounted for a member of staff might be responsible.'

The reporters sat in silence as he went on.

'This is the first ever example in this country of a nurse attacking her infant patients. We hope that the inquiry, and its recommendations, will help minimize the risk of such a terrible thing happening again.'

Sir Cecil was speaking at the end of an exhaustive, independent inquiry into a trail of murders and attempted murders on Children's Ward Four of the Grantham and Kesteven Hospital. He revealed how there had been talk, before his report was published, that it might make scapegoats of some staff for what had happened. 'But those who read the findings will see that many months ago we warned ourselves against the danger of laying the blame merely to assuage the grief and anger of innocent people at the wrongs done to them by Beverly Allitt,' he said.

'Where we have found fault we have plainly said so, without fear or favour. Where there was cause for commendation we have noted that too. We have made a number of recommendations aimed at making it more difficult for someone like Beverly Allitt to get into a position to commit her terrible crimes.'

Sir Cecil sat down. In just a few words he had spoken about the most famous and prolific serial killer in Britain this century.

Beverly Allitt was an unstable and insecure young woman who, in her muddled mind, would seek attention and comfort from men or women. She had a few male lovers but they found her cold and unresponsive. With women, she found a more satisfying response to her physical and mental needs.

Allitt resorted to childish pranks and self-mutilation to gain the attention she craved. The flaws in her character were evident from an early age. As a schoolgirl she would turn up in class wearing bandages or plasters on a wound she would be reluctant to have examined. As a student nurse she was suspected of smearing the walls of the nurses' home with human excrement, even putting some in a fridge for her colleagues to find.

Allitt was one of four children, the second-born of Richard, a tractor factory worker, and Lillian, a cleaner and dinner lady. The family, who lived in a neat, red-brick semi in the quiet Lincolnshire village of Corby Glen, set in the valley of the River Glen, near Grantham, seemed outwardly to have a happy and normal existence. From Allitt's local village school, Corby Glen Primary, there were two routes for girls. Those fortunate enough to pass their eleven plus went on to former prime minister Margaret Thatcher's old school, Kesteven and Grantham Girls'. The rest went to Charles Read School, the local secondary modern, which catered for around 230 pupils.

Beverly went to Charles Read, with a report from her primary school saying she had above average ability and was a friendly and helpful pupil. By this time her ambition to be a nurse was shining through and she was uninterested in some subjects. She hated sport and would find any excuse not to participate. However, mothers in her home village always knew where to look for a babysitter, for the overweight pupil who wore baggy jumpers was ready, willing and apparently extremely able to look after their children. She had taken her confirmation vows at fourteen and was often seen walking to the village church with her family.

Allitt eventually went to Grantham College, where she was a very ordinary pupil who repeatedly failed the exams she needed to qualify for nursing college. She found it difficult to make friends and became shy, quiet and introverted. During her second year she missed most of the course through sickness, and her illnesses became a cause for concern. She was given special permission to take longer over her exams that summer because of an injury to her wrist. Altogether she missed fifty-two days out of a possible 180. She sat her exams time and again before managing to pass. Finally, she obtained an O-level in food and nutrition and CSEs in maths, English, biology and French. But around this time her character began to change. She began to hang around with gangs of girls on street corners, drink heavily and get violent. She enjoyed a good fight. At the same time her injuries and illnesses became more frequent. She often showed her wounds to her tutors and appeared to be using them to draw attention to herself.

Allitt returned to Corby Glen and the dole. She did not have enough O-levels to train as a registered general nurse, so she applied to train for two years as a pupil at the South Lincolnshire School of Nursing with a view to becoming an enrolled nurse. She did not name a tutor from her pre-nursing course at Grantham; instead, references were provided by her school and a local businessman. In November 1987 she was accepted, and it was a proud moment for her parents. But during her two-year training a physiotherapist complained about her attitude and her time off with real or imagined illnesses. She missed a total of 126 days during her 110-week course. Nothing was done. Later came a fascination with the occult. When staying with friends, she said she discovered a carving knife stuck in a pillow, the bathroom curtains on fire and the family Jack Russell spitting out tablets. She blamed it all on a poltergeist. But the real insight into Allitt's twisted mind at this time comes from her only boyfriend, Stephen Biggs. The couple met when Allitt was eighteen and doing a course in child psychiatry. Soon they were seeing each other every night and before long Allitt had proposed. Stephen, taken aback, accepted. It was to be a stormy two-and-a-half-year relationship. Allitt was bubbly and cheerful at the outset of their romance, but she degenerated into violence, lies and bitter recriminations. Stephen held on, seeing that she was always good with children – and she desperately wanted kids of her own. This was surely a sign of goodness and caring. But he became suspicious when she started to lie about being pregnant. Allitt would talk endlessly about her nursing ambitions and how she wanted to be a midwife. After a while they began to argue about silly things as couples sometimes do. By now their arguments would always end in violence.

'She really let rip when she kicked me,' Stephen admitted later to reporters. 'She had me in tears once.

She used to hit me when I was driving. She would hit me in the groin and in the head. I told her one time that it was finished. She reacted by pulling my hair and dragging me to my knees!'

Stephen found his fiancée a compulsive liar. 'She shouted to everyone that I had AIDS,' he said. 'She told them I gave it to her. There was even talk that she had an abortion and that the baby was mine. But she wasn't pregnant. She said a friend of ours raped her. But she didn't go to the police, she just said it for effect.'

Allitt was always talking about euthanasia and that worried Stephen. 'She was always on about drugs and how hospitals killed old people for their own good,' he said. 'But she claimed it was never talked about outside the wards. She told me that when people were very old doctors used morphine or some drug like that. Their families were left in the dark because it would upset them. It seemed a strange thing to say.'

Stephen's sexual relationship with Allitt was difficult and he was soon to realize why. Allitt became infatuated with another student nurse. They got drunk together at a hospital social club. She went back to her new friend's digs, they went to bed together and suddenly the world changed again for Allitt. That affair was to last until her arrest. After that, pictures of her female lover were to adorn the walls of her cell.

On 5 March, just two weeks after the murder of Liam Taylor on Children's Ward Four of Grantham Hospital, an eleven-year-old cerebral palsy victim, with a mental age of three months, was admitted into Allitt's care.

Timothy Hardwick had suffered an epileptic fit at a special school he was attending. His mother, Mrs Margaret Hardwick, and teachers saw him gently settled into the four-bed room at the end of Ward Four, an area for children considered not too ill. The little ward was like the others, bright with big cartoons, joke boards and toys. But Timothy, although in no distress, would never be able to play with the other children. He could not talk, walk or see because of his condition. He was a loving little boy entirely dependent on carers. As he lay silently recovering from his fits, everybody was impressed by the calm, caring quality shown by Allitt. Perhaps, after all, she would be allowed to stay on at the hospital. There were many other people around at the time, nurses bustling about with the drugs tray, and doctors in the treatment area. But the unusual layout of Ward Four, with its central core of offices and treatment rooms, meant that those on the other side of the corridor could not see what was happening as Allitt bent over her little charge. She needed privacy for just a few minutes.

Two nurses, Mary Reet, in charge of the ward, and Heather Skayman, were on their drug round at the bottom of the corridor when they were shocked to see Allitt race round the corner shouting: 'Quick, quick, cardiac arrest! Cardiac arrest!' They discovered Timothy very pale, cold to the touch and going blue around the mouth. Again, children's specialist Dr Nanayakkara was the man who tried to save a little boy whose heart had stopped beating.

All he could say later was: 'His death was unexpected.'

Again, despite a post-mortem examination, the cause of death was – and is – still unexplained. At the time it was put down to epilepsy and cerebral palsy. As his parents grieved, no attempt was made to call in the police.

Timothy's mother, Margaret, who was wheelchair-bound following a stroke, was beside herself with grief. 'There was so much love in that little boy it shone through him,' she said. Such shining love was something Allitt would never understand.

A few feet away from where Timothy had died lay little Kayley Desmond. The fourteen-month-old toddler with blonde hair and blue eyes had been admitted on 3 March with a minor chest infection. Kayley was a strong, healthy baby and nobody was too worried about her, but on 10 March, in Mr Happy's cubicle, where Liam Taylor had been murdered, she had a cardiac arrest while being treated by Allitt. The crash team managed to revive her but there were worries that her brain had been starved of oxygen and she was transferred to the intensive care unit at the Queen's Medical Centre in Nottingham. There doctors discovered an unusual mark under Kayley's right armpit. It was a needle puncture and behind it was a small air bubble. Somebody, probably by accident, had injected air into her body. However, Kayley had been born with a cleft palate and always had trouble feeding. Combined with her chest infection, it was believed that this had caused her to vomit some milk and inhale it, which in turn caused her breathing to stop.

Things went back to normal on Children's Ward Four. But by now the hospital authorities were concerned that something was wrong. The horror of what was really happening, however, was too evil to contemplate. Then came three potentially murderous attacks in four days.

Five-month-old Paul Crampton was brought into Ward Four with mild bronchitis on Wednesday, 20 March. He responded well to treatment and plans were made to discharge him the following Sunday. Again, only Allitt was present when his condition suddenly and inexplicably deteriorated. On three separate occasions his insulin level suddenly soared so high that he collapsed with hypoglycaemia, a critical lack of sugar in the body. His lips turned blue, he broke out in sweats and rolled his eyes. Doctors saved him by pumping glucose into his body. Allitt, quiet and cool, watched the proceedings, telling the doctors she too thought it was hypoglycaemia. Doctor Nelson Porter could not understand why Paul's blood sugar kept dropping so dramatically. He considered various explanations and ordered blood samples. On 28 March, after his third attack, Paul was rushed to Queen's Medical Centre with Allitt in the ambulance. The youngster was again found to have a high level of insulin in his blood. Although in children the body sometimes produces insulin naturally in erratic amounts, the results of another blood sample were later to shock the police.

On 29 March, five-year-old Bradley Gibson, who had gone into hospital suffering from pneumonia, suffered a massive, unexplained heart attack. The crash team battled successfully for half an hour to save him. Pathologists later discovered that he too had insulin in his body. During the night, Bradley had complained twice that his arm was hurting where his antibiotic drip was attached. On both occasions Allitt checked the drip site. Soon after she went the second time, Bradley suddenly slumped forward suffering cardiac arrest. He was also taken to Queen's.

On 31 March, two-year-old Yik Hung Chan, called Henry by his family, collapsed and was revived close to death. He had been playing with his mother earlier that day. But at 9pm Allitt called on other medical staff to come and see him because he was crying. They found him blue with his back arched but he was quickly revived with oxygen. Allitt was left alone with Henry once more and about an hour later she raised the alarm again. Doctors found the same scene, Henry blue and stiff with his back arched . . . but he quickly recovered and was taken to Queen's. It was generally believed that the fall that had landed him in Ward Four was the cause of him nearly dying. He had plunged twenty feet out of his sister's bedroom window, fracturing his skull on the patio below. Henry had a history of asthma and eczema, for which he had previously been treated. All three children had been in the direct care of Allitt. Still police were not called in. It was a private matter, of concern only to the regional medical authorities.

Death number three followed within five days and it was close to being a double murder.

Becky and Katie Phillips were identical twins, born prematurely to their mother, Susan, by Caesarean section on 31 January 1991 at Nottingham City Hospital. Becky weighed 3lb 2oz, Katie 2lb 12oz. At thirty-three days the twins, who had been in ventilation chambers, finally went home to Sue and husband Peter's new five-bedroom home in a quiet cul-de-sac half a mile from Grantham Hospital. The family made a great fuss of the two babies dressed in identical pink and white dresses, pink cardigans and white frilly socks. Everyone was overjoyed. Everything was working out well in their lives. Sue and former lorry driver Peter's car valeting business was going well and now they had these wonderful additions to their family. Peter already had two girls from a previous marriage and the couple had a son, James, born three years earlier. But things began to go wrong. Becky and Katie suffered from suspected acute gastro-enteritis and on 1 April, Becky was admitted to Ward Four. Doctors wanted to keep her under observation. They felt her milk feed might be the cause of the trouble, and Susan was asked to bring some to the hospital for tests.

Allitt had been off for two days and when she returned she made a point of spending a lot of time with Becky in Cubicle Five – Mr Tickle. Sue had been at Grantham College with her at the same time, although they didn't know each other well, but Allitt did not acknowledge the young mother as a former student. Sue thought she hadn't recognized her.

On 3 April Allitt ran from Mr Tickle and urged another nurse to have a look at the child.

'She is cold to the touch and she looks hypoglycaemic (very low blood sugar),' she said. 'I think we should call the doctor.'

The nurse felt the child was perfectly well, and told Allitt to stop being paranoid. The next day, after Becky had been fed by Allitt, she was taken home. The milk given for testing was found to be clear and returned to Susan. During the night, however, Becky woke up sweating, twitching and screaming in pain and suffered repeated convulsions. Susan, tending her, noticed her eyes drop in their sockets. The doctor was summoned again. He found her heartbeat and pulse normal and believed she was suffering from severe colic. The parents took her into their own bed and dozed off, reassured. At 3am they woke. Becky was dead beside them. She had died in under an hour. They tried desperately to resuscitate her themselves then rushed her to the hospital, but efforts to revive her failed. No reason for Becky's death could be found in the post-mortem examination or in the routine biochemical analysis, so it was attributed to cot death. But a blood sample taken from her heart later showed high levels of insulin in her body. The following evening the family's mystified doctor was worried about Becky's twin sister, Katie. As a precaution she was sent to hospital and into the care of Allitt in Cubicle Two, Mr Noisy. There appeared to be nothing wrong with the baby but that night, for some reason, Allitt decided to move the bed without explanation, and within ten minutes she ran out holding the baby in her arms shouting: 'Cardiac arrest, cardiac arrest!' Katie was dark blue in colour and had stopped breathing, although none of the emergency alarm systems had sounded. Only hectic treatment in intensive care saved her. Katie's condition deteriorated two days later when again she had convulsions and her lungs collapsed. This time it took longer to restart her breathing. Air was leaking from her lungs into the chest cavity. As soon as she was stable she was transferred to Nottingham, thirty miles away, but she had suffered serious brain damage. Katie was also found to have five broken ribs, as if somebody had squeezed her. Medical staff agreed that the broken ribs could have been the result of the resuscitation procedures. Katie was the fifth child to be transferred from Ward Four to Nottingham in less than a month.

Susan felt Allitt had saved her baby's life . . . and asked her to be godmother to her surviving daughter. The smiling nurse readily agreed.

How could they have known that Allitt had murdered eight-week-old Becky and tried four times to kill Katie, squeezing her until her ribs broke and injecting her with large doses of potassium?

It left Katie with cerebral palsy, her right side paralysed, her hearing damaged and her eyes partially blinded.

In the following eleven days there were four more unexplained collapses involving perfectly fit children.

On the evening of Sunday, 7 April, six-year-old Michael Davidson was admitted to Ward Four after an operation to remove an airgun pellet from his stomach. He had been shot accidentally. Two days later Allitt helped a doctor prepare a dose of antibiotic for him. While the doctor was administering the drug intravenously, Michael's limbs stiffened and he became blue around the mouth. The doctor could not feel him breathing and gradually Michael's heart stopped beating. He came round quickly when they began to resuscitate him.

Dr Nanayakkara, who was on the ward at the time, decided that Michael had been overbreathing and it had led to a fit. A blood sample was taken, but surgeons in charge of Michael's treatment told him that what had happened was not unknown in children recovering from an operation. Michael was discharged on 12 April.

That same day, two-month-old Chris Peasgood was admitted for a persistent cough and chest problems, believed to be bronchiolitis. He was put in an oxygen tent. His worried parents, Creswen and Mick Peasgood, who had lost their ten-month-old daughter Michelle to a cot death two years earlier, were by his side when Allitt suggested they take a break for a cup of tea. They returned ten minutes later to find the crash team fighting to save their son. Creswen was beside herself with grief, fearing she would lose Chris just as she had lost Michelle. Allitt led her out of the cubicle, telling her everything would be all right. The alarm indicating that he had stopped breathing had been turned off and a staff nurse had rushed in to find Allitt doing nothing. Chris had almost suffocated but he pulled through. Later that night, however, Chris suffered another cardiac arrest. This time things looked worse than before. A chaplain was sent for and the little boy was christened in front of his distraught parents. There was just one chance – Queen's Medical Centre. But the journey was dangerous for him, he might not survive. It was up to Creswen and Mick. They decided to take the gamble – and it paid off. He pulled through. It was believed that Christoper's collapse could have been the result of him inhaling some milk and choking.

Alternatively, it was possible that his existing breathing problems had deteriorated to a point where he could not maintain the proper level of oxygen in his blood. Or was he suffocated?

Next came little Christopher King. Chris experienced breathing difficulties following his birth in 1991. When he was a month old he began vomiting repeatedly and was admitted to Ward Four to determine the cause. A few days later Allitt shouted to medical staff that he had inexplicably turned grey. He recovered quickly with oxygen, and an operation to correct a narrowing of the muscular outlet in his stomach was performed on Monday, 15 April. The following morning Allitt was allocated to look after him – and drama was to follow. A few hours later she raised the alarm again. This time Christopher had turned blue and more or less stopped breathing. He was given emergency treatment and he improved. A short time later, Allitt rushed out of his cubicle shouting that it was happening again. Doctors raced to his side and he revived quickly. But at 10.30am the doctors were called back. It was the same frightening problem. He couldn't breathe properly and had turned blue. He was revived and sent to Queen's Medical Centre, where he recovered.

Patrick Elston, just seven weeks old, was in Ward Four for a check-up after he had developed a cold and stopped taking his feed. Days later Allitt came running out of Cubicle Six carrying him in her arms. He had stopped breathing. He was rushed to Queen's but he had suffered brain damage. Hours before, when his parents had left him, he had been playing and laughing.

In every case the only common denominator was Allitt. On each occasion she had been alone with the children. Still the police were not called. But at Queen's questions were being asked. Why were so many seriously ill children suddenly being sent into their care?

The final killing was that of Claire Peck, fifteen months. By now Allitt seemed prepared to take unbelievable chances. Claire, an asthmatic, had been admitted to Ward Four on 18 April but discharged two days later. Then on 22 April, after a coughing fit, her mother, Susan, and husband, David, of Balderton, Notts took her back on doctor's advice. One of the first people Sue saw was Allitt and the worried mother was not pleased. She had taken an instant dislike to the nurse the last time she had brought Claire in, finding her cold and unfriendly. She felt that Allitt had ignored her daughter.

Meanwhile a consultant paediatrician sent Claire to the treatment room for nebulizing treatment and an intravenous drip. Susan squeezed into the small room and saw that Claire was wheezing but that she was bright-eyed and not too unwell. There too was the chubby nurse with mousy hair she disliked so much. Unable to watch her little girl have a tube put down her throat, Sue agreed with ward sister Barbara Barker that it would be better to wait in the TV lounge. The Pecks were then quietly ushered away. The doctor attending Claire left the treatment room for a few minutes to check with a colleague on the dosage of a new drug for the toddler, and another nurse left too, leaving Allitt alone with her charge. The other nurse had gone just a few steps down the corridor when a cry rang out from the treatment room: 'Arrest! Arrest!' The nurse ran back, joined by doctors and nurses nearby who had heard the cry. Claire had suffered respiratory failure and was having trouble breathing. After being given oxygen, however, she quickly recovered. When the tube was inserted into Claire's throat, everything seemed in order and the doctor and nurse left again. Only Allitt remained with Claire.

A minute later the cry rang out again: 'Arrest, arrest!' This time Claire had suffered heart failure.

When David and Sue arrived back at the treatment room they discovered a full medical team working on their daughter, giving her chest massage, electric shocks, and injections into her heart. Allitt stood among them, watching in silence. They fought in vain. Minutes later, grief-stricken Sue and David were saying goodbye to their baby for the last time. Distraught Dr Porter sat with his head in his hands. 'This should never had happened,' he said.

Allitt had stood coldly watching the proceedings.

To this day Susan is haunted by the nightmare. She later told newspaper reporters: 'I sat there holding Claire and looked around as if to say: is that it? I knew my baby was dying but did not know if she was going to die in my arms or if it had already happened. Everybody either looked away or looked at the floor but Allitt just stood, staring vacantly. I will never forget it. She was just staring, staring, staring at me!'

It was Claire's tragic death that finally made the authorities realize that something terrifying was happening on Ward Four. A post-mortem blamed natural causes and Claire was buried four days later. But even if the alarm bells had not been going off in the cots, they were going off in the minds of some medical experts. And, as David and Sue demanded to see the hospital managers, rumours were rife that an airborne virus such as legionnaires' disease was at work in Ward Four. After exhaustive tests, however, no virus was found. Nevertheless Ward Four was swabbed inch by inch and the walls scrubbed. Then the police were called in.

A poisons expert had found that Claire had traces of the powerful drug lignocaine, an anaesthetic substance used on victims of cardiac arrest. This was one substance that had no right to be in any baby's body. It was clear evidence of murder.

In this final killing Allitt had had only a few minutes to administer a fatal dose, and she did it while more than a dozen staff members, doctors and nurses, and the child's family were only yards away. It was the beginning of the end. Detective Superintendent Stuart Clifton and his men had arrived.

The first case the detective and father-of-two looked at was five-month-old Paul Crampton. In the space of eight days in March, Paul had collapsed three times. No one could understand why. After the third collapse it was discovered that he had been injected with virtually the whole of an adult syringe of insulin. Experts at Cardiff University had never seen so much insulin in a child. Could Paul have been injected with insulin by a nurse who thought it was something else? Or was he injected deliberately? Suspicions grew when Allitt herself reported that the key to the fridge containing insulin was missing. Now the inquiries centred on staff working on the ward, because only they had access to the babies and drugs and could move around without arousing suspicion. Clifton sought the opinions of Nelson Porter and Dr Charith Nanayakkara. Porter suspected that something untoward could be going on but Nanayakkara was not so sure. Porter even told the detectives about Munchausen's Syndrome and wondered if there was a sufferer in the hospital. Parents of victims were interviewed, medical experts were called in, records checked and a security video camera installed in the ward.

The twelve-man police team had their first break-through when they discovered that pages had been cut out of a notebook kept on the ward for nurses to comment on their treatment of patients. The missing pages covered the period of Paul Crampton's stay in hospital.

They drew up a chart of the twenty-five attacks on the thirteen victims and pinned it to a wall. They were looking for a common threat – a pattern. Then they began to check the staff rotas. As they ticked off the medical staff at each emergency, one name was there every time. Allitt.

On the morning of 21 May, three weeks after the start

of the investigation, she was arrested. For two days she rigorously denied the charges. She was cool, calm and collected. But after her arrest, another ward diary which had gone missing was found in a wardrobe at her home. Allitt was suspended by health chiefs, but even then Katie's mother and father were so taken in by her that they employed a private detective to try and clear her name.

Police, however, were struggling to find a motive. There was only one: Allitt's deep-seated desire to impress and seek attention.

Finally the evidence was overwhelming. Allitt was charged and sent to trial at Nottingham Crown Court. Most of her colleagues couldn't believe it. A few had noticed that she was unemotional and never cried when children died. Some noticed too that she did not pick babies up just to cuddle them in the way most nurses did. One sister said: 'I just thought that was her way of handling the stress we all felt.'

On Monday, 15 February, 1993, Beverly Allitt was led into the dock at Nottingham Crown Court and a silence fell over the courtroom as the roll call of dead and injured babies was read out. In a calm voice the prosecutor called out one name after another. Four dead, nine injured, all on Ward Four. As the list went on a look of bewilderment crossed the faces of the people sitting huddled together in the public gallery. They were the parents of the children attacked by Allitt. They listened quietly as the court heard that it was not until the death of victim number twelve, Claire Peck, that hospital chiefs called in the police.

The jury heard that the one thread linking the victims was that Allitt was on duty when each one became dangerously ill in bizarre circumstances. The collapses stopped after her arrest.

Allitt, pale and thin after suffering anorexia nervosa while awaiting trial, sat impassively in the dock. Her hair was clipped back and she wore a patterned cardigan over a white blouse and navy skirt. Her parents had bought her new clothes because her weight had fallen from 13 stone to a mere 6 stone 13lb, bringing her dress size down from a sixteen to an eight. She denied four charges of murder, eleven of attempted murder and eleven alternative charges of grievous bodily harm. But the court was told how in some cases she injected insulin into her tiny victims, in others a mixture of drugs. Sometimes they were put into a drip feed, on other occasions a hand over the baby's mouth and nose was all it took. Or even a push of a switch on the oxygen supply.

Professor Roy Meadow, a consultant paediatrician at the St James Hospital in Leeds, told the court that Allitt had shown the symptoms of Munchausen's Syndrome and Munchausen's Syndrome by Proxy. The first condition was where the sufferers inflicted pain upon themselves in order to gain hospital treatment. The second, most commonly found in mothers, was a form of child abuse where factitious injury is inflicted on infants. Allitt's medical records between 1985 and 1991 showed that she had inflicted a whole series of injuries on herself. She convinced doctors she needed her appendix removed, but after the operation it was found to be normal. The surgical wound refused to heal because she had plucked at it. She also reported unusual wounds to her hands and feet, caused herself with a hammer. In another incident she pushed glass into her feet. Allitt also tampered with catheters being used to drain her bladder, so that they broke inside her and had to be surgically removed.

In the summer of 1991, when she was on bail following her arrest, her medical history became even more bizarre. She was admitted to hospital in Peterborough, where she manipulated thermometer readings to temperatures incompatible to her medical state. At the same time she complained of an enlarged right breast. No cause was found, but doctors discovered three small puncture marks in the tissue. She had injected herself with water. Munchausen's Syndrome was suggested.

Professor Meadow told the jury that Allitt was an extreme case of a condition in which mothers had been known to kill two or three of their own children. It was very rare to find someone who suffered from both Munchausen's Syndrome and Munchausen's Syndrome by Proxy. The court heard that he dealt with about forty severe cases of the proxy condition each year. Asked if Allitt could be described as evil, he said: 'What happened was extremely evil, and all the children suffered very greatly, as did their families.' But sufferers seemed to 'be able to shut off their minds to their crimes'.

Allitt had never admitted what she had done in the two interviews he had with her at Rampton Hospital. He said her very abnormal personality would be with her for the rest of her life and could not be cured, although it might be modified. She had described her mind to him as being like a box in which she could only see the top layers.

Doctor James Higgins, a Home Office consultant forensic psychiatrist, said he had interviewed Allitt five times. She was not willing to admit to harming or killing children. But she had confessed to him that she had low self-esteem and had told him: 'I had to prove that I was better than other people thought.'

Fifty-one days later Britain's most prolific female serial killer this century was given thirteen life sentences for murders and assaults on children. It was a record punishment for a British woman in modern times. Mr Justice Latham told the court there was no chance Allitt could ever safely be released. As Allitt, gaunt and frail with cropped hair, wearing jeans, a flowery shirt and a purple jumper, turned to walk from the dock, relatives of her victims hurled abuse at her. But she remained expressionless, as she had done throughout the evidence by doctors on her personality disorder. She raised her eyes only when she stood unsteadily to be sentenced. Because she was suffering from anorexia nervosa, Allitt had not been in court since the sixteenth day of the trial.

The judge told her: 'You have been found guilty of the most terrible crimes. You killed, tried to kill or seriously harmed, thirteen children, many of them tiny babies. They had been entrusted to your care. You have brought grief to their families. You have sown a seed of doubt in those who should have faith in the integrity of care their children receive in hospital. Hopefully, the grief felt by the families will become easier to bear, but it will always be there. You are seriously disturbed. You are cunning and manipulative and you have shown no remorse for the trail of destruction you have left behind you. I accept it is all the result of the severe personality disorder you have. But you are and remain a very serious danger to others.'

The judge sentenced Allitt to life imprisonment for murdering Liam Taylor, Claire Peck, Becky Phillips and Timothy Hardwick. He also gave life terms for the attempted murder of another three children: Paul Crampton, Bradley Gibson and Becky's twin sister, Katie Phillips. Life sentences were given for causing grievous bodily harm with intent to six more youngsters: Kayley Desmond, Yik Hung Chan, Christopher King, Patrick Elstone, Christopher Peasgood and Michael Davidson.

Allitt was taken to London's Holloway gaol, where she was placed in the psychiatric wing known to inmates as the Muppet House, because its furniture was made of cardboard and there were no naked lightbulbs which could be used as weapons. Later she was transferred to Rampton.

The nearest Allitt ever came to an apology was when she admitted to a psychiatrist: 'I hate myself.'

The tortured inner world of Beverly Allitt was revealed in a series of letters she wrote to her friends during her trial. They made no mention of her crimes and were often jokey and light-hearted, proving how she had taken refuge in a syndrome that allowed her to seek the limelight while absolving herself from any feeling of guilt. In one letter, written from Rampton Hospital the day after the jury heard harrowing evidence about the murder of Becky Phillips and her attempt to kill her twin sister, Katie, which had left her permanently brain-damaged, she wrote: 'Well, court hasn't been too bad – but I'll be glad when it's all over.'

In another she talked of joining her friends on their new patio. 'I want to be able to come and sit out on it, supping lager and eating a chinky when I get out, OK?'

And another: 'I just can't wait until I get out of all this shit to be able to spend a lot of time with you and really make up for all the lost time. It'll be one hell of a long piss up!'

Allitt also talked about her anorexia, saying: 'I'm not going too well with the food, it's coz I've got too much on my mind at the moment. And I can't think about anything other than court, but believe me I will try to eat again one day when I feel able to keep it down.'

In another note she talked about her weight and said: 'I'm going to get mum to get me some nice new clothes – as mine are far too big and I need to impress someone . . .'

Who was that someone?

While Allitt was awaiting trial inside top security Rampton, newspapers were running stories that she had confessed in other letters to being besotted with a 'macho' female arsonist. Snatched pictures were circulating of the couple kissing and cuddling. The families of her victims were devastated. They were hurt, angry and grieving. Allitt was enjoying herself. Perhaps at last Allitt was getting the attention and affection she had always craved.

The letters revealed that she adored the arsonist's skinhead hairstyle and muscular body. Was it the fact that she needed to be the centre of attraction in her new world again – and someone was opening the stage door? Or did she have a physical need for love like normal people? That question, along with why she became a serial killer, will never be answered.

Three months after conviction Allitt was treated for self-inflicted stab wounds. Staff at Rampton found her mutilating herself with metal paper clips she had straightened. She was the centre of attention again. In another incident she poured scalding custard over her hand and on one occasion even tried to eat glass.

Five months after being jailed, Allitt finally admitted killing three children and injuring six more. Detectives did not reveal the names of the victims in the hope that she would finally confess to all thirteen.

The trail of murders prompted Health Secretary Virginia Bottomley to set up an independent three-member inquiry, headed by Sir Cecil Clothier, QC. It met thirty-five times, and interviewed ninety-four witnesses.

In February 1994 it found that a combination of overworked doctors, shortage of nurses and weak hospital managers was to blame for the nightmare on Ward Four. Vital clues were neglected that would have revealed Allitt as a serial killer. Fragments of medical evidence, including autopsies, blood tests and X-rays pointing to her as the 'malevolent cause of the unexpected collapses of children' were missed altogether.

The report stated: 'The principal failure lay in not

collecting together those pieces of evidence. The initiative and energy to do this were not forthcoming at Grantham and Kesteven Hospital. This is the true and ultimate criticism.'

However, no single person was to blame. It was down to a collection of staff failures. All the staff on Ward Four were discussing what caused a series of children to collapse with heart and breathing stoppages, but no meeting was ever called to pool their ideas. An emergency resuscitation team was summoned to the ward seven times in three months – an unprecedented rate – but no one suspected a crime. Four times alarms mysteriously failed to go off when children collapsed, but no one asked why. Allitt stood out as a nurse who did not pick up babies to cuddle them when they cried and showed no emotion when children died.

Failures highlighted by the report included:

Sloppy appointment procedures. Allitt missed 126 days in her two-year training through sickness, but this was never made known when she was employed.

Inadequate staffing. Only three full-time nurses and one part-time qualified sick children's nurse were on the ward. The complement was more than ten. This meant that Allitt was often one of only two nurses on duty performing tasks beyond her capability. 'Her colleagues noted she was invariably present when a child collapsed. Some of them teased her as an agent of bad luck.'

The two consultant paediatricians Doctor Nelson Porter and Doctor Charithnanda Nanayakkara were over-worked. On call all day and on alternative nights, they had unsuccessfully sought extra staff for years. Under less pressure they might have been in a better position to see the broader picture.

Senior management was said to have poor operational procedures and was indecisive in the crisis. There was a delay of over two weeks in following up a vital clue that ultimately pointed to criminal behaviour. Another child died in that time. Allitt rarely attended the fourteen-week hearing because of illness.

The report made twelve recommendations for safeguarding children in hospital, including the need to check all nursing applicants' sickness records. It called for specialized paediatric autopsies to be carried out in every case of unexpected or clinically unaccountable death. Hospitals should also be able to order a specialist post-mortem without the coroner's permission, it said. The report highlighted the fact that a Grantham coroner had refused a specialist autopsy of Allitt's first victim. A specialized pathologist, however, might have been able to discover that the baby had been killed. Two other mistaken causes of death were recorded after post-mortem examinations. The Government planned to act on all the recommendations.

But the Press conference did nothing to silence the anger of the victims' parents, and that same day they confronted the hospital's managers demanding to know why senior executives had not been disciplined.

Creswen Peasgood, whose baby son Christopher was attacked twice by Allitt, said: 'They have only told us what they want us to know. We still feel the truth is being hidden from us. It is a cover-up which we feared all along. They have got rid of the nurses and the doctors but we have not seen anything happen to the management.'

The children's families, who were still demanding a public inquiry which was turned down by the Government, called for heads to roll after hearing Sir Cecil's conclusions.

The management of the ward has now been transferred to Queen's Medical Centre, Nottingham.

The 122-page report found that the two consultant paediatricians should have grasped sooner the significance of the 'cascade of collapses' they had to deal with. Meetings should have been held.

But at a news conference later Dr Nelson Porter and Dr Charith Nanayakkara, who were both made redundant following the transfer of the hospital's management to Queen's, attacked Sir Cecil for holding the inquiry behind closed doors and for not taking evidence from paediatric experts. The doctors still felt that the report had failed to take account of the extreme staff shortages on their ward.

Doctor Nanayakkara, close to tears, said that the report had had a devastating effect on his life.

'It has destroyed me and my family,' he said. 'My reputation is at stake and my future uncertain. Here I am, a competent, fully qualified clinical paediatrician, wasting my skills at home.'

Dr Porter said: 'We were working in such circumstances that the clinical demands of caring for our patients consumed our qualities of leadership, energy and drive.

These demands were compounded by the lack of staffing and resources.'

Sister Barbara Barker, the senior nursing sister on the ward, was also made redundant and Mrs Moira Onions, the clinical services manager, took early retirement.

The month after the report was published the harrowing Allitt story rolled on – with at least one ray of sunshine through the dark clouds of despair. Little Katie Phillips, left brain-damaged after Allitt's attack, was given new hope after a trip to the seaside. She flew 4,000 miles to Florida with her parents Peter and Sue to try revolutionary dolphin therapy, a system that stimulates youngsters' brains and bodies as they touch, play and swim with the magic mammals. In less than thirty seconds, Katie, who has difficulty moving her arms, was giggling with delight as Sandy, an Atlantic bottle-nosed dolphin, splashed her and let her stroke his grey snout with her foot at the Dolphin Research Center in the Florida Keys. Just one little smile in the trail of tragedy and heartbreak.

Chapter Eight

AILEEN WUORNOS

'I have gone through at least 250,000 guys in my life, maybe more, and never hurt any of them. Matter of fact I became very good friends with them, you know, and they really liked me.'

Deland, Florida, 1992

The woman on the television screen waved her hand in a gesture of dismissal. 'I just kept shooting him,' she said calmly. Fourteen jurors leaned forward, looking and listening intently. One slowly shook his head, another flinched and a third shut her eyes in thought for a moment. For thirty-three minutes they sat staring fixedly at the face of Aileen Wuornos on the small screen as she described to detectives how she shot and robbed a man named Richard Mallory.

The videotape clip was exhibit 121 in the State's case against the thirty-five-year-old highway hooker who always dreamed of being a movie star. Now she sat alongside a judge, jury and lawyers, watching herself play the leading role in a drama centred around Interstate 1–95, one of the American highways that was her killing ground.

Pictured in an orange gaol jumpsuit and blue sweater, Wuornos puffed cigarettes and recounted to detectives how fifty-one-year-old video and TV repair man Mallory picked her up as she was hitchhiking outside Tampa. They parked the car, drank vodka and talked most of the night on a dirt road of 1–95 near Ormond Beach, she said. The judge, with his own small TV monitor in front of him, stared intently at the screen as Wuornos told how Mallory agreed to have sex with her. Then her account became vague. For a moment Wuornos, sitting watching herself in the courtroom, fidgeted in her seat and one of her court-appointed attorneys whispered in her ear as the TV drama hotted up. On screen she claimed she and Mallory started to wrestle, either because he wouldn't remove his trousers – or because she thought he wouldn't pay her any money. She ran from the car and lunged for her purse, snatching out a .22 calibre revolver.

'I shot him in the front seat,' she said. 'He just went like "Ooooo" you know? I think I hit him on the side. He got out of the car and started to run towards me so I shot him again, I think in the stomach or in the chest or somewhere around that area. Then he fell to the ground – I just kept shooting him!' The camera panned in on her as she stood and indicated where the bullets hit her victim. Then she gestured with her hand as if she was firing a pistol. 'I don't care about me,' she told detectives. 'I deserve to die.' The screen went blank.

For a moment the court sat in silence. One of the jurors aimed a long, hard stare at the accused hooker, who took a pink tissue from her maroon jacket and wept into it. Her attorneys, Tricia Jenkins and Billy Nolas, embraced her and patted her back before leading her away.

The videotape they had all watched had been chopped from three hours of film to thirty-three minutes to remove any reference to six other highway killings Wuornos had confessed to. Under Florida law evidence of a defendant's other crimes was allowed as long as it did not become a feature of the main trial. In the case of Wuornos, the prosecution felt that their case might be overturned on appeal if they showed the other confessions. The defence had already objected to the showing of any part of the tape. While Wuornos had confessed to killing seven men during 1989 and 1990, she was charged with only five.

The next day, the sad, wandering blonde of the highways sat before the jury and gave a more detailed version of the murder that sparked her on a trail of killings across Florida.

After years of abuse from truckers she had thumbed down by the roadside, she claimed she finally reached her limit when Mallory tied her up, sodomized and tortured her. She had no choice but to kill him, she said. It was a case of self-defence. 'I had to kill or die.'

She looked across at the jury, clenched her fist and told them: 'Mallory had agreed to pay me $100. But after I undressed he said he didn't have enough money. I said: "No way! I'm not here for my health!"

Mallory, she claimed, then threw a cord around her neck, shouting: 'You're going to do everything I want you to do and if you don't I'll kill you.'

For a moment Wuornos lost her composure, and there was a stillness in the court. Then, under gentle questioning by her attorney, Tricia Jenkins, she told how Mallory had tied her hands to the steering wheel and raped her.

'I was crying my brains out,' she said. 'He tore me up pretty well.'

When he finished, she said he washed himself down with rubbing alcohol and eye-wash, then forced the liquids up her nose.

'He was saying he loved to hear me in pain,' she claimed. 'I said to myself this guy is going to kill me. He was strange, totally weird.'

After resting for an hour, Mallory untied her from the wheel with a warning: 'You had better be a good girl or I'm going to kill you!'

He lashed the cord around her neck again and tried to have more sex. 'I jumped up real fast and spat in his face. He screamed: "You're dead, you bitch!"'

They began to struggle and she broke free, reaching for the .22 calibre revolver she carried for protection. Then she shot him, again and again.

The Florida hooker covered his body with a red carpet. 'I didn't want the birds to be picking at him,' she said. She drove off in his car, which she used to move into a new apartment with her lesbian lover Tyria Moore. Later she abandoned it near Ormond Beach.

State Attorney John Tanner walked slowly up and

down the courtroom in front of Wuornos before beginning two hours of cross-examination. The hatred between them was soon to boil over into the court. The prosecution portrayed her as a grasping, power-hungry prostitute who lusted for the ultimate revenge over men – their deaths.

There was no physical evidence found at the murder scene to corroborate her story, he told the jury.

He asked Wuornos why she had not discussed details of Mallory's brutality when she made her initial confession to the police.

Investigators, she said, cut her off when she tried. She was confused and incoherent and suffering from alcohol withdrawal. She also accused the police of threatening her and using her lover as a tool.

'They coerced me to talk, saying they were going to arrest Tyria Moore if I didn't tell them about the case,' she said.

She claimed her lover Moore had lied 289 times in her statement to the police. Her motive was to capitalize on the massive media attention her case had gathered.

'Tyria Moore is interested in making $500 million,' said Wuornos. 'These people that are involved in books and movies must have my blood to get their money.'

Moore had already testified that while Wuornos had told her about murdering Mallory, she had never mentioned rape.

Tanner let Wuornos ramble on about her life as a prostitute, her upbringing and how much she had loved Moore. She had never loved anyone so much in her life.

Every now and then she would explain the reasons for her actions.

'Hard to keep the stories straight, isn't it?' Tanner interrupted.

'No, it's hard to remember what you're talking about,' she retorted.

The longer the testimony went on, the more agitated and worn Wuornos became. Tanner was slowly chipping away at her story. She nervously flicked her blonde hair with her hands, twisted her face, raised her eyebrows and nervously gestured him away. The questions and answers began to speed up into rapid-fire exchanges.

'I wasn't hurting anybody out there,' she asserted.

'That's not true, is it?' Tanner shot back.

'I'm the victim as far as I am concerned!' she shouted.

Wuornos worked, she said, as a prostitute and never posed as either a hitchhiker or a motorist in distress. She described herself as an 'exit-to-exit' hooker who worked all the roads in Florida. She claimed to have earned up to $200 a day having sex with at least three men four days a week. Some weeks she could earn more than $1,000 picking up between forty and fifty men.

When Tanner asked if she knew she was breaking the law by carrying a gun and being a prostitute, she became even more belligerent.

'Everybody breaks the law – I bet you do too! You drive a car and pollute the earth!' she shouted.

'And some people shoot men in cold blood,' Tanner continued.

'I never shot anyone in cold blood,' she responded.

The police questioned her claim that she was an 'exit-to-exit hooker' working all the Florida highways. If she propositioned up to fifty men a week, why was she never convicted of soliciting? For prostitutes with such a high turnover of clients, convictions were an occupational hazard. Yet Wuornos had no such charges against her during the eleven-month period in which the men were murdered. Wuornos was a 'hustler and prostitute only in the last resort', detectives said.

The ten-day trial ended with the thought in the minds of the jury that the prostitution, the robbery, the killing, seemed to be everybody's fault except Aileen Wuornos's.

On Monday, 28 January 1992 the jury took just ninety-one minutes to decide her fate – guilty of the robbery and murder of Richard Mallory.

Moments after being convicted her composure cracked.

'I was raped,' she shouted to the departing jurors. 'I hope you get raped too, scumbags of America!'

Her attorney, Nolas, tried to calm her down as she was led away to a holding cell, facing the death sentence.

The jury were returning later that afternoon to weigh aggravating and mitigating factors in the case before recommending either the electric chair or life in prison with no chance of parole for twenty-five years.

What they didn't know was that Mallory was a convicted sex offender. He had been described to them as an average guy who probably did nothing to deserve his fate. But new information has come to light that in 1957 he had pleaded insanity to charges that he tried to rape a

Maryland woman. Court records revealed that Mallory was a sexually-disturbed man who entered a woman's house, grabbed her from behind, fondled her and tried to rip her blouse off. He was sentenced to four years in jail. But after a psychiatric evaluation he was transferred to a prison mental institution where he spent ten years.

Did the events leading up to Mallory's killing happen the way Wuornos claimed? There are some who believe they did. Whatever the truth is, Mallory made something snap inside Wuornos. He ignited her psyche and put her on the road to becoming a serial killer. If the jury had known this perhaps they would not have recommended the death sentence.

Nevertheless it was the end of the highway for the ninth-grade school dropout who left home at fifteen and embarked on a career of prostitution and dead-end menial jobs. Raped five times, her life was one of misery and spiralling desperation that finally led to mental illness.

As with all female serial killers, along with the anger of her victims' relatives, there was a large measure of public sympathy for her. But at the end of the day dead men cannot tell their tales. Was the testimony of Aileen Wuornos true or false? The public debates rages on.

It was a fine sunny April evening when my taxi driver, John, sped down the sliproad and on to Interstate 1–75, the highway that cuts through the sunshine state of Florida. This wide stretch of concrete carries Buicks and Pontiacs, six-wheel trucks and Greyhound buses from the green fields and sprawling housing complexes of Orlando to the white sands of Daytona Beach and Miami. We were on our way to Daytona to visit the bar where Aileen Wuornos, incorrectly described by some newspapers as America's first female serial killer, had made her home on a car seat on the front porch.

'There's a lot of sympathy here for her, man,' John said. 'You have to understand people like Aileen Wuornos. Don't think Florida is all about Disney World and swimming pools. A lot of drifters, including families, come here from all over America in search of the good life. They think the streets are paved with gold. Few realize their dreams and they end up living in the woods – in tents, abandoned cars or even old crates. No wonder they turn to crime. Florida is a hard place when you are down and out. The only thing that is going to help you is the weather. At least you won't freeze to death. No, man, not everybody is privileged enough to see the duck walk at the Peabody Hotel.'

John laughed as he recalled the media circus that had surrounded the Wuornos trial. 'You have to understand America,' he said. 'Sometimes it is like living in a giant movie set.'

Perhaps he was right. The losing lawyer in the Wuornos case, Steve Glazer, had picked up his guitar and sung about the electric chair, police who interviewed the convicted female serial killer had tried to sell movie rights along with her friends, and many tabloid headlines had focussed on her kinky sex romps. Even Britain's Channel 4 TV station was forced to defend plans to screen an interview with Wuornos from her death cell. A stampede for profit was the motive behind many of the films, books and documentaries on the twelve-month killing spree that had thrust Wuornos into infamy.

The trail began on a warm sunny afternoon in December 1989 when the body of Richard Mallory was found. He had been shot four times with a .22 calibre revolver.

The police sealed off an acre-wide area of woodland near the Florida resort of Daytona Beach as forensic experts placed the rubber-backed red carpet his body was wrapped in into a plastic sack and took it away to the laboratory. Mallory's camera, jewellery and money were missing. His abandoned beige Cadillac coupé had been discovered days before by a police officer on routine patrol miles from the scene. It had been backed up thirty feet into a narrow, wooded dirt road. Nearby in a sand dune were two expired credit cards and Mallory's car ownership papers. At first the officer thought the Cadillac had been stolen. Then he discovered a blood stain on the back rest of the driver's seat.

In the eleven months that followed the discovery of the TV repairman's crumpled body, five other murdered men were found dumped in remote areas across north central Florida. All had been killed with carefully aimed shots from a .22 calibre revolver. The youngest was thirty-nine, the oldest sixty. They had been robbed. Some were partially clothed, others were naked. Their clothes had been removed to prevent easy identification. Their abandoned cars were found up to eighty miles away, all cleaned of prints. Their licence documents and log-books were missing. By the time the body of the last victim, security guard Walter Gino Antonio, was found in November 1990, police were certain the deaths were linked and a serial killer was on the loose.

Taxi driver John pulled up outside Aileen Wuornos's favourite bar, the Last Resort, nestling in the centre of Daytona's sunbaked walkways. In a little room at the back was the old car seat she had slept on before her arrest. It was decorated with a small air-brushed portrait of her. Beneath the portrait on a placard were the words: 'Here lied Aileen (Lee) Wuornos on her last night of freedom.' It was a ramshackle reminder of the girl who dreamed of being a movie star and had to kill before her dreams came true.

Thwack! The brown, steel-studded leather belt whipped through the air and cut into the buttocks of the naked, sobbing girl, spreadeagled on the bed. She bit into the blanket as the belt came down again and again, the weals turning white in her crimson, bleeding flesh.

'You're evil, what are you?'

'Evil!' she screamed.

'You're worthless!'

'Worthless!' she screamed.

'You should never have been born . . . you're not worthy of the air you breathe!'

The belt came down again.

'Fuck you!' she sobbed. 'You old man!' Her father left her crying and shaking on the bed, slamming the door behind him. He ritualistically hung his belt on a peg in his room. He would get her to clean it with saddle soap in the morning, he thought. Time for a bottle of wine.

The sun went down over the little one-storey ranch house in Troy, Michigan. But Aileen Wuornos didn't rise from the bed. Her spine and legs were numb. The world didn't want her. Perhaps there would be someone one day, a white knight who would take her away and protect her. One day she would be a movie star, a rock singer – or maybe a nun. She just knew it, she really did. She had the feeling of destiny.

In the morning when she woke, things would be the same. One day, though, they wouldn't be. One day she would learn that he wasn't her father.

Aileen Carol Pittman was born on 29 February 1956. It was an unlucky start. Her mother, Diana, abandoned her before she was a year old, leaving before dinner one day and never returning. Aileen was the younger of two children. Her brother, Keith, was born in 1955. She never knew her real father, a car-bumper worker named Leo Pittman, and he never knew her. Perhaps it was just as well. Strangely, he had had a life much like hers was to be. Leo never knew his parents either. They abandoned him when he was five months old and he was adopted by his grandparents, who ran the local rubbish tip. He had sex with an elderly woman neighbour when he was ten and was cold and indifferent to his grandparents, who doted on him. They put his attitude down to his bad start in life. When his grandfather died of throat cancer, his grandmother spoilt him even more, baking him cakes and giving him money. In his teens he returned her love and kindness by beating and abusing her. One of his favourite games was to tie two cats together by their tails and throw them over a clothesline to watch them fight. Long-haired Leo had an insatiable sexual appetite and would demand sex from Aileen's mother six times a day. She asked friends if this was normal. There were other women, too, during his brief marriage to Diana. But six years after he had left her he abducted a seven-year-old girl from a school, drove her to a quiet, remote spot, and brutally raped and sodomized her. Later, after his arrest, he was diagnosed a paranoid schizophrenic. In January 1969, when he was thirty-three years old, he was found hanging from a rope made of bedsheets in his cell. At the time he was being investigated for indecent assaults on two ten-year-old girls and a child murder.

Aileen and Keith were adopted by Diana's parents, first generation Finnish immigrants Lauri Jacob Wuornos and Aileen Britta Wuornos. Aileen Pittman then became Aileen Wuornos. Her real mother remarried and surfaced in Texas. She became Aileen's 'sister' but they later lost contact. Her mother's sister Lori and brother Barry became Aileen's brother and sister. Aileen grew up believing her grandfather Lauri was her father. It was a complicated start for the girl destined to kill.

Lauri was a strict disciplinarian who drank until he was comatose. Each evening he would sit in his armchair, smoke a cigar and polish off three bottles of cheap wine. Then he would fall into a deep, drunken sleep, inexplicably coming to in time to stumble into bed. His dependence on alcohol was so great that he kept a bottle of wine in his car – and another in his desk at work.

Aileen's only escape from his world was through her bedroom window. When she was eleven she would sneak out at night and run across the family's huge, messy backyard, home for an assortment of dogs, cats, ducks, pigeons and fish. Clambering over the rickety wooden fence, she would head for nearby woodland. There, in a makeshift den of timber, twigs and old petrol cans, she learnt that sex meant money. For the price of a pocketful of loose change or a single cigarette, she would take off her clothes and perform sexual acts for a never-ending stream of teenage boys. Love and sex did not go together in her life. Love was something she read about in fairy tales. Sex was business.

Soon the little den was not enough. Next came car seats, front rooms, street corners, garages and even dirt tracks. When one of the boys got a job at the petrol station there was sex in the storeroom, the bathroom and the little office. There was no sexual pleasure in it for her, no conversation afterwards, just the ritual handing over of dollars and Marlboro cigarettes, sometimes from three boys at a time. The money was never spent on condoms. Aileen lived in a dangerous world of coitus interruptus. The money went on cigarettes, beer and drugs – uppers and downers, acid and pot. Anything to make the world seem a better place. The Marlboro and the packs of Budweiser and Buchs were to be a strand of her life that would eventually give police one of their biggest clues.

At thirteen, Aileen's sexual reputation had spread. Boys

called her a whore. Girls called her a slut. Both sexes called her the Cigarette Pig. Few boys would admit to having sex with her but most of them had. She began to dream about having a boyfriend, someone she could be seen on the block with, go to dances with, but there weren't any offers. Aileen was isolated until the next packet of Marlboro changed hands in the woods. So Aileen turned her attention to her brother Keith, then fourteen, and they had an affair.

Keith was embarrassed by his sister's reputation as the local whore, but in the quiet, lonely hours between the beatings in the Wuornos home he took advantage too. Aileen knew about sex, and he suggested that she teach him about it so that girls wouldn't laugh at him. She showed him the ropes, sometimes while his friend looked on. But looking on meant nothing to Aileen. Often there would a line of boys waiting, urging whoever was on top of her to get on with it because they were next. But it wasn't all sex in those early days, there were fantasy times too. Aileen, her hair swept back like a boy's, would often prance around the living-room, holding a beer can as a microphone, pretending to be a rock 'n' roll singer on stage.

These, then, were the beginnings of the girl who dreamed of being a movie star – and one day would be, when Hollywood snapped up her story as she sat on Death Row nicknamed the Damsel of Death.

During Aileen's teenage years the beatings by her stocky, five foot nine inch tall father, Lauri, went on. Sometimes she was made to pull down her knickers and lean over the kitchen table as he bent the belt double so that the buckle would tear at her skin. His discipline knew no mercy. Once when he discovered that she and Keith had skipped school they were grounded for a month. No friends, no phone calls, no playtime.

Lauri's relationship with his wife Britt was cool. They rarely went out together and never displayed affection. She would remain quiet when he dished out his disciplinary sentences. She just wanted a quiet life. But she was a desperately unhappy woman who held a terrible secret from her children. She had once told Aileen's mother that sex was an unpleasant chore a woman had to do for her husband. This was the backcloth of Aileen's early years.

As they grew older though, Keith and Aileen rebelled against the old man. They would argue about their chores, get more lippy. They hated the house. It was dark and gloomy. The curtains were always closed and there was never enough food. They were lucky if they got a bowl of breakfast cereal. Often at school, teachers would lend them money or they would beg a sandwich from a friend. Aileen would even offer sex for a coke and ham on rye.

Lauri was a Jekyll and Hyde character, however. There were times when he was friendly to the kids. On weekends he would sometimes chauffeur them to a movie, or go tobogganning and ice-skating with them. Every summer he would take them on a two-week camping vacation in the north and sit late into the evening telling them how he had won his Purple Heart in the Army. There were good family Christmasses too. The house would be festooned with decorations and there were carols around the fire. Britt would take Aileen and Keith to church, while Lauri stayed home with the wine. But there were more bad times than good, and Aileen's memories of her childhood years were of being locked in her bedroom. The most haunting memory of all, however, was of the day a family of wild kittens were found in the attic. All but one had been taken to the pound. Aileen was playing with it and it scratched her face. The next day, as she was tickling the little bundle of fur, Lauri appeared and shouted: 'Is that the damned thing that scratched you?' When she replied 'Yes' he grabbed the kitten and made her follow him into the sauna.

In strong Finnish tradition, Lauri had built the sauna in the garage. An old metal barrel was the stove, which had been topped in rocks. A barrel of water stood in the corner for the required steam. Lauri made Aileen stand and watch as he held the struggling kitten under the water until it drowned. That wasn't the only reason Aileen was to hate the sauna. Sometimes she and Keith would be locked in it as a punishment.

Hatred was something Aileen was an expert on. She hated school and school hated her. She was noted for her anti-social behaviour. She had low grades and poor relationships with teachers and classmates. The young misfit also had poor hearing and vision, which didn't help. She was prescribed glasses but her vanity would not let her wear them. Aileen was by now a skilful shoplifter. At first she sneaked records out of stores under her coat. Bigger items were to follow, and once she was caught raiding her local K-Mart where her mother worked. Britt quit over the embarrassment.

Friction at home got worse when Lauri and Britt finally revealed to Aileen and Keith that they were not their real parents. From that day on things changed. Aileen would taunt her grandfather. 'You're not my real father – bugger off!' she would scream. But he would always come back with the belt.

Near the end of her fourteenth year Aileen became pregnant. It was at the height of her incest with Keith. Whether he was the father is still not clear. At first she claimed she had been raped at gunpoint by an Elvis Presley lookalike. Then she claimed it was Keith, then Lauri, then a string of other men. Lauri was beside himself with anger. Distraught Britt referred the case to the Michigan Children's Aid Society, and the Department of Social Security finally paid for the birth in an unwed mothers' institution in Detroit. Lauri dropped her off at the door and she stood alone, staring up at the concrete steps with just a small bag. Aileen had no visitors. Lauri allowed Britt only one telephone call a week.

Aileen had just one peek at her child when he was born on 24 March 1970. She stared through a cubicle window at the bouncing baby boy, who had two little front teeth and long fingernails. He had weighed into the world at 7lb 11oz.

'Sorry, young 'un,' she said quietly, 'but if you knew my situation, you'd understand why I have to give you up. You'll be ten times better off!' The boy was adopted.

Aileen returned home in shame and things grew worse.

Her relationship with Lauri hit an all-time low. She would often run away and sleep rough in the woods or in abandoned cars. The men she had sex with were older now, and she lurched from one motel room to the next, spending the money she earned on drugs and drinking binges. Once or twice she tried to straighten herself out, going home and even re-enrolling in Troy High School. But she soon dropped out again. Britt seemed to grow quieter and quieter, shutting herself away for hours on end. But she wasn't alone – she had a bottle with her. Through the years she had kept her heavy drinking a secret.

Neighbourhood crime was growing. Cars were stolen, houses burgled, stereos and TVs sold on the black market. Drug-dealing Keith broke into houses, stole hi-fis and sold them. He injected himself with heroin and drove around in stolen cars. Aileen pill-popped from one high to another, money flowing in from prostitution. She rolled from one acid party to the next, sitting quietly stoned in parlour corners watching the friends she had grown up with kissing and cuddling on the sofas. No one ever kissed and cuddled her. Many of the boys had given her Marlboro cigarettes for a trip to the woods. Now they left her on her own lonely trip in the corner. As the sounds of Led Zeppelin, the Rolling Stones and the Moody Blues thudded into her ears, the Cigarette Pig began to feel even more unloved. There was no white knight after all.

On 7 July 1971, Britt died from cirrhosis of the liver. She had been secretly suffering the DTs for years in her alcoholic quest to blot out the realities of life at home.

Aileen was woken to be given the news – by relatives who found her sleeping rough on the back seat of an old Ford in the woods. Dressed in blue jeans, she went to the funeral parlour and was thrown out for lighting up a cigarette and blowing smoke in her adoptive mother's face. On the way out she switched nameplates on the men's and ladies' toilets to get her own back.

Five years later, on 12 March 1976, Lauri committed suicide. He went into the garage after downing his bottles of wine, closed the door, turned on the car engine and sat in the front seat. Aileen didn't attend his funeral. Neither did Keith, who was fighting a losing battle against cancer. The disease had spread to his throat, brain, lungs and bones. His shady friends would bring drugs into hospital and put them in his intravenous drip when the nurses weren't looking. He died on 17 July 1976, aged just twenty-one.

It was an eventful year for Aileen, who by now had taken to hitch-hiking for her prey. One day a car pulled up alongside her on the highway and it was love at first sight for sixty-nine-year-old Lewis Gratz Fell, a wealthy yacht club president from a long line of good Philadelphia stock. They married in Kingsley, Georgia. Slim, attractive Aileen was twenty. The wedding was announced in the society pages of the Daytona press and Aileen was at home riding around in a cream-coloured Cadillac. She was the talk of Troy. Fell had a beachside condominium and lavished his new wife with jewels. But it wasn't enough for his volatile young partner and before long she was slipping away to satisfy her needs, going on drunken, bar-hopping binges into the early hours. The seedier the bar, the better she liked it.

The marriage was over in a month. Fell walked out, filing a restraint order claiming his wife had beaten him with his walking stick. He went back to his yacht club and Aileen found a new way to earn a living, hustling for money in pool clubs. No one realized she was such a good shot. By the time the divorce came through, however, she was on the road again, turning up on the doorstep of an insurance company to collect $10,000 left to her by her brother Keith in his will. She blew it on a black Pontiac, later repossessed, and a collection of antiques, even though she didn't have a home. She later pawned them.

Aileen worked as a motel maid, a labourer and a waitress, drifting from town to town persuading ministers to take her in because she was in need. Truckers were only too willing to give her a free ride to her destination providing they got a free ride too. She adopted the aliases of Susan, Lori and Camme March Green after getting involved in petty crime. She even used her aunt's married name, Laurie Grody. She was fined for assault and battery and sentenced to three years in jail for holding up a Daytona convenience store at gunpoint. She served one. She was also jailed for disorderly conduct and arrested for a string of offences including drunk driving, weapons violations and cheque forgery. At one time she even joined a biker gang in Colorado.

On a muggy September evening in 1986, Aileen walked into the Zodiac, a gay bar near Daytona Beach. She swung her hips to the music and sipped from a can of Budweiser. It was an area she felt at home in. Sex and Daytona went together like tablespoons on top of each other. The bars, arcades, cheap motels and boardwalks blistered by the sun were her playground. When the haze of the sun went down, everyone went down in a haze of alcohol. It was just that kind of place. Aileen had already had several lesbian affairs along the way and now she needed comfort again. There on a bar stool sat the woman who would change her life, twenty-four-year-old Tyria Jolene Moore. The short, stocky, strawberry-blonde motel maid, with deep brown freckles, laughed and joked with the girls around her. She seemed easy going and fun to be with. Tyria was the child of a middle-class family from Cadiz, Ohio. Her mother had died when she was two and she had been raised by her father Jack, moving to Daytona in 1983 after coming into a family inheritance. She had loved basketball at high school and liked playing softball and watching football on TV. In fact, Tyria loved TV period. But she was confused both spiritually and physically. She would talk openly of her lesbian relationships but deep down wanted to live by the Scriptures, which made it clear that homosexuality was 'an abomination'. Her only criminal record was a 1983 misdemeanour charge for breaking into a former lover's houseboat. Tyria was tough. She had to be. She was just about to embark on a love affair with a physically powerful woman prone to deep, aggressive mood swings. After being evicted from her apartment in Florida, Tyria had moved in with a family who had befriended her. She would do odd jobs around the house for them and was good with the kids. She was a regular churchgoer, attending services three times a week at the local Baptist church. After work at the nearby motel she could be found sitting in her bedroom with her head stuck in the Bible. That evening in the Zodiac, however, Tyria had not long ended a stormy relationship with another woman. Aileen couldn't take her eyes off the girl in shorts, T-shirt and baseball cap. She looked just like a chunky guy. They were lovers that first evening. Days later they were shopping for sex toys. Within weeks they were living together, Aileen leaving on a Monday morning with a large brown vanity case, returning by Friday with hundreds of dollars, which they would blow in bars over the weekend. Aileen told everyone she worked for a pressure cleaning company.

Tyria soon stopped going to church and Aileen didn't like her working, so she gave up her motel job too, preferring to lie in bed watching TV until midday instead. Tyria cooked burgers and chips while Aileen, the male in their relationship, walked around smoking and drinking beer. They believed they were the perfect couple. For the first time in her life Aileen felt needed and loved. She would do anything for Ty . . . even kill.

One morning, while Aileen was out shopping for her beer, one of Ty's curious friends looked inside Aileen's vanity case and discovered a huge stock of condoms, an assortment of executive business cards and several men's rings and watches. The friend suspected Aileen was a hooker and confronted Ty.

'She could be,' Ty answered, acting dumb.

'But you know she hitchhikes everywhere?' said the friend.

'Yes.'

'Isn't she scared of riding with strangers?'

'No, she's very careful. She only rides with older guys!'

Ty knew that her lover sold sex for money. It didn't bother her. She wasn't jealous of other men. And anyway, they needed the cash.

At that time Aileen had a use for her empty beer cans. She and Ty would practise shooting at them in the back yard. Aileen admitted she carried a gun for protection. Ty wasn't worried. Life was magic. True, they had their fights. Aileen was volatile and her temper always erupted in violence. She smacked Ty around. But Ty gave as good as she got and making up was fun. One thing was clear to outsiders, however, Aileen was the boss.

One sunny afternoon a moped turned into the drive of the Pierre Motel in Zephyrhills. The two blondes on the bike had only one backpack between them and had arrived hoping to find work. They checked in for two days. At the end of the second day Ty had persuaded the motel owner to give her a job. She had the right qualifications – she knew the business, was warm and friendly and got on well with the mostly elderly guests. Aileen kept herself to herself at first. But no one seemed to like her.

For some reason at this time she was constantly seeking people who believed in God to talk to. She would tell whoever would listen that she had been verbally abused and hit by her parents. She claimed she went on the streets as a prostitute to survive when she was just eleven, and missed her brother terribly. She felt alone. Ty was all she had. After a few beers Aileen would talk about how she could have been a nightclub singer and would break into song. People around her were impressed. She had quite a good voice, they agreed.

'There's gonna be a book about my life one day,' she would boast.

When she returned to her room drunk, she would find Ty writing to her family back in Ohio. It upset Aileen. She had no one to write to. Life just wasn't fair. She wanted Ty to feel as lonely and isolated as she did. That way they would have a bond.

As the months went on the motel became a real home. They ate hamburgers, drank beer and practised their shooting out the back. They both got fatter and fatter. But their world changed again when they were asked to move on. They had been flaunting their gay relationship, holding hands and kissing by the pool, and it had upset some of the guests. They were broke and had sold their moped. Slowly they walked into the sunset carrying a bag each. They slept in the woods, in orange groves, by the railway tracks or in old barns. When they had some money they motel-hopped. For Aileen it was like the good old days. But she had a desperate need to provide for Ty and Ty wasn't happy sleeping in the woods. Aileen didn't want to lose her. They were sometimes so desperate for food they stole bread from bakery trucks.

*

Richard Charles Mallory had his own TV repair shop, Mallory Electronics, in the shopping mall at Palm Harbor, near Clearwater, Florida. The fifty-one-year-old, moustachioed loner with wire-rimmed glasses liked the good-time girls and was a regular visitor to the topless bars along the West Coast of the sunshine state. Many of the hookers and go-go dancers knew him by sight but not by name. Paying for sex with cash, TV's or videos was a way of life for the divorcee. He drank, smoked pot and would often unwind by watching two women make love together.

On 30 November, at 6.10 pm, Mallory, clutching his black attaché case, closed up his shop as usual, checking the door locks time and again. Robbery was something he was paranoid about. He had had the locks changed on his own apartment eight times in three years.

Things weren't going too well for the trim, 5ft 11in tall TV repair man. He was depressed. He had money troubles and was $4,000 in arrears with the rent. Now the Inland Revenue Service was on his tail. He needed a break, a bit of rest and relaxation. He climbed into his beige two-door 1977 Cadillac Coupé with dark-tinted windows, turned the ignition key and headed for Daytona to sort out his depression. Fuck the world, he said to himself. Better still, fuck women.

She stood on the highway, edging back and turning her face when the young guys slowed down alongside her. She told them what to do with their tongues. She was looking for someone older. Someone she could handle. She had a fistful of dollars, it had been a good day around Fort Myer. Ty would be pleased with the money. She walked slowly on, waiting, waiting for the right time. The beige Cadillac pulled up. She wasn't sure, the windows were tinted. He wound the passenger glass down and she looked in. Seconds later they were driving towards Daytona.

They stopped off for beers, then again for more beers and some vodka. She admitted she was a hooker. They talked money. It was still dark in the woods. Mallory switched the car light on to get a better look after she had taken off her clothes like she had done so many times before. He wanted his money's worth. But this time something inside her snapped. She missed Ty. Something. He didn't even take off his jeans. What if he beat her up and took her money, or raped her? Men did that. Mallory sensed something was wrong, but then that was his normal paranoia, he reasoned. This time though, he was right. He was still behind the wheel when she blew him away.

'You sonofabitch! You were gonna rape me!' she screamed, pumping four shots from a .22 into him. She stood watching him die. There was some carpet nearby. She dragged him out of the car and wrapped him in it. Still naked, she drove for miles and miles before dumping the car down a dirt track and wiping the steering wheel with a cloth as the sun came up.

David Spears finished his beer and waved goodbye to his workmates at Universal Concrete. Minutes later he was heading down the highway on his way to Winter Garden near Orlando, about 100 miles away. It was Saturday, 19 May 1990 as he headed north from Sarasota on 1–75. He spent every weekend with his ex-wife and childhood sweetheart and had told her to expect him around 2.30pm. He had plenty of cash on him, around $80. It was his daughter's birthday the following week and her forthcoming graduation, so he was going to shop for a special present. She would never receive it. Somewhere, around thirty-six miles from his destination, David stopped his cream pick-up truck and opened the door to a hitchhiker. When they found his naked body, in woods a long way off his route to Orlando, he had six bullets in him. Two had been fired from behind. Beside him were empty Budweiser beer cans and cigarette butts. His body was naked except for a baseball cap.

Ty noticed the cream truck through the motel window. Aileen said she had borrowed it. It was gone the next day. The highway hooker stripped off the licence plate and dumped the truck in a woodland ditch. She had ripped out the radio and taken all her victim's tools.

Thirty-year-old rodeo rider Charles 'Chuck' Carskaddon loved the 1975 brown Cadillac he had painstakingly restored. As he sped south through Kentucky heading for Tampa, Florida on Thursday, 31 May, he felt the car was going well. In fact, everything was going well in his life. He had just landed a job as a press operator in Missouri and was picking his fiancée Peggy up to join him. But Peggy never got to Missouri, for Chuck made a date with death on Highway 1–75. He was barely short of his destination when he leant over and opened the passenger door to a woman in hot pants. When they found his naked body he had nine bullets in him from a .22 calibre handgun. There was no sign of his wallet, rings or watch. Ty noticed the old Cadillac through the window. The next day it was gone. Ty also noticed a .45 automatic with a pearl-white handle grip in a holster on the table. That belonged to Chuck too.

Retired merchant marine Peter Siems, sixty-five, stacked the Bibles neatly into his silver-grey Sunbird. The bespectacled part-time missionary from Jupiter was going north to New Jersey to visit his mother. His wife of twenty-five years, Ursula, was away, working in Europe with their son Leonard. It was a bright, sunny morning on 7 June when the proud member of the Christ is the Answer crusade drove north with $400 in his suitcase. Only one person was ever to see him alive again, the hitchhiker he picked up on 1–95. They found a spot about ten miles off the highway. Both naked, he opened his sleeping bag – and she opened her murder bag. There was a struggle but minutes later his body was full of lead from a .22 handgun.

Ty was asleep when the Sunbird rolled into the parking bay outside. This time, though, the car would stay and lead to the downfall of the killer hitchhiker.

Aileen was alone in her mind again. Ty was always having fun, going about with friends to Universal Studios and MGM. Aileen threw jealous rages, fueled by her deadly secrets. She wanted Ty to be alone with her. She couldn't stop the killing now. Soon the apartment began to fill up with an odd assortment of goods – cameras, a fishing rod, tools, even a Bible. Aileen knew she would have to get a lock-up garage.

It was a hot afternoon on 4 July 1990 when the silver-grey Sunbird pulled up at the liquor store. Aileen, in jeans and a baseball hat, stumbled in to buy some more beer. They had been drinking all day.

'You drive, I'm too drunk,' she told Ty when she came out. Ty, wearing a baseball hat too, wasn't much better but she agreed. They sped away, sipping their Budweisers. Half an hour later they spotted a sign for an Indian reservation. Curious, they turned off and raced down the dirt track. The hours of drinking had taken their toll. Ty took a bend too fast and lost control. The car crashed through a gate, spun over a barbed-wire fence and smashed into a tree on the passenger side. They sat dazed for a few minutes, steam billowing from under the car bonnet.

'Get yer butt outa here!' screamed Aileen, dragging herself from the car. Ty didn't need telling twice. She thought the petrol tank was going to explode. Or was it? Why was Aileen tearing off the number plate?

'Why are you doing that?' she shouted.

'We can't let the cops know anything right now. This is the car of a murdered guy. I killed someone!' Aileen screamed back, throwing the licence plate into some bushes.

'Are you crazy?'

At that moment two local residents appeared on the

scene. They had heard the crash. Aileen, her head and shoulder bleeding from cuts, pleaded with them not to call the police, saying her father lived up the road. As the man and woman walked away, she got back in the rammed car and tried to start the engine. Amazingly it spluttered into life. Ty clambered into the back seat and they somehow drove off. But within minutes a front tyre burst and they were grounded again. Aileen grabbed the car keys and threw them into a bush.

The couple who had heard the crash were suspicious and called the police. Detectives found the Sunbird along with Siems's registration documents and a pile of empty Budweiser cans on the back seat. A computer check revealed that Siems had been reported missing. An artist was brought in to draw sketches of the two women seen staggering from the car. The drawings were circulated across the state. They were uncannily accurate.

By now things had got bad between Aileen and Ty. Aileen had lost interest in sex with her lover and was quick to anger, often violently. Ty wanted her to find a nine to five job and stop working the highways. Aileen refused. They became distant. Aileen drank night and day. Ty worked night and day – often just to pay for the beer. Something bad was going on and Ty knew it. She wanted to leave but underneath she didn't want to hurt Aileen. She knew her partner loved her deeply – well, as deeply as she could ever love anyone.

Ty began to filter out the bad in her lover, trying to see only good. She had a choice between getting her relationship with Aileen back together or going to the police. Her emotions won.

Eugene 'Troy' Burress was glad he didn't have his own company any more. He was fifty now and didn't need the headache of running a small business like Troy's Pools. It would have given him a heart attack in the end. Driving for a sausage company in Oscala was carefree. He would live longer, or so he thought. There were money worries though. He had never expected to be well-off again driving a truck but he was really feeling the pinch. Troy was a proud family man. He had two grown-up daughters from his first marriage and three stepdaughters from his second wife.

The truck pulled over on the highway on its way to Daytona and the hitchhiker climbed in. She left Troy dead, with two bullets in him. Strangely, she left his wedding ring and the gold chain around his neck. Perhaps she was happy enough with the $310 she found in his truck cash box. She covered him with leaves and ferns and drove away half-naked in his van, stopping for a moment to throw his credit cards and clipboard into a field and put her clothes back on. The truck later ran out of petrol and she simply walked away from it, thumbing a lift back to her motel and Ty.

On a muggy day six weeks later, Aileen turned up the air-conditioning in the little blue Oldsmobile Firenza and put her foot down on the accelerator. Seventy miles on in southern Lake County she pulled into a desolate stretch of marshland. Checking that there was no one around, she methodically began to strip the car of Dick Humphreys' possessions – an ice-scraper, maps, personal and business papers, warranties, even his pipe and tobacco pouch. All were thrown into the wild. Then she drove on, pulling into a service station where she carefully cleaned the inside of the 1985 car with a cloth and a spray before abandoning it.

They found the body of fifty-six-year-old health worker and retired police chief Charles Richard Humphreys in sparse woodland. He had been shot seven times on 11 September with bullets from a .22 His pockets had been turned inside out.

Ty was bored. All she did since losing her motel job was lie on the bed, eat and watch TV. Sure she liked TV, but enough was enough. The news came on. Someone had been murdered – a man called Humphreys. A little blue car popped up on the screen. It was the Firenza Aileen had parked in the drive. Another shot showed a crashed and abandoned silver-grey Sunbird. Next came an artist's impression of two women in their early thirties they were hunting. Ty moved closer to the screen and then gasped. One was blonde, about 5 feet 6 inches, the other dark-haired, shorter and thick-set.

As she made plans to leave her lover the police net was closing in. That day detectives from several forces were having the biggest brainstorming session in the murder hunts so far.

Walter Gino Antonio was found naked except for his

socks. He had been shot four times with bullets from a .22 calibre firearm. His Pontiac Grand Prix was miles away. His fiancée gave detectives a list of belongings he had with him – his police badge from his days as a reserve deputy with the Brevard County Sheriff's Office, a police-style club with a black, plaited handle, a black flashlight and a pair of handcuffs, a Timex watch, a few suitcases, a red metal tool box and a gold diamond ring.

That same day Aileen quietly, almost sheepishly, strolled across the room to Ty and put Antonio's gold diamond ring on her finger. Now they were man and wife. But it was too late. Another dream would soon turn sour.

A few days later Aileen ran out of beer and went to buy some. When she returned to their room at Dayton's Fairview Motel, Ty was gone. The gold ring was on the bedside table. Aileen was devastated. She turned to the one thing that had always given her comfort – alcohol. She began drinking heavily, throwing herself into a five-day affair with a man she met at a bar whose wife had walked out on him.

She moved out of the Fairview and began sleeping on a dirty yellow car seat on the front porch of her favourite bar, the Last Resort in south Daytona. She was arrested there on 8 January 1991. Police had managed to trace a camera belonging to her first victim, Richard Mallory. It was found in a pawn shop. Anyone who pawns an item in Florida must show ID and leave a fingerprint. Wuornos used her aunt's name, Laurie Grody, but she couldn't fake her fingerprint.

After her arrest detectives went in search of Ty. They found her with her sister in Pennsylvania, where she was taken into protective custody. Ty told the police she had left because she was scared Wuornos might kill her. Wuornos gave her presents, she said – a camera, jewellery, clocks and a briefcase. All had belonged to murder victims but detectives established that Moore was at work at the time of the killings.

They flew her back to Daytona Beach and put her up in a motel. On 12 January 1991 she sent Wuornos, in prison on remand, a note asking her to telephone. Wuornos called Ty ten times in four days. The police taped all the calls. Ty assured Wuornos that the calls were not being recorded and told her that the police were trying to pin the murders on her. The news touched the little bit of conscience Wuornos had left. On 16 January she rang again. 'I'm going to confess,' she said. 'I will not let you be involved. You are not the one. I am the only one. I am the one who did everything. I did it all by myself. You were at work every time I did one.' Moore put down the telephone and sobbed into the arms of a detective.

Wuornos never wavered from those words but later she claimed that Ty knew about some of the killings and lied to stop herself being charged as an accessory.

The next day the highway hooker made her video-tape confession to killing seven men.

The murders had preyed on her mind, she told police. She wanted to be right with God. She felt bad about the shootings and deserved to die. She was charged with six murders. She admitted shooting Peter Siems but she couldn't be charged with his killing because his body had not been found. Wuornos couldn't remember where she left it.

An assortment of the victims' belongings – clothes, car stereos, clocks, briefcases and jewellery – were found at a garage Wuornos rented near Daytona Beach. She had kept them to pawn.

In January 1992, Wuornos was convicted of the robbery and murder of Richard Mallory. The sentencing phase of her trial began with a psychologist explaining that the hooker's denial of responsibility for the killings was part of her twisted and angry outlook on life. Dr Elizabeth McMahon, who spent twenty-two hours interviewing the serial killer, testified: 'How does she choose to see the world? It is malevolent. It is persecutory. She is a victim. Her paranoia is frequently sky high. It is an angry, unpleasant, out-to-get-her kind of place.'

Clad in a beige coat, Wuornos sat composed throughout the testimony, sometimes smiling at the psychologist's description, sometimes glancing at jurors. Once she flung an arm over the back of her chair, turned around and glared at spectators, forcing some of them to look away.

For the defence, Dr McMahon picked apart Wuornos's psyche, diagnosing her as a borderline personality, almost a psychopath. Her sad life had left her emotionally scarred. She was 'self-destructive, and impulsive with roller coaster emotions'. She had a 'great fear of loneliness and alienation and had trouble with intense anger'.

Borderline personalities, Dr McMahon said, generated negative reactions wherever they went. 'They are difficult people to deal with. They are unhappy and they tend to project that unhappiness on the world.'

Wuornos also suffered an organic dysfunction in the brain cortex. 'Her brain is not working in concert,' she said. 'Everything is structurally intact, but not functioning right.'

The doctor added that Wuornos's mental condition could have warped her comprehension of what was really happening. 'Wuornos saw herself as in severe, imminent danger – whether that was a distortion of what was really going on at the moment, I don't know. Her behaviour was determined by her perceptions.'

Aileen seethed as Barry Wuornos, her uncle and adoptive brother, claimed that she came from a happy, well-adjusted home. She glared at him across the courtroom as he swore on oath: 'We were a pretty straight and narrow family. There was very little trouble.'

Statements by Aileen that her grandfather Lauri, Barry Wuornos's father, was an alcoholic who beat her were untrue, he claimed. 'I never saw any spankings!' he said. 'It was just a moral upbringing for all of us.'

As he left the stand Aileen flew at her lawyers. 'I had questions I wanted to ask!' she screamed, stabbing her finger at the empty witness stand. Spectators in the court could still hear her shouting as she was led down a hallway to a holding cell.

Her anger was to no avail. The jury recommended the death sentence.

Aileen, wearing a hot-pink turtleneck jumper and black skirt, was given one last chance to speak to the judge before being condemned. She proclaimed her innocence and insisted she was railroaded by a police conspiracy. 'I have been labelled a serial killer and I'm no serial killer,' she said. 'I had no intention of killing anyone. I would not do that. They want me convicted to get money from books and movies!'

Circuit Judge Uriel Blount looked across at Wuornos standing in the dock at Deland County Court and listened impassively. Minutes later he announced: 'You, Aileen Carol Wuornos, will be electrocuted until you are dead,' he said. 'May God have mercy on your soul.'

And so the curtain came down on the serial killer of the highways, the woman nicknamed by the Press the Damsel of Death. An uncharacteristically subdued Wuornos stood before the judge, surrounded by ten police officers. She accepted her sentence without emotion. Now the appeals process would start, but she had decided not to contest the five other murder charges against her. The more guilty findings, the more chances of her going to the electric chair.

After the hearing reporters crowded into the chilly alley outside the courthouse to catch Wuornos as she left for the drive to women's Death Row at the Broward Correctional Institution. Prosecutors, too, stood waiting.

Her lawyer Nolas walked away. 'This is morbid,' he said.

As she entered a patrol car, Wuornos shouted: 'Bust these crooked cops and their conspiracy please, I'm innocent!'

Now the full details from the Aileen Wuornos confession could be released. Here is some of the story she told to detectives on the videotape that was to convict her.

> I have gone through at least 250,000 guys in my life, maybe more. I have never hurt any of them. Matter of fact, I became very good friends with them, you know, and they really liked me.
>
> I would hitchhike. A guy would pick me up, and I would ask him if he was interested in helping me out, 'cause I'm trying to make rent money, you know. And then they'd say how much and I'd say thirty for head, thirty-five straight, forty for half and half, or a hundred an hour.
>
> Ty was my only friend in the whole world, and that's why I loved her so much. She's in love with me, you know what I'm saying?
>
> We didn't even have sex hardly. We had sex, I'd say, the first year, maybe three times and the next years, we didn't even have sex together. We were just friends, just good friends, hugging, kissin' and all that.
>
> I'm not a goody-goody girl as I might think I am but I know in my heart I'm a good girl. I knew that I had problems and I was scared and everythin' and so I guess, I've done a few crooked things.
>
> I really do believe in God. And I really, am really religious. But I just, I don't know, I guess I was basically drunk.
>
> I didn't really have any parents. I sort of raised myself ever since I was fourteen. If I had a proper

family I'm sure I wouldn't be in this predicament. That's for sure, I wouldn't have been a hooker or nothing. But I was.

I was pretty much trusting-like. And so I would always take my clothes off first so they would know I'm not gonna take off, take their money and run or anything. So it was pretty stupid on my behalf to get undressed first considerin' what happened.

'I'd normally get my money and then go on my way, my merry way, and then try to go to the next car. And then some cars would pick me up and I'd say, OK, have a nice day, and I'd go. It wasn't just kill somebody. It was because they physically attacked me. Or they were tryin' to get free ass because they said they were a cop or something', which I didn't think they were.

I'm confessing to what I did, and go ahead, put the electric chair to me. I shoulda never done it.

I wanna get right with God and if I get sent to the electric chair . . . let me die a normal death and you know, I'll just . . . I'll get to heaven. I know inside, right inside me, I'm a good person.

I'm possibly lookin' at life imprisonment, I don't know what I'm lookin' at.

I'm willing to give up my life because I have killed six people, which maybe it was self defence, maybe it was stupid, just off the wall. Shoot, maybe I could've got away with it . . . I feel guilty. I am guilty. I'm willing to pay the punishment for that.

> If it was in Western days they'd put me in a noose and watch. Let the town watch me die.

In April that same year Wuornos pleaded 'no-contest' to charges of murdering Dick Humphreys, Troy Burress and Dave Spears. She said God forgave her for all the killings.

'I hope I'll get the electric chair as soon as possible,' she told a judge. 'I want to get off this planet, go to God and be up in heaven. I can't wait to leave.'

When she was sentenced to death she yelled at the court: 'Thank you, I'll go to heaven now – and you will all rot in hell!'

Today Aileen Wuornos still lives on Death Row.

Chapter Nine

KARLA HOMOLKA

'Paul is the greatest influence in my life. My wildest dream is to marry him and see him more than twice a week.'

St Catharines, Ontario, Canada, 6 July 1993

A reporter put his hand to his face and wept openly, his shoulders shaking uncontrollably. Hardened police officers stared at the courtroom floor with watery eyes, their jaws firmly clenched, biting back the tears as the two mothers described in aching detail how their lives had been shattered by the sadistic deaths of their young daughters.

The judge, Mr Justice Francis Kovacs, remained expressionless as the terrible legacy of Karla Homolka was unveiled to a captive audience of reporters he had banned from writing about the case.

But someone else was crying in the courtroom too – twenty-three-year-old Karla herself, sitting with her back to the packed public galleries. Up until now she had remained poised, elegantly groomed, her honey-blonde hair perfectly styled and her body as motionless as a mannequin. Sometimes she stared at the portrait of Queen Elizabeth II on the wall. Sometimes she stared at the judge's ornately carved hardwood bench. Now she dabbed her eyes with a white tissue as she sat just a few feet away from the grieving mothers. It was a rare display of public emotion by the woman at the centre of one of Canada's most horrific criminal cases.

Prosecutor Murray Segal stepped up to the lectern, cleared his throat and read the statement of facts – a twenty-seven-minute litany of asault, rape and torture that stunned the room. Karla's lawyer, clearly shaken, took off his glasses and put his hand to his head as the details of his client's involvement in the brutal sex slayings of two teenage girls were revealed.

Karla and her husband Paul Bernardo were known as Barbie and Ken by their friendly, middle-class neighbours, but beneath their doll-like smiles lay a terrifying story. Behind the front door of their pretty, pink clapboard home they tortured, raped and butchered their victims, committing their vile deeds to film with a home movie camera.

Just like Britain's Moors murderers, Ian Brady and Myra Hindley, they had captured the agonizing screams of their victims for their own pleasure. No one would ever have thought it of this apparently perfect couple. Could this really be the legacy of the high school girl who loved animals and got mad if someone even killed a fly? She cared, she loved, she worked hard at whatever she did, she was beautiful and fun to be with – a kind of friend anyone would be grateful for. But that was a long time ago. Now no one could properly explain why a pretty, middle-class girl from a nice, quiet family home had become entangled in such heinous crimes. Crimes where she had lived out her darkest fantasies.

At recess, Karla's sister Lori hung back in the court as Karla walked alone to the cell below the dock. Up until then Lori had hugged and comforted Karla in the dock at every break. This time, though, she was unable to bring herself to stand up – the terrible roll call of torture, sexual assault and death still ringing in her ears.

At about 6pm, Mr Justice Kovacs sat solemn-faced and handed out his sentence – two concurrent twelve-year terms and a curious lifetime ban on owning firearms, explosives and ammunition. Karla was led away in handcuffs. The unmarked police van which had carried Karla, her family and their luggage from their home to court each day now passed an angry crowd waving placards proclaiming 'Rot in Hell Karla!' as it made its way east to Kingston's Prison for Women.

Even as the van disappeared in a haze of dust the crowd would not go away, turning its attention on Kovacs, hurrying from the steps of the court with a police escort.

'I thought you stood for justice,' screamed a mother clutching a baby girl. She didn't know if justice had been served because no one knew for sure what had happened. Karla's case had fascinated the country, partly because the crimes she and her husband had been accused of were so horrible and partly because obtaining the facts of the case had become a sport.

Kovacs had ruled that the full story of Karla could not

be legally published in Canada until her husband was tried because it would prejudice his fair trial.

Residents of Canada's Niagara peninsula, a region of family farms and small industrial cities that skimmed Lake Ontario and the US border, had sought the details of the trial through computer bulletin boards, dinner-party gossip, stolen satellite television signals and secret faxes of a few articles in overseas magazines. Customs officers had seized foreign newspapers covering the story and censors had cut TV bulletins. When the *Washington Post* ran a report on the case, demand for the details was so high that 2,000 Canadians crossed the border into America to buy a copy. Vendors who ran out of the edition sold photocopies. The Canadian media meanwhile remained gagged and nervous about Kovacs's threat of an unlimited jail sentence for editors in contempt of court. One British newspaper printed a story that included banned material and 1,000 copies destined to be sold in Toronto were voluntarily shredded by the distributor.

Now, as Karla was driven away to prison, her dreams were in tatters. Her world had changed as dramatically as it had done five years earlier when she met Paul Teale, as he was known then, for the first time. From that moment she felt as though her life had been transformed. She had never felt as light or as happy. It was impossible to explain or describe but it was almost as though she would never be afraid again, or unhappy. Boring school work, rows with friends, family tiffs didn't matter any more. She felt overwhelmingly calm, in love and at peace with the world around her. Paul was her fairytale knight in shining white armour. She would do anything for him. Anything.

Niagara Falls, 29 June 1991. The sun beat down on the horse-drawn carriage at the Queen's Landing Hotel as the bride stepped out, clutching a pink and green bouquet. Flowers adorned her blonde hair and fluffy veil, and the crowd sighed in admiration as she waved to family and friends like Cinderella arriving at the ball.

It was one of those perfect, deliciously warm afternoons when the air felt like silk. Everyone agreed that Karla's white lace and pearls made her pale skin look even more fragile and delicate than usual. There wasn't a man or woman standing on the lawn that day who didn't admire her beauty. But little did they know that there was never more truth in the saying that beauty was only skin deep than at that moment. For behind Karla's Barbie doll looks lay an evil secret that would soon shock the small, tightly-knit community and traumatize a nation.

As the champagne glasses tinkled all the men were in agreement – Paul Bernardo was indeed a lucky man. He certainly seemed proud of Karla as he held her arm and steered her through the throng of guests and well-wishers, resplendent in his white tie and tails.

But his grip on Karla's arm was hurting her, because underneath the white lace she was covered in bruises from the beating he had given her the night before. And behind his smile was a burning anger that his parents had not, in his mind, contributed as much as they should have to the expensive reception. Even the wedding presents weren't what he had expected; after all, didn't people realize they were a designer couple of the 1990s? A couple who were going places? A couple who should be looked up to and treated in a special way?

'I'll never forgive them for this,' he said to Karla under his breath as he waved to friends.

A bridesmaid moved alongside Karla and asked how her arm was. She had seen the bruises while dressing the bride.

'I told you, I'm fine! You know I work with animals and they are always jumping over me. It's part of the job, stop going on!'

There wasn't much else Karla could say. Underneath she wanted to strangle Paul for hurting her. She was so mad. But a part of her was sad too. Everything had gone wrong between them so quickly last night. It was almost impossible to understand it. It must have been because of the pressure they were under over the wedding. Paul had wanted everything just right. All she could think about was their future together, the honeymoon in Hawaii. Other images began to creep into her mind. Dark images, evil images, a girl screaming . . . she blocked out such thoughts. After all, this was her wedding day.

Paul downed a glass of champagne and snapped his fingers at the waiter, who hurried over and gave him another from his silver tray.

They were the couple who had everything – good looks, promising careers and money. The sun shone, the bridesmaids looked like fairies in fuchsia dresses, the ushers in pink bow ties could have stepped out of a Hollywood movie, the guests were served pheasant and the bride and groom were toasted and cheered in the sunshine.

'I love you, Karla,' said Paul in front of everyone. 'I love you too, so much,' she replied, her lips wet with champagne as they kissed and friends cheered. Everyone agreed . . . a wonderful wedding, a wonderful day, a wonderful couple. It was indeed a fairytale and the icing on the cake was the honeymoon in Hawaii. If only the guests had seen the bruises on her arm, then perhaps they would have realized some of the nightmare behind the dream.

The sun shone down that same day on the bonnets of two police cars as they pulled into the gravel parking space looking down on the shallow south-east waters of Lake Gibson in Thorold, near St Catharines, twenty miles away. Waiting for them were two shocked anglers, who led the officers to their find.

There was no doubt about it. They were parts of a human body. Hours later the area was sealed off as divers pulled up seven lumps of concrete encasing the body parts of missing fourteen-year-old schoolgirl Leslie Mahaffy from the murky water bed. She had been torn apart by a power saw.

As the last lump of concrete was laid on the green plastic sheeting, surrounded by detectives and forensic experts, Karla and Paul had their head in the clouds – 39,000 feet up in a Boeing 757 on their way to Honolulu.

Karla's father was a refugee from Czechoslovakia and she grew up on a trailer park at the end of an old pot-holed road on the industrialized outskirts of St Catharines, Ontario. Her father, Karel, and mother, Dorothy, moved to the city from the Toronto area in the mid 1970s. Karel started a picture-framing business with some relatives who also lived on the sprawling trailer park. It took off after they began to sell framed black velvet paintings outside shopping malls.

After a few years the business was doing well and Karel and Dorothy moved their family – Karla and her younger sisters Lori and Tammy – into a pretty brown clapboard townhouse north of the city. They seemed a happy, normal family. Karel would boast to neighbours of how he had escaped from the oppressive regime in Czechoslovakia and was so happy to see his daughters grow up in the West. Later they moved again, this time into a comfortable semi-detached home in Merritton. Karla appeared to love her sisters, even if at times Tammy did get on her nerves.

At the Sir Winston Churchill Secondary School, Karla was a leading member of the choir, appeared in stage shows and even did some tutoring. Everyone liked her, pupils and teachers alike. She was known to be an ardent animal lover who particularly doted on cats, and it was this love of the animal world that led her to work part-time in a pet store and later for a veterinary surgeon. No one ever saw her get angry – unless someone tried to kill a spider or a fly. One thing was certain, though. Teachers saw her as an intense teenager who never did things by halves. She had a reputation for being an all or nothing girl.

Karla's dress sense was as startling as her looks. While other girls dressed in pink, red or blue, and wore frills, Karla wore all black or all white.

In every respect she was a normal, healthy, well-behaved schoolgirl. But her sweetness turned sour in her third year at Sir Winston's. Her personality changed and her interest in class activities waned. She began hanging out with a small clique of close friends who would occasionally skip school and drive around parking lots listening to their favourite song by the Beastie Boys rock group: 'You Gotta Fight for Your Right to Party'.

Karla's parents put her attitude down to adolescence. It was a difficult time for her, as it was for every girl her age. But their close relationship as a family would see them through. There was no doubt she had the right outlook on life. For she belonged to an élite band of friends called the Diamond Club. Its motto was 'When you Marry – Marry Rich!'

Then along came the man who qualified for entry into this hallowed circle. His name was Paul Bernardo and her love for him did indeed sparkle like a diamond – but that diamond was to shatter like glass.

*

Paul Bernardo was born on 27 August 1964, the last of three children for Kenneth and Marilyn Bernardo. The blond boy with the cherub smile grew up in a modest home with his brother David and sister Debbie on Sir Raymond Drive, Scarborough, a comfortable Toronto suburb.

Paul's upbringing was the portrait of ordinary middle-class life. His father was a chartered accountant and his mother was a Girl Guide leader who made jams and canned fruit and always had home-baked cookies waiting for her children after school. There were yearly vacations, summer camps, a pool in the back yard, nice clothes and new bikes. All seemed prosperous and normal. Only close neighbours saw the paint beginning to crack. For as the years went on the family rows grew and constant screams from the house pierced the night air.

Paul would appear smiling and waving the next morning, however, as if nothing had happened, but he would sometimes confess to his school buddies that he longed for love in his life.

His mother and father had long ago stopped sleeping together. She told Paul she had moved into a basement room because she felt more comfortable that way. As the years went on Paul grew to dislike her. He sided with his chauvinistic father, who believed women should be kept in their place. Paul began to treat his mother the same way. He complained about her cooking and how she treated him. He also grew resentful towards his sister, whom he constantly accused of being the family favourite.

Few people were allowed past the Bernardo front door.

The family almost never entertained and the children's friends were not made welcome. Paul's father made it clear he did not want kids hanging around the pool when he got home from work. He was essentially a quiet man, only loud when he was cracking chauvinist jokes.

Paul's only visible problems, however, were asthma and an early stutter which later cleared up. He was a polite, good-looking boy who loved to play the drums and excelled at his school work. Of the three children Paul appeared to be the happiest.

But it was at high school in 1981 that his true character began to come out. He had three passions – music, cross-country running and chasing girls.

He planned to become a chartered accountant like his father, but not for long. He wanted to use the training as a stepping stone to becoming a partner in a business, and in the fall of 1983 he began business and commerce studies on the Scarborough campus of Toronto University. From that day on he treated what few old friends he had back home with disdain, adopting a superior attitude to them. He became even more of a loner and a chauvinist, like his father.

The Scarborough bus drew to a halt in the darkness at the corner of Centennial Road and Lawrence Avenue and a young girl got off. She pulled up the collar of her coat against the wind and hurried along the tree-lined path towards her parents' home two roads away, unaware a man was following her.

For a moment, the early morning moonlight flashed off the blade of his knife. Only for a moment. For within seconds he had dragged his prey away.

It was May 1987 and the Scarborough rapist, who was to stalk most of his victims after they got off buses, had made his first attack. Others were to become his victims after he watched them through their bedroom windows.

For years he was to terrorize the Scarborough area. Detectives had no leads. They knew he was white, in his twenties, around 5 feet 9 inches tall and of medium build with curly brown hair. There was no photofit, only a psychological profile from the FBI, who believed the attacks were based on 'retaliatory anger'. The rapist, they said, was probably involved in a confrontation with a woman – a female boss, his sister, spouse or mother.

Paul Bernardo's carefully planned life was on course. While still living at home he graduated from Toronto University in September 1987 with a Bachelor of Arts degree. He then enrolled in the student chartered accountancy programme run by the Institute of Chartered Accountants of Ontario and began work at the Scarborough offices of Price Waterhouse. Life was on the up and up.

The reception area of the Howard Johnson Hotel in Scarborough was packed with vets and their assistants for the pets convention.

Paul Bernardo, now twenty-three, looked across at the seventeen-year-old bubbly blonde sitting at the restaurant table with her friends. She was stunning and looked even younger than her age. He caught her gaze for a few seconds – and that was all it took to open the door into a world of evil for Karla Homolka.

Hours later a hallway conversation sparked their romance. They exchanged telephone numbers. She was smitten with the handsome young chartered accountant. Like many girls of her age when they finally discover their sexuality, there was no stopping her new-found adultness and there was nothing her parents could do to stop her ruining her school studies with the obsession of her new love. They only hoped it would be a passing fad – or something good for her future. They were to be wrong on both counts. But it would take many years for them to find out.

Paul showered Karla with gifts and she was charmed by his easy manner. At school she gushed about her handsome, blue-eyed boyfriend and proudly displayed his photograph.

'This is a guy who is going places,' she told friends.

Paul travelled to Karla's home in St Catharines several times a week and her parents finally grew to love him like a son. At the time Karla was still at Sir Winston's and worked part-time as a veterinary assistant at a local animal clinic. She was a natural. Her boss quickly encouraged her to work in all areas of his surgery – animal diets, operations and anaesthetics – and she soon became knowledgeable on all types of animal drugs. Most of her money, however, was spent on $300 telephone bills to her lover's home in Scarborough.

Paul, who was obsessed with younger women, quickly took Karla under his wing, and before long he found it easy to manipulate the dizzy young schoolgirl who had opened her heart to him. He would boss her about, arrive late for dates, make her fulfil his every sexual whim. He had always secretly wanted somebody he could have control over, like his father had over his mother. Now he had the perfect package.

Karla's schoolwork began to suffer even more. It was as if she was living in a fantasy world. All she would talk about was getting gifts from rich, older men. In her 1989 graduating yearbook she wrote: 'My wildest dream is to marry Paul and see him more than twice a week.' Under the heading 'My Chief Distraction' she wrote: 'A certain chartered accountant in Toronto'. Under the heading 'My Greatest Influence in Life' she wrote: 'Paul'.

The die was cast. But behind the scenes the fairytale romance was sinking into a cauldron of evil.

The fairy lights twinkled on the deck of the *Garden City* as she sailed out of Port Dalhousie. The tables were covered with pink and white lace, silver trays, champagne bottles in blue ice buckets and vases of flowers that seemed to throw out waves of rose-scented perfume. Karla laughed and joked with her friends and the drink flowed. It was a wonderful graduation party.

But Paul was quieter than usual. He didn't know

anybody, didn't want to and felt he didn't belong. He was also conscious of being much older than his partner. They were all just kids. Silly juveniles. He downed his drink and got another, wondering why he had come. He didn't like them and they certainly didn't like him, he could tell. And the guy in the red jacket was getting too fresh with Karla. Didn't he know she belonged to him?

'Tell that guy to keep his hands off you, or I will,' he told her, drinking heavily now.

'But Paul . . .'

'All right, I ruddy well will!'

Before Karla could stop him he went over to the boy. There was a row, and in a split second Paul had been punched to the floor. As he lay writhing in agony, his nose bleeding, Karla waded in handbag flying, knocking a classmate down. How dare anyone hurt the most beautiful thing in her life. The party was over.

When the boat docked Karla turned on her friends and called the police, then pressed for assault charges, but officers refused. Life wasn't so perfect now for the blonde Barbie doll, in more ways than one. For Paul not only had a hot temper, he also had a huge sexual appetite that she couldn't satisfy. But she would do anything to keep him – and she did. Karla began to help him find young girls to have sex with. Some were friends of her sister Tammy.

On 26 May 1990 the Scarborough rapist made a fatal mistake. In the early hours of the morning he pounced on his eighth victim. The nineteen-year-old girl was beaten, slashed with a knife, brutally raped and left bound in twine. But in his lust he allowed his sobbing victim a close look at his face.

Days later detectives issued a computer composite of the blond boy-next-door they were hunting. When some of Paul's friends and neighbours saw the picture in the newspapers and on TV they cracked jokes about the similarities between him and the attacker. At first he laughed it off. As the jokes went on he got angry. He was more of a loner now than ever before.

Meanwhile the trail went cold again for the police, but four months later they called Paul in for questioning following a tip-off over the similarities between him and the picture. Detectives took body samples from the young accountant, who seemed credible enough, and sent them to a forensic laboratory for testing. And there they were to sit for more than two years.

A month after Metro police had questioned Paul over the Scarborough rapes, detectives called him in again. But this time it was the police in Niagara and this time it was about a death.

Karla's sister Tammy was one of her school's most popular pupils. Everyone liked her. She was athletic and outgoing and excelled in gymnastics, track and field events. But her real passion was soccer, a game she had begun playing when she was just six years old.

Tammy was bubbling with excitement when she and

her mother, Dorothy, met her friend at the Pen Centre shopping mall in the early afternoon two days before Christmas, 1990.

It was cold but it was sunny and the light was clear. All she could talk about was the Christmas holidays and how great it was to be off school. She had helped her mother decorate the house with pine cones and holly and scattered silver stars over the fir tree in the hall.

'I just want to spend my time at home with my family,' she told a friend.

Tammy was doing some last-minute shopping with her mother, and the three chatted for a few minutes before Tammy took her friend aside and whispered in her ear.

'I've got to ditch my mom because I have to buy her a present,' she said, giggling. 'I want to get her some perfume.'

Tammy gave her friend a big kiss, wished her a merry Christmas and rushed off. She didn't know that hours later she would be Karla's Christmas present to Paul.

It was seven o'clock in the evening as Karla stood before her bedroom mirror, trying to decide which dress to wear. She was tired and desperately in need of sleep, but she knew that Paul needed her so she washed her face and combed her hair then listened to her favourite cassettes. How could he do this to her? Why couldn't they just go to bed or enjoy the family celebrations together? She knew there was no way. There had to be sex – if only to keep him. Sometimes she even had to dress up in Tammy's clothes for him.

That evening the three of them, Karla, Paul and Tammy, went into the basement to watch a video. Karla slipped an animal tranquillizer into Tammy's rum and egg nog. While she was unconscious both Karla and Paul had sex with her, each videotaping the other. The rest of the family were upstairs, unaware of what was happening.

But Tammy suddenly began to vomit and the sex orgy turned sour. Karla and Paul carried her into a bedroom and laid her on the bed, then hurriedly called an ambulance. When it arrived they did not tell the medical team about the drug she had swallowed. They only told how Paul had desperately tried to resuscitate her.

Tammy died the next day, Christmas Eve. The cornoner ruled that she had choked on her own vomit.

Her teammates from the St Catharines Girls Soccer Club all attended her funeral. On her gravestone was a carving of a soccer ball.

In the weeks that followed Paul and Karla appeared to go into depression. They both lost a lot of weight and were noticeably drinking heavily. Paul seemed particularly devastated. Friends felt sorry for both of them; after all, they had been at the scene, they had tried to save her, it must have been terrible. On the face of it the tragedy drew the couple closer together.

Paul quit Price Waterhouse and went to work for the accounting firm of Goldfarb, Schulman, Patel & Co. But he left a few months later, declaring himself bankrupt. His reasons for going broke were unemployment, financial mismanagement and over-extension of his credit cards. His only asset, he claimed, was his mobile telephone. But he had another asset – Karla. They got engaged, and in February 1991 Paul finally left his Scarborough home for St Catharines, where the couple planned their fairytale wedding.

On the evening of 15 June 1991 a pretty young girl with long blonde hair and teeth braces arrived with her friends at the Rock bar in Burlington, a small city half-way around the west end of Lake Ontario between Toronto and Niagara Falls. They had a few drinks and played their favourite songs on the juke box. Hours earlier they had staged a wake in the woods for four schoolmates who had died in a car crash.

It turned out to be a memorable evening, and fun too, for all the sadness in their hearts. When it was over fourteen-year-old Leslie Mahaffy said goodbye to her classmates and walked to a pay phone at the nearby Mac's Milk Store to call a girlfriend. The roads were quiet and well lit. There was hardly anyone about.

It was dark around the pay phone and Leslie didn't notice the man watching her. She put the receiver down and turned. Leslie was never seen alive by her family again.

No one saw her arrive on the driveway in the gold car an hour later because the fences and trees shielded the house from view. Inside the pink clapboard house a torture chamber was waiting.

Days later the police released an indistinct picture of

the slight, missing teenager and asked the public for help in tracing her. Although detectives viewed her as a runaway because she had twice bunked off school, once for seven days and another time for ten, her parents insisted that this time it was different. They were right. The Press however, listening to police contacts, relegated the story to the inside pages.

Two weeks later, fishermen in the shallow waters of Lake Gibson stumbled on the concrete-encased body parts of a young woman. Identification was difficult because her body had been hacked to pieces by a power saw. Detectives had one hope . . . her teeth. Dental records finally identified her as the missing Leslie.

On that same bright, sunny Saturday, Paul and Karla were riding in their horse-drawn landau to church for their wedding in Niagara-on-the-Lake.

After the honeymoon in Hawaii, Karla moved into Paul's quaint, pink clapboard Cape Cod style home in a pretty, tree-lined street in fashionable Port Dalhousie, just three kilometres from the old trailer park where she had grown up.

It was truly an upmarket house. Karla's friends in the Diamond Circle would have been proud. The owners had tried to sell it for $300,000 but when they failed had rented the renovated duplex to Paul for $1,200 a month. Karla kept it immaculate. There were photographs of the couple on the mantelpiece and a special spot in the kitchen for the couple's purebred Rottweiler, Buddy.

The big, fresh stripes on the lawn always made it look as if it had just been cut, and the scent of the old bush roses along the brick wall mingled with the sappy smell of the grass was a pleasure to inhale. The borders of blue, purple and silver leading to the front door looked as if they had been sprayed on with a giant hose.

After a while, however, the few chosen friends who visited Karla in her little dream home found her reserved, and couldn't understand why Paul had pictures of himself with young girls in their bedroom. Some made jokes about it and Karla laughed with them – but only when Paul wasn't there, and they understood why. Paul's hot temper was no secret. When he and Karla were together he seemed to do all the talking. He would often snap his fingers and his wife would hurry to get him a drink. One day he would treat her like a slave and the next like a queen, buying her a new dress and taking her out on the town. He was totally possessive about her. Karla was totally possessive about him too, and they were becoming more isolated from her friends. Karla knew Paul didn't like her to spend time with them. But so what? Paul was her life, not them.

Karla went to work full-time as a veterinary nurse at the Martindale Animal Clinic in nearby St Catharines. Neighbours tried to be friendly but gave up. Sometimes they would wave to her as she took Buddy for a walk. But few ever saw her husband.

Paul never accompanied his wife to her office social functions or visited her at work. People were curious, and when they bumped into him asked what he did. He began to tell neighbours he was self-employed, but they were never really sure he was telling them the truth.

Some thought he was a salesman because he was often seen talking on his mobile telephone in his leased gold Nissan 240SX car. Others thought he was a freelance chartered accountant. But the truth was that Paul had never qualified. In fact, he was making a living smuggling tobacco and alcohol from New York into Canada.

By this time Karla's character had hardened even more. The girl who once couldn't even kill a fly now had a different view of life.

The couple had a pet iguana. One night in the kitchen it bit Paul on the arm. He was so incensed he grabbed the pet, held it down and chopped its head off. That evening he barbecued the animal and ate it with Karla.

Days later he punched Buddy as hard as he could squarely in the face because he had been disobedient. Karla could do nothing and didn't want to. Whatever Paul did was right.

At 3am on 30 March 1992, two sisters were buying doughnuts at a local St Catharines store when they realized they were being filmed by a man in an imported gold sports car.

When they left the shop the man put the video camera down and followed their vehicle home. As soon as they got inside their house the young women telephoned Niagara police, telling them the man had parked down the street. They described the car as Japanese, probably a Mazda RX7, plate number 660 NFN or 660 MFN. But nothing was done. Bernardo's Nissan number plate was

660 HFH. Sixteen days later, a sixteen-year-old girl was abducted.

The sixteenth of April 1992 was the day before Good Friday, and Holy Cross Secondary School was dismissed for the Easter holidays.

In the grey, relentless rain, sixteen-year-old figure-skating hopeful Kristen French waved goodbye to her schoolfriends and began her short walk home, oblivious to the gold car following her.

She was looking forward to a party with her parents that weekend, and wondered where they had hidden her Easter eggs. As she crossed a church parking lot, the vehicle slowed beside her. A blonde-haired woman opened the door and asked for directions. Minutes later Kristen was dragged into the car by a man and snatched away. Seven people saw the scuffle. There was no doubt it was a kidnapping. Police arrived at the scene within minutes.

Detectives and the media were soon working closely together. Kristen's long record as an excellent student, her close relationship with her middle-class parents and the possibility that she was still alive mobilized the detectives, the public and the media. She made front-page news, and money was set aside for the investigation. But sadly the kidnap car was wrongly identified as a 1982 cream or beige Chevrolet Camaro or Pontiac Firebird. Karla and Paul breathed a sigh of relief at the news bulletins.

Five days later police announced the formation of a sixteen-officer task force. They nicknamed it the Green Ribbon Squad because Kristen's classmates were wearing green ribbons as a symbol of hope. While everyone searched, hoped and prayed, Kristen was being held captive in a soundproof room behind the doors of a pink clapboard house and being sexually assaulted. Her videotaped ordeal lasted thirteen days, during which time she was shown tapes of Leslie Mahaffy suffering her fate.

Karla was now completely in her husband's power. She was almost zombie-like in his company, terrified that if she didn't do his bidding he would reveal her role in her sister Tammy's death.

By now the police were desperate in their hunt for Kristen and turned to the community for help. People responded in their hundreds, trudging through the damp spring rain searching forests and woodlands. They kept watch for the elusive off-white Camaro car seen near the spot where the much-loved schoolgirl had disappeared. They too had daughters. They cared. She had to be alive. She just had to be.

On the morning of 30 April they were shattered to wake up to the news bulletins that Kristen's naked body had been found dumped in a ditch less than a kilometre from where Leslie Mahaffy's body had finally been laid to rest. Kristen, they heard, had been alive until shortly before her body was found. Her long brown hair had been hacked off. A hunt for a serial killer was underway.

Two weeks later, on 12 May, Paul was again interviewed by the police, following a tip-off – and then released. Despite the expensive Green Ribbon Task Force, detectives had yet again drawn a blank.

Karla and Paul's lives had always been so carefully glued together for the outside world. They looked so perfect, so ordinary. But the dream was falling apart. Paul now regularly beat Karla, sometimes throwing her down the stairs, sometimes pinning her to the floor in their kitchen. His mother, Marilyn, was seeing a psychiatrist because she was unable to deal with the death of her father. She was estranged now from both Paul and his sister, Debbie. Paul's father, Ken, was convicted on a sex charge and jailed for nine months. Karla's world was crumbling.

Then came the turning point.

On 5 January, eighteen months after their wedding, Paul exploded with rage during an argument with Karla and beat her black and blue with a flashlight. Full of pain, guilt and shame, she could take no more. She'd been so badly beaten that one of her eyeballs was almost dislodged from its socket. After she was discharged from hospital she moved in with her parents and called the police. When they arrived they found a woman on the verge of a nervous breakdown.

On 6 January, Paul was charged with assault. As he had no previous record he was released on bail, returning to his home. The next morning he called a hardware store and had the locks changed.

Weeks after Karla filed charges against her estranged husband the jigsaw of their evil past slowly began to come together. Strangely, the results of the DNA test given voluntarily by Paul to detectives hunting the Scarborough rapist two years earlier were finally returned to the Metro police sexual assault squad, with no explanation for the long delay. Hours later the squad descended on the sleepy lakefront community where Paul lived. For days they shadowed his midnight prowlings.

He had apparently changed his image. His interests had swung to rap music. He had installed a synthesizer and other equipment in a soundproofed bedroom and planned to record an album. He told those who could be bothered to listen that he wanted to be the white MC Hammer and began wearing earrings and wearing his hair in ringlets.

Finally the Metro squad decided to contact Niagara police because they were about to swoop.

The Niagara police, startled by the allegations, cross-referenced Paul's name on a computer holding 30,000 tips that had poured in from the public since Kristen had been abducted on 16 April. They were amazed to discover that they had visited the twenty-eight-year-old freelance accountant two days after the schoolgirl's naked body was found. A tip from someone who claimed to know Paul well had come to them through a police officer in southern Ontario.

The friend revealed to the officer that Paul had been a suspect in the Scarborough rapes, had been questioned by Metro police and had moved to St Catharines in February 1991, two months before an attack on a fourteen-year-old rower on Henley Island and six months before Leslie Mahaffy's dismembered body was found in Lake Gibson.

Police returned to the home of Karla's parents and slowly the shocking story came together. The information Karla now willingly gave them was enough to compile a 900-page document and gain a search warrant. They were even told that Karla had to dress up and pretend to be the murdered schoolgirls when the couple had sex. As Karla was taken to a psychiatric hospital the police moved in on Paul and arrested him at gunpoint.

For ten exhausting weeks detectives combed the house where Kristen and Leslie had been kept prisoner, taking away the horrific videos of their ordeals. There were videos of Karla in lesbian sex orgies. Officers took pictures of the specially soundproofed rooms upstairs and pulled up every floorboard. Police believed Karla had been lured into the killings by her husband. He had totally corrupted her. But they needed her evidence.

Meanwhile the coroner reopened the files on the death of Karla's sister Tammy, and her parents lost no time in finding legal representation for their daughter. They hired lawyer George Walker and almost immediately discussions began between him, the police and the Crown.

At the end of February, Paul was charged with forty-three counts of sex-related offences. A few months later he was accused of the murders of Leslie Mahaffy and Kristen French as well as kidnapping, forcible confinement and aggravated sexual assault. There was also a charge of committing an indignity to Leslie's body.

After seven weeks in a psychiatric wing battling against severe suicidal depression, Karla Bernardo became Karla Teale. The name change had been legally approved by the provincial government. Paul had applied to change his name to Teale because he suspected the police in Scarborough were seeking him under the name of Bernardo.

Meanwhile Karla's guilt and shame had finally come out. She admitted privately that she had never forgotten the family's newspaper tribute to Tammy two years after her death.

It read:

> Homolka – Tammy Lyn.
>
> In loving memory of a dear daughter and sister who left us two years ago today. It was such a sudden parting. Too shocking to forget. Those who love you most, Tammy, are the ones who can't forget. Our hearts and eyes still weep for you and think of how you died. To think you couldn't say goodbye before you closed your eyes. We miss you Tammy. Love Mom, Dad, Lori, Paul and Karla.

Inspector Vince Bevan loosened his tie, stroked his black moustache and chose his words carefully as the reporters in the crowded room fired one question after another over the murders of teenagers Leslie Mahaffy and Kristen French.

Now that Paul had been arrested, were there any other suspects?

Bevan, head of the Green Ribbon Task Force investigating the killings, looked thoughtful for a moment.

'Yes, we are watching a second suspect,' he told the packed news conference. 'That person is not at present a threat to the public. I know where that person is twenty-four hours a day. We are continuing to watch this suspect.'

Bevan didn't give the sex of the suspect. He didn't need to. The media was out in force. Reporters and cameramen were already watching Karla's parents' home in St Catharines night and day. Two US TV networks had offered to buy her story, a publishing house wanted to do a book, a Canadian film company offered movie rights. But Karla was nowhere to be found.

The woman in the ill-fitting black wig, sunglasses and tight blue jeans stepped out of the front door of the condominium and glanced around as if she was looking for someone. For a month she had been staying in the quiet complex in Brampton, suburban Toronto, relaxing in the building's hot tub or shopping at a nearby mall. The warm waters of the tub soothed her aches and pains. Sometimes she slipped under the water for a moment before appearing again and massaging her swollen face, made black and blue by the beating she had suffered at the hands of her husband.

Karla had moved into Unit 130 in Brampton, where her favourite aunt and uncle, Patti and Calvin Seger, lived. They seemed to understand. They showed her love. But today it was not the kind of love she so desperately needed. Today she needed Johnny.

They had met in a city bar owned by Johnny's friend a few weeks after Paul had finally been arrested. Tonight, though, was the night. They met at around eight o'clock and danced and drank the night away. At 3am Johnny locked the bar and they made love on a seat in the corner. Karla was in love again.

From then on she saw Johnny when she could. But the world was closing in on her.

Residents in the condominium, mostly retired couples, knew little about Karla Homolka, the quiet woman with the bruised face, when she first arrived. They had no idea her husband was making headlines across Canada and she was being sought by the media wolves. They assumed she was staying there because of a split with her husband or lover.

Karla was pleasant but distant. She always wore a hat and dark glasses, even on the cloudiest of days. But they didn't realize she was trying to disguise herself. Then their lives began to change. Strange men started coming and going. People sat in cars outside staring in. Policemen were seen wandering through the complex. Some residents wondered if the visitors, many of them shabbily dressed, were drug dealers. Unknown to them, however, was the fact that one newspaper had rented an apartment across the street. Telephoto lenses were snapping Karla sunbathing and walking around the neighbourhood wearing shorts, hats, sunglasses and halter tops. One irate retired banker rang the police to complain about the comings and goings. A police car turned up to investigate, unaware the complex was surrounded by officers from another force watching Karla. A row broke out because they had not been told.

Now Karla's cover was blown, she returned to her parents' home to face manslaughter charges, the police surveillance team in close pursuit.

Later Karla's aunt and uncle were to appear on a TV show, where they told how Karla had admitted to them her involvement in the killings and that the public was going to be outraged when the truth was known.

It was 5.30am on Monday, 28 June and the sun had come up over St Catharines. The streets were normally deserted at this time of day, but not that morning. Already a cluster of TV vans had surrounded the courthouse, a modern, four-storey building of concrete, metal and glass, and scores of people were milling about. By 9am more than 200 people were lined up four abreast from the court entrance to the street. A man in a Spiderman outfit marched up and down carrying banners in support of the police. Behind the courthouse was another crowd, photographers and local residents being held back by uniformed officers. They were waiting for the arrival of Karla, her parents and her younger sister, Lori, who were being driven the five kilometres from their home to the building.

Someone spotted an approaching grey Dodge van.

'Here they come!' he shouted. The crowd surged forward. 'Bitch!' screamed a young woman in Levi jeans. Seconds later the van disappeared into a dark opening and a steel door closed behind it.

The public gallery in Court 10 was packed as Judge Kovacs, the sixty-three-year-old son of Hungarian immigrants, entered at 10 am. Before his ornately carved hardwood bench a portrait of Queen Elizabeth II looked down on Karla, who appeared frail but well dressed. The parents of murdered teenagers Leslie Mahaffy and Kristen French sat quietly to the left of her. Karla's parents, Karel and Dorothy, sat with their twenty-one-year-old daughter, Lori, in the front row near the prisoner's box. To them Karla, dressed in a navy-blue dress with her long blonde hair in a ponytail, had always been a dutiful daughter, an animal lover, gentle and caring, a nurse to sick cats and dogs. That's how they and her friends saw her. Nothing could ever change that.

It was a demanding day. Crown Attorney Murray Segal argued for three hours for a publication ban on evidence. He contended that Paul Bernardo's right to a fair trial would be jeopardized if the media reported facts used to convict his estranged wife. Segal brushed some hairs off his flowing black robe and addressed the court: 'Freedom of expression does not exist in a vacuum,' he said. 'If there is a conflict between freedom of expression and the right to a fair trial, then the right to a fair trial is held to be paramount!'

Next came Timothy Breen, representing Paul. The young lawyer's strong voice and dramatic style were in stark contrast to the barely audible monotones of Segal. Breen cleared his throat, adjusted his glasses and began with a surprising line of argument.

His client, who had originally applied for the publication ban, now wanted the evidence against Karla made public. He claimed that the police had deliberately leaked information portraying his client as the perpetrator of the crimes and Karla as the victim. How else could anyone explain Karla's release on bail under such serious circumstances?

However, the evidence against Karla would reveal that she had taken an active part in the deaths, he said. He wanted the public to hear how 'a deal' had come together. It was his client's right and the public's.

The following day Karla's lawyer, George Walker, stood before Kovacs and supported Segal's application for a publication ban.

'Forget about case law and legalese,' he told the court. 'Instead think about the psychological damage that publication of the evidence would inflict on the community.' In a voice so low that many in the court strained their ears to catch his words, he added: 'I care about this community. I care about the trauma that will be inflicted on the Mahaffy family, the French family and on my client's family!'

Next came a battery of Toronto lawyers representing some of Canada's largest media organizations, arguing that the public was entitled to hear all the evidence.

On Monday, 5 July, Leslie Mahaffy's mother Debbie wasn't in the packed courtroom to hear the groans of anger as Kovacs announced his decision to enforce a publication ban. It would have been too painful for her. That day her daughter would have been seventeen. For three hours Kovacs defended his ruling, responding to each of the lawyer's arguments and citing previous cases and precedents to support his position. Paul Bernardo's right to a fair trial superseded the media's right to freedom of expression, he said. 'The gravity of the charges against him reinforces society's interest in ensuring that justice is done!'

His next move was to bar American reporters from the court because he could not enforce such a publication ban in the United States. Karla, who had sat motionless up until then, turned and grinned at the public gallery. Anger filled the courtroom. Canada wanted to know about the evil crimes. The local community wanted to know. Friends of Leslie and Kristen wanted to know.

Late that afternoon Karla was driven to her parents' home for the last time. Such was the loyalty of her friends that they shielded her from Press cameras. Some held flattened cardboard boxes in front of her as she went into the house her father had put up as bail.

On Tuesday, 6 July, the general public was excluded from the room as the clerk of the court read the charges against Karla. There was more anger outside the court. People told pressmen they had come to hear the truth – they were entitled to after two years of innuendo and rumour. Had Karla made snuff movies? They demanded to be told.

Then Segal rose to read the statement of facts agreed

to by the Crown and Karla's lawyers. The twenty-seven-minute litany of rape and torture was graphic and sordid. Karla's sister, Lori, slumped in her chair weeping. Hardened police officers and the fifty-four Canadian reporters stared hard at the floor, holding back their tears. Karla, sitting rigidly in the dock, showed little emotion. Kovacs, sensitive to the trauma that the French and Mahaffy families were enduring, ordered a recess until they were ready to continue.

Forty-five minutes later everyone filed quietly back to their seats as the judge registered convictions against Karla on both counts. She had pleaded guilty to the manslaughter of Leslie and Kristen. But even that fact the public wasn't allowed to know.

The next stage of the trial was equally harrowing. Leslie's mother, Debbie Mahaffy, appeared frail and tormented, sometimes weeping, sometimes choking with emotion as she read a statement describing the impact of her daughter's death on her family. Many in the court now openly wept. Kristen's mother, Donna French, was next, and the ordeal was repeated. Kovacs ordered the statements to be sealed for ever.

At 4.30pm that afternoon he stared hard at Karla, who sat motionless as always, and lectured her for seventy-five minutes on the gravity of her crimes and the horrendous damage she had inflicted. Karla seemed unmoved, showing no emotion.

She was charged with manslaughter because she bore responsibility for the deaths of Leslie and Kristen French, even though she did not personally kill them.

'The maximum sentence for manslaughter of life imprisonment is reserved for the worst offenders,' he said. But Karla was not the worst conceivable offender. She had cooperated fully with the police and provided information that was not normally available in abduction cases. 'She has also spared everyone the expense and trauma of a long trial,' he said.

Kovacs then sentenced Karla to concurrent twelve-year terms on each charge.

'The penalty is harsh enough to deter others who might be tempted to commit such deeds and to protect the safety of the community,' he added.

He expressed the hope that Karla could be rehabilitated.

But in one crucial respect he admitted the sentence was inadequate. 'No sentence I can impose would adequately reflect the revulsion of the community for the deaths of two innocent young girls who lived their lives without reproach in the eyes of those around them.'

For Karla the trail to the perfect marriage that began at the end of a pot-holed road now led down the highway to the Kingston Prison for Women.

When Debbie Mahaffy left the court for the last time she was in a state of despair. She had spent nights at home curled up in a chair. She had scarcely slept, haunted by the memories of her daughter. The noises of the courtroom had kept her awake in her mind. Was she to blame? Should she have been with Leslie on her way home?

'It was like my daughter had died all over again,' she

said. 'I met a couple of reporters who were genuinely moved and, for a fleeting moment, my grief was magnified. For me there is a constant sense of loss, the overwhelming loss of your child. When my brother died I lost part of my past. When my daughter died I lost a part of my future.

'Any memories of Leslie have become bitter-sweet. In my court statement I didn't mention the little signs of her that are gone – the chair where she used to slouch, the hairs in the sink, the phone never being where I left it. Those are not major things but they matter to me.

'I can't sit now at the kitchen table because that's where Leslie would always sit. The family room – well, it is just not a family room any more. Everything has changed.'

Things had changed for Karla as well. But did the memories of her past haunt her like the memories of Debbie's past?

Was there any remorse? Was there a future? For Leslie's mother there didn't seem to be much of either.

Debbie and her daughter had become another statistic in the heartbreaking trail of crime in North America. Karla had become a chapter in the terrifying annals of world evil.

As the iron doors were slammed shut behind the blonde Barbie doll she began a new life – one which was in her heart a life of hope.

And, true to what friends had believed, she was a child in a woman's body. That soon became evident as she built her new life behind the bars of her gaol.

Karla covered the walls of her cell with Mickey Mouse posters and her bedsheets were embroidered with the fantasy characters from Sesame Street. It was as if she was living in yet another fantasy world, away from the videos of horror that had taken over her life.

Her looks were all important to her and she remained obsessed with her appearance, dieting, exercising, manicuring her nails, plucking her eyebrows and highlighting her honey-blonde hair.

'I'm trying to change myself back into a newer, better version of the person I was before I met Paul,' she told her friends and family.

In August 1993 she filed for divorce from Paul, citing physical and mental cruelty. He didn't challenge the petition and it was granted in February 1994.

Karla was no ordinary convict.

From the moment she passed through the prison gates in the back of an unmarked police van stuffed with a colour TV, toys and other gifts from her family and friends, she had been kept apart from mainstream prisoners, cocooned in the gaol hospital or in the segregation block, where she enjoyed munchies from the canteen, wore her own clothes and worked out in the gym. For Karla was being counted on to perform as the prosecution's key witness against her ex-husband when the most sensational criminal trial in Canadian history started the following year.

Karla, earning 6 dollars a day by doing menial tasks in the segregation unit, was trying to build a new life and plan her future as Paul spent day after boring day listlessly lying in his bright orange prison overalls in a bleak, windowless isolation cell at Niagara's detention centre in Thorold.

The authorities meanwhile were keeping Karla sweet. She enjoyed family visits at a cottage in the grounds, where even her Rottweiler, Buddy, was brought to see her.

Karla's only major problems were disagreements with her psychiatrist and stress brought on by Paul's prosecutors, who interviewed her day after day, week after week.

For the second time in her life Karla was in bad company. If the influence of Paul wasn't bad enough now, she was banged up with 120 fellow women convicts, 41 per cent of whom were serving time for murder or manslaughter. Most were chronic alcoholics and drug addicts with lengthy criminal records. Society meanwhile was looking for some kind of remorse. Many today say they have not seen it from Karla. But in some way that is part of her treatment programme. She is learning to face the future.

So far during her time in jail, Karla, sometimes heavily medicated with anti-depressants, had shrugged off death threats and had a telephone and dressing-table thrown at her.

She was among killers . . . but being a killer of schoolgirls was frowned on by most of the inmates.

Karla has set her heart on winning early parole. She is eligible for release in July 1997. Her aim, she says, is to work with abused women. She is studying for a BA through a correspondence course. But she has revealed to friends that in her heart she wants to return to Brampton. The city holds something very special for her.

At her first Christmas party in gaol, Karla and the other girls from the segregation unit toasted the future with egg-nog.

She said later to a friend: 'Christmas has always been my favourite time. Of course since Tammy died things haven't been the same. But one thought I have always held is that Tammy wouldn't want us to live in misery over the holiday she always enjoyed.'